James Cox

Old and New St. Louis

Vol. 1

James Cox

Old and New St. Louis
Vol. 1

ISBN/EAN: 9783337293413

Printed in Europe, USA, Canada, Australia, Japan

Cover: Foto ©ninafisch / pixelio.de

More available books at **www.hansebooks.com**

OLD AND NEW ST. LOUIS:

A CONCISE HISTORY OF THE METROPOLIS OF THE WEST AND SOUTHWEST, WITH A REVIEW OF ITS PRESENT GREATNESS AND IMMEDIATE PROSPECTS,

BY

JAMES COX,

Author of "St. Louis Through a Camera," "The Carnival City of the World," "Missouri at the World's Fair," "Our Own Country," &c.

ST. LOUIS, 1894:
PUBLISHED BY THE AUTHOR.

PUBLISHERS' NOTICE.

THE PUBLICATION of "Old and New St. Louis" has been delayed far beyond the wishes of the publishers by the immense amount of work which had to be done, not only in securing data concerning the lives and achievements of prominent men in the city, but also in having the necessary steel plates made. A large number of gentlemen who could not possibly be excluded from a work of this character have been absent from the city, and neither photographs nor biographical data could be obtained until they returned. The completeness of the work and the unprecedented and uniform excellence of the plates is ample justification for the delay.

The introductory and historical chapters have been in print for upwards of a year, and since they were written a number of events have taken place which have greatly affected the city's standing and its prospects. The financial depression of 1893 has been succeeded by a period of healthy reaction. No city in the United States withstood the panic in such a thoroughly satisfactory manner as St. Louis, which has the proud record of no bank failure for a period of nearly nine years. St. Louis generally is in a much better condition financially and commercially than it was when the earlier chapters of this work were prepared, and it now stands before the world a model of financial strength and of conservative progressiveness.

The largest Union Railroad Station in the world, described in Chapter V., was completed during the summer of 1894 and opened with befitting ceremonies at the commencement of the fall festivities season. In every respect the depot has proved to be superior to expectation, and the words of praise written in anticipation of the completion of the work seem feeble and inadequate in view of the magnificent realization.

The Planters Hotel, also described as in course of construction, was completed shortly after the New Union Station and was opened to the public immediately. Like the magnificent structure fourteen blocks farther west, the Planters Hotel—referred to in this work as the New Planters House, its exact title not having been determined upon until a recent date—far exceeds expectation. It is declared by experts to be one of the finest hotels in the world, and in many most important respects it is absolutely unsurpassed and indeed unapproached. In the Biographical Appendix a record will be found of the lives of some of the men who have given to St. Louis this noble hostelry, and more particularly should credit be given to Mr. Isaac S. Taylor. This accomplished architect not only conceived the unique plan upon which the hotel is constructed, but also superintended the work in every detail, preparing special designs on every possible opportunity and earning the praise and commendation, not only of the owners of the hotel, but also of the public generally and of the traveling fraternity.

The Autumnal Festivities Association, whose work is described in Chapter VII., having completed its program, went out of existence on October 9, 1894, to be succeeded by the Business Men's League, another organization which is justly entitled to be included in the list of "aids to progress." The Veiled Prophet made his annual visit in October, preceded a few days by King Hotu, who, with his Funny Fellows, gave the first of a series of annual daylight parades. The city's record as a convention gathering place has been more than maintained, and the Trans-Mississippi Convention, held at the Exposition Building in November, brought to the city representative men from all the Western States.

Another event of importance to St. Louis, not referred to at length in the historical chapters for obvious reasons, was the launching of the Steamship St. Louis at Philadelphia on November 12, 1894. This magnificent steamship, the largest ever constructed in America, will carry the American flag between the United States and Europe. As soon as work commenced on this vessel, the Bureau of Information of the Autumnal Festivities Association entered into communication with Mr. Griscom, president of the International Navigation Company, and suggested to him that the ship be named "St. Louis," in honor of the great metropolis of the West and Southwest. The suggestion was favorably entertained, and subsequently a meeting was called at the mayor's office which resulted in a committee being appointed to visit Philadelphia. On their arrival at the City of Brotherly Love the committee found that the request already made to President Griscom had been complied with. It accordingly pledged the city to make a suitable presentation to the ship in recognition of the courtesy extended. A large party of St. Louisans went to Philadelphia to be present at the launching, and when the great ship commenced to glide gracefully into the water, Mrs. Cleveland broke a bottle of St. Louis champagne upon it and christened it in due form.

During 1894 a practical test has been made of the new water-works, which come up to every expectation. The street car equipment of the city has also been vastly improved. The table of mileage given on page 77 does not now represent the actual mileage of St. Louis street railways. Thus the Union Depot system, which is credited with fifty-five miles of track, has now seventy-six miles. The most important addition to its service has been the Grand Avenue division, the work on which is now nearly complete, and which will provide a most important north and south road. The Lindell company has increased its mileage from forty-one to fifty-five miles. The most important addition to its service has been the Compton Heights division, with a total mileage of eleven. This line connects the Eads Bridge and the new Union Station with a district in the southwest which is very thickly populated. The Baden Railway Company has ceased to exist, and the old horse-car line has been replaced by a double-track electric road, operated by the owners of the Broadway cable. The total mileage of track in the city is now 208, with forty-five additional miles authorized and about to be constructed. At the present time the percentage of cable to electric road is as one and eight. This percentage will be still further decreased by the substitution of electricity for cable power on the Citizen's road, or Franklin Avenue cable, as it is more generally called, the change being now nearly complete.

ST. LOUIS, December, 1894.

TABLE OF CONTENTS.

OLD AND NEW ST. LOUIS.

CHAPTER I.

OLD ST. LOUIS.

FROM THE FOUNDING OF THE TRADING POST IN 1764, TO THE ADOPTION OF THE CITY SCHEME AND CHARTER IN 1876.

THE TRADING POST from which has grown the fifth largest city in the United States was established in 1764, in which year Auguste Chouteau, with about thirty followers, landed at the foot of what is now known as Walnut street. The founders of the city erected a few log cabins on the ground subsequently occupied by Barnum's Hotel, and here they were joined by Pierre Liguest Laclede (or Pierre Laclede Liguest, as he seems to have signed his name), by whose directions the settlement had been made. Authorities differ concerning the origin of the name by which the city has been known from the first. The theory generally accepted to-day is that Laclede christened the settlement "St. Louis" in honor of the canonized monarch of France, though quite a large number of well-informed writers assert that he gave it the name as a mark of respect and loyalty to Louis XV., who then occupied the French throne, and whose patron saint was Louis IX. In explanation of this latter theory, it is argued that Laclede was not aware that the territory west of the Mississippi River had been ceded to Spain, and that he only learned of his error the following year, when, to his intense grief and disgust, he became acquainted with the terms of the treaty of Paris of 1763. But, however this may have been, the early settlers were almost exclusively French; and, although the territory was nominally under Spanish government, little effort was made to assert authority or to introduce the Spanish language or customs. The history of the trading post during the eighteenth century has been written at length by several competent authorities. The adventures of the hardy pioneers were more thrilling than important, and for the purposes of this review it is sufficient to state that when the famous Louisiana purchase was completed in the year 1803, the population of St. Louis was still less than a thousand, with Carondelet as a separate trading post or town, with a population about one-fifth that of St. Louis itself.

An excellent pen picture of St. Louis at the time of its passing into the hands of the United States is given by Richard Edwards in his "Great West." "There was," we are told, "but one baker in the town, by the name of LeClerc, who baked for the garrison, and who lived in Main street, between what is now known as Elm and Walnut. There were three blacksmiths, Delosier, who resided in Main street, near Morgan; Recontre, who lived in Main, near Carr, and Valois, who resided in Main, near Elm, and did the work for the government. There was but one physician, who was

Dr. Saugrain, who practiced many years after the territory passed into the possession of the American government, and who lived on Second street.

"There were but two little French taverns in the town, one kept by Yostie, and the other by Landreville, chiefly to accommodate the *couriers des bois* (hunters) and the *voyageurs* (boatmen) of the Mississippi. These little taverns, visited by the brave, daring and reckless men, who lived three-fourths of the time remote from civilization, in the wild solitudes of the forests and rivers, and in constant intercourse with the savages, were the very nurseries of legendary narratives, where the hunters, the trappers and the boatmen, all mingling together under the genial excitement of convivial influences, would relate perilous adventures, hair-breadth escapes; deaths of comrades and families by the tomahawk, starvation and at the fire-stake; murders by the pirates of Grand Tower and Cottonwood Creek; captivity in the wilderness and cave, and protracted sufferings in the most agonizing forms incident to humanity. There is no record of these wild narratives, which could have been preserved for future times, had there been an historian, who, by the embalming power of genius, would have preserved them in an imperishable shape for posterity. Both of these taverns stood upon the corners of Main and Locust streets.

"The principal merchants and traders, at the time of the cession to the United States, were Auguste Chouteau, who resided in Main street, between Market and Walnut; Pierre Chouteau, who resided on the corner of Main street and Washington avenue, and had the whole square encircled with a stone wall—he had an orchard of choice fruit, and his house and store were in one building—the store being the first story, and the family residence the second; Manuel Lisa lived on Second street, corner of Spruce; Labbadie & Sarpy; Roubidou lived at the corner of Elm and Main, and Jaques Clamorgan corner of Green and Main. The Debreuil family occupied a whole square on Second street, between Pine and Chestnut."

THE FIRST INCORPORATION. The town of St. Louis was first incorporated on November 9, 1809, in accordance with the provisions of an act passed the preceding year by the Legislature of the Territory of Louisiana. The boundaries as then defined correspond with present lines and names as follows: On the north a line from the river, between Biddle and Ashley streets, to the vicinity of Seventh and Carr, thence south to Seventh and Cerre streets, and thence east to the river. The population of the town on its budding into corporate existence was 1,400, and its wealth, according to the first assessment, was $134,516. Auguste Chouteau was the heaviest tax-payer, his town assessment being $15,000, independent of about $61,000 worth of real estate which was situated beyond the limits of the little town, but which is now in the heart of the great city. There had been a great deal of land speculation prior to this, and values had gone up every time the tide of immigration gained strength and impetus. There were a few other wealthy men in the city, as wealth went in those days, including J. B. C. Lucas, John O'Fallon, William Clark, William Christy and Henry Von Phul.

After its incorporation the town of St. Louis began to grow rapidly, and in the year 1822, when it was advanced to the rank and dignity of a city, its population was 5,000. The boundaries were extended in December of that year as far north as Ashley street and as far south as Labbadie and Convent streets, the western line being on Broadway, between Ashley and Biddle streets, and on Seventh, between Biddle and Labbadie streets. The area of the town was thus increased to 385 acres, on which there were to be found about 650 houses, 419 of which were frame. The taxable property had not yet reached a million dollars, and the annual income from taxation was a trifle less than $4,000.

Several additions were platted out during the '30s, including the Lucas addition, between Seventh and Ninth and Market and St. Charles streets; the Soulard addition, between the river and Carondelet avenue and Park and Geyer avenues; O'Fallon's 1836 addition, between Seveuth and Eighth streets and Wash street and Franklin avenue; Langham's addition, between LaSalle and Rutger streets and Second and Fifth streets; Christy's addition, between Ninth and Twelfth streets and Franklin and Lucas avenues; O'Fallon's 1837 addition, between Seventh and Fourteenth streets and Franklin avenue and Biddle street; and Soulard's second addition, between Carondelet avenue and Decatur street and Park and Geyer avenues, including a reserved square, subsequently the site of the Soulard Market.

In 1839 the city limits were again extended. In the meantime the population had increased rapidly and was now 16,000, with taxable property assessed at $8,682,000. In 1841 the limits were again increased, this time to take in a total area of 2,630 acres and to increase the taxable property to twelve millions. Additions were laid out in large numbers during the next fifteen years, including William C. Carr's third addition from Eighteenth street to Jefferson avenue, between Franklin avenue and Biddle street. The conditions of the dedication of this addition were unique. It was declared that there "shall be no butchery, tallow chandlery, soap factory, steam factory, tannery, nine-pin alley, or any other offensive business or occupation, set up or carried on in any part of said addition, whereby the dwellers or any lot-owners, proprietors or occupants may be in any way annoyed or disturbed." Nine-pin alleys appear to have been a special menace to peace and quietness half a century ago, for the dedication of several other additions contain specific references to and restrictions against them.

In December, 1855, the city limits were again extended, and most of the additions of the last ten or twelve years were taken in. The southern boundary was extended to Keokuk street, and a line 660 feet west and north of Grand avenue became the western and northern limits. The area of the city was increased to seventeen square miles, and the assessed valuation to $59,609,289. The town of Bremen, incorporated in 1845, and the town of Highland, incorporated three years later, were absorbed by the exten-

sion. The former has preserved its name and individuality to this day, but the latter is known only to history and the proverbial "oldest inhabitant." It included the five squares between Jefferson and Leffingwell avenues, from Laclede avenue to Eugenia street. Among the numerous subdivisions which became portions of the city in 1855, the Stoddard and Compton Hill additions are the only two which have preserved their identity to any extent, or whose names are familiar to any except title examiners and realty agents.

After another interval of fifteen years, in April, 1870, the limits were again extended, and Carondelet became a portion of St. Louis. Our southern neighbor, which at one time had been looked upon as a possible rival, had not been able to keep up with us, though it had grown into a prosperous little city, first incorporated in 1833, and advanced to city rank eighteen years later. In 1872 the limits were extended north and west so as to include Tower Grove, Forest and O'Fallon Parks, but in 1874 the Legislature repealed the act and restored the limits of 1870.

On August 22, 1876, the scheme and charter was adopted, and the city of St. Louis was separated from the county, it being thus made a free city in local government; an advantage possessed by no other city in the Mississippi Valley.[*] The area was increased to sixty-two and one-fourth square miles, and the assessed value of real estate to $181,345,560. The new territory made part of St. Louis included the towns of Lowell, incorporated in 1849; Rock Springs (1852), Cheltenham (1852), Quinette (1859), Mount Olive (1854), and Cote Brilliante (1853), as well as McRee City, Fairmount, Rose Hill, Evans Place and College Hill additions. Some of these towns and additions still retain their names, while others have completely lost their identity, and become entirely merged into the general street nomenclature. Every one has heard of, and may have

---

[*] As far as the writer has been able to ascertain, there is but one other town in the United States which is practically a county as well as a city.

smelt, Lowell, but comparatively few could locate Quinette or McRee City. Twenty years hence, few, if any, of these distinctive names will exist in anything but a pleasant memory.

EARLY FINANCIAL DIFFICULTIES. St. Louis kept pace with its increase in territory. A post-office was established soon after the Louisiana purchase, and Rufus Easton, a lawyer and title examiner, was the first postmaster. In July, 1808, Joseph Charless commenced the issue of the *Missouri Gazette*, the first newspaper published west of the Mississippi. It was necessarily a very primitive newspaper, but its growth has been on a par with that of the city, and, as the *Missouri Republican* and the *St. Louis Republic*, it has acquired national importance and influence. In 1811 there were two schools, one French and one English, and during that year a market was erected on Centre Square, between Market and Walnut streets and Main street and the river, the site of the old Merchants' Exchange. In 1816 the first bank was incorporated, with Samuel Hammond as president and John B. N. Smith, cashier. Prior to this there had been little or no circulating medium in St. Louis, trading being conducted by means of exchanges of lead and skins for groceries, dry goods and other merchandise. This financial institution, the Bank of St. Louis, soon had a rival in the Bank of Missouri, established in 1817, with Auguste Chouteau as president, but neither of these banks enjoyed a lengthy career of prosperity. Even in those days bank officials were not proof against the temptation of over-speculation.

While the inhabitants of St. Louis were worrying over financial problems, Missouri was admitted to the Union, and in December, 1822, the newly-formed State Legislature passed an act incorporating St. Louis. In April of the following year the first corporate officers of the city were elected. Mr. William Carr Lane was the first mayor of the city, and Messrs. Thomas McKnight, James Kennerly, Philip Rocheblane, Archibald Gamble, William H. Savage, Robert Nash, James Loper, Henry Von Phul and James Lackman were the first aldermen elected after the city's final incorporation. The size and importance of St. Louis at this period are easily ascertained, because, in 1821, the first St. Louis directory was published, and, although compared with publications of to-day the book appears crude and imperfect, it gives information of a very valuable character, and settles a great many questions which would otherwise be in dispute.

From this directory it appears that in May, 1821, or about eighteen months before the incorporation, there were 651 dwelling houses in St. Louis; of these, 232 were of brick and stone and 419 were of wood, and rather more than half the structures were in the northern portion of the town. In addition to the dwelling houses, there were, to use the words of the directory, "a number of brick, stone and wooden warehouses, stables, shops and outhouses." Among the buildings, the steamboat warehouse, built by Mr. Josiah Bright, is described as a large brick building, which would do credit to any of the Eastern cities. Mention is made of "the Cathedral," which, when the directory was compiled, was forty feet high, with a frontage of forty feet and a depth of one hundred and thirty-five, and also of the elegant and valuable library of Bishop Du Bourg. The St. Louis College, we are told, had sixty-five students and several teachers. As to the other educational and mercantile establishments, the following extract from the directory tells the story concisely and with evident accuracy.

A PEN PICTURE IN 1821. "St. Louis likewise contains ten common schools, a brick Baptist church, forty feet by sixty, built in 1818, and an Episcopal church, of wood. The Methodist congregation hold their meetings in the old court house and the Presbyterians in the circuit court-room. In St. Louis are the following mercantile, professional, mechanical, etc., establishments, viz.: Forty-six mercantile establishments, which carry on an extensive trade with the most distant parts of the Republic in merchandise, produce, furs and peltry; three auctioneers, who do considerable business—each pays $200 per annum to the State for a license to sell, and on all personal property sold is a State duty of three per cent, on real estate one and a half per cent and their commission of five per cent; three weekly newspapers, viz., the *St. Louis Inquirer, Missouri Gazette* and *St. Louis Register*, and as many printing offices; one book store; two binderies; three large inns, together with a number of smaller taverns and boarding-houses; six livery stables; fifty-seven grocers and bottlers; twenty-seven attorneys and counsellors-at-law; thirteen physicians; three druggists and apothecaries; three midwives; one portrait painter, who would do credit to any country; five clock and watchmakers, silversmiths and jewelers; one silver plater; one engraver; one brewery, where are manufactured beer, ale and porter of a quality equal to any in the Western country; one tannery; three soap and candle factories; two brickyards; three stonecutters; fourteen bricklayers and plasterers; twenty-eight carpenters; nine blacksmiths; three gunsmiths; two copper and tinware manufacturers; six cabinetmakers; four coachmakers and wheelwrights; three saddle and harness manufacturers; seven turners and chairmakers; three hatters; twelve tailors; thirteen boot and shoe manufacturers; ten ornamental house and sign painters and glaziers; one nail factory; four hair-dressers and perfumers; two confectioners and cordial distillers; four coopers, block, pump and mastmakers; four bakers; one comb factory; one bellman; five billiard tables, which pay an annual tax of $100 each to the State and the same sum to the corporation; several hacks or pleasure carriages and a considerable number of drays and carts; several professional musicians, who play at the balls, which are very frequent and well attended by the inhabitants, more particularly the French, who, in general, are remarkably graceful performers and much attached to so rational, healthy and improving an amusement; two potteries are within a few miles, and there are several promising gardens in and near to the town."

A great deal more information of a valuable character is given. Thus, we are told that

eight streets ran parallel with the river, intersected by twenty-three streets running east and west. The streets in the lower part of the town were narrow, varying from thirty-two to thirty-eight and one-half feet in width, but the streets on "the hill" were much wider and more handsome. On the hill in the center of the town was a public square 240x300 feet, reserved for a court-house. Mention is made of two fire engines, with properly organized companies, one in the northern and the other in the southern portion of the city, in addition to which every dwelling and store had to be provided with good leather fire buckets. Much space is devoted to the Missouri Fur Company, whose capital was "supposed" at the time to amount to about $70,000, the company having in its employ twenty-five clerks and interpreters, and seventy laboring men. The Indian trade of the Missouri and Mississippi Rivers amounted to about $600,000 a year; and the estimated imports of the town to about $2,000,000. The commerce by water was carried in by steamboats, barges and keel boats, and the principal articles of trade were fur, peltry, lead and agricultural products. Two miles above town, at North St. Louis, there was a steam saw-mill, with several common mills on neighboring streams. "The roads leading from St. Louis," the directory notice continues, "are very good, and it is expected that the great national turnpike leading from Washington will strike this place, as the Commissioners of the United States have reported in favor of it."

The population of the town was estimated at 5,500 by the compiler of the directory, and the alphabetical list of householders contains about 800 names. It is interesting to note the first name on the list is "Abel, Sarah, seamstress, North Fourth, above C," and the last "Young, Benjamin, baker and grocer, 81 South Main street."

THE CITY'S FIRST MAYOR. The salary of the first mayor of St. Louis, Mr. William Carr Lane, was fixed at $300 per annum, but he applied himself most zealously to the city's interest; and among the first acts of his administration were the division of the city into wards, the straightening and more accurate defining of the streets, the appointment of assessors and health officers, and the grading and partial paving of Main street.

In 1826 an ordinance was passed authorizing the building of a court-house, and in the following year work was commenced on the arsenal. A forward step was taken in the direction of city improvements by the systematic naming of the streets. At first, all the streets of St. Louis bore French names. Main street, from Almond to Morgan, was "La Rue Principale," and Second street was "La Rue de l'Eglise," or Church street, so called because of the first church of the city being built upon it. These French names had continued until 1809, when another system was adopted. Market street, which was even then the dividing line between north and south, was the only east and west street with a distinctive name. Other streets were, for the most part, distinguished by letters of the alphabet. In 1827 a much better system of nomenclature was adopted, and during the same year ordinances were passed for raising funds for the erection of a market and town-house, and also for the grading and paving of Chestnut and Olive streets as far west as Fourth.

In 1829, Mr. Daniel B. Page was elected mayor, and much activity was manifested by the municipal authorities in the way of street grading and paving. Fourth street was surveyed from Market to Lombard street, and Seventh street was extended to the then northern limits of the city. Locust street was also graded and paved as far west as Fourth, and the city began to put on metropolitan airs in other ways. In the following year a bridge was erected across Mill Creek, at Fourth and Fifth streets, and a large amount of enterprise in the way of brick-making was manifested. As a result, the primitive one-story houses of the French and Spanish *regime* began to give place rapidly to brick buildings, and the building lines were much more carefully observed.

In 1831, more attention was paid to manufacturing, and the steamboat and river traffic began to increase rapidly. The work of paving and grading the streets was continued actively, and the government of the city was generally regarded as excellent. In 1832 the city's progress was checked by an attack of cholera, but in the following year the temporary set-back was overcome, and marked progress was made. Mr. Edwards, in his "Great West," says of this period: "Since the first arrival of a steamboat, every year they have increased in number, and at this time there was not a day but numbers of steamers landed at the levee, or departed for Ohio, Illinois, Missouri, and the upper and lower Mississippi. There was also a line of stages for Vincennes and Louisville. The time of performing the journey by coach between St. Louis and Louisville was three and a half days. There was also a stage line between St. Louis and Galena, via Springfield. There was, as yet, no railway to destroy the impediments of distance, and a journey through the interior of the Western country, that could not be assisted by river navigation, if performed in early spring, was associated with every idea of discomfort; the horses floundering in mud-holes, and probably not being able to extricate the vehicle, and then the traveller had to step out, ofttimes in the very middle of the sink, which held to his legs with such quicksand pertinacity that it frequently required considerable effort to disengage himself."

ENTHUSIASM AND METAPHOR IN 1835. Despite these apparent difficulties, the city's growth was rapid, and much foresight was manifested by the authorities. In 1835, the Commons were sold and one-tenth of the proceeds was devoted to the support of public schools, the remainder of the proceeds being used for city improvements generally. Much enthusiasm was aroused by the success of the sale, and a local writer of the day says of St. Louis: "She already commands the trade of a larger section of territory, with a few exceptions, than any other city in the Union. With a steamboat navigation more than equal to the whole Atlantic seaboard; with internal improvements, projected and in progress; with thousands of emigrants spreading their habitations over fertile plains which every-where meet the eye, who can deny that we are fast verging to the time when it will be admitted that this city is the lion of the West?"

The same writer goes on to enthuse over the proposed erection of a theatre, and shortly after his prophecy was issued, the corner-stone was laid of the St. Louis Theatre on the corner of Third and Olive streets, on the site now occupied by the old post-office. The ground cost fifty dollars a foot front and the expense of the building was about $60,000. The enterprise appears to have been somewhat in advance of the requirements of the times, and the early history of the theatre shows that the projectors met with a great deal of discouragement.

A year later work was commenced on the Planter's House, which was subsequently completed by the St. Louis Hotel Company.

In 1836, about twenty-five of the leading merchants formed the "St. Louis Chamber of Commerce," not for the purpose of buying and selling grain and trading in options, but to generally further the interests of the city in commercial matters. Edward Tracy was the first president, Henry Von Phul, vice-president, and John Ford, secretary. Meetings were held after office hours at regular intervals, and substantial good was effected. The Merchants' Exchange was not established until 1849, and in 1850 it was joined by the Millers' Association. In 1837, the Bank of the State of Missouri was incorporated with a capital stock of $5,000,000. The need of banking facilities had been much felt in St. Louis, and the new institution was heralded with much rejoicing and satisfaction.

It was at about this period that the absolute necessity of railroad facilities between St. Louis and the East and West began to be appreciated, and Mayor John F. Darby called the first railroad convention held in St. Louis. Although some years elapsed before practical results were manifest, the building of the roads now known as the Iron Mountain and the Missouri Pacific was practically decided upon. Delegates were present at the convention from eleven of the best counties of the State, and the influence of the meeting was felt in many ways. The years 1836 and 1837 were also memorable in the history of St. Louis for the first appearance of a daily paper, the *Missouri Republican*, commencing its daily issue at about the time of the railroad convention.

The financial panic of 1837 does not appear to have affected St. Louis as much as other cities of the Union, and even at this early stage of its existence, the "Future Great" established a reputation for solidity and financial soundness which has so marked it during the last half-century. The recovery from the depression was so rapid that the year 1839 was distinctly a boom year. The Mechanics' Exchange was formed, the steamboat trade grew enormously, a mayor's court was established and the population increased to upwards of 16,000. During the year more than 2,000 steamboats arrived at the port — no less than 659 during the month of March.

In 1841, the Planters' House was opened, and that the city had attained considerable importance as a manufacturing point is shown by the record of factories and business establishments to be found within it. There were, according to Mr. Edwards, two foundries; twelve stove, grate, tin and copper manufactories; twenty-seven blacksmiths and housesmiths; two white-lead, red-lead and litharge manufactories; one castor-oil factory; twenty cabinet and chair factories; two establishments for manufacturing linseed-oil; three factories for the making of lead pipe; fifteen tobacco and cigar manufactories; six grist-mills; six breweries; a glass-cutting establishment; a britannia manufactory; a carpet manufactory and an oil-cloth factory. There were also a sugar refinery; a chemical and fancy soap manufactory; a pottery and stoneware manufactory; an establishment for cutting and beautifying marble; two tanneries, and several manufactories of plows and other agricultural implements.

In the following year the foundation stone of the Centenary church at the corner of Fifth and Pine streets was laid, and in 1843 immense activity was manifested in the building of commercial structures. Eighteen hundred and forty-four was the year of the disastrous river flood which did immense damage, but which did not prevent 1,146 buildings being erected during the year.

THE GREAT FIRE AND ITS INFLUENCES. In 1846 the Mercantile Library was organized, and the foundation laid for the splendid institution which has done so much educational work for the city in every way. In 1849 the city's progress was checked by a calamitous fire, resulting in a loss of upwards of $3,000,000. The entire area between Locust and Market streets, and from Second street to the river, was devastated, and this catastrophe was followed by another attack of cholera, this time more serious than the first. During the months of May, June and July the number of deaths attributed to cholera amounted to 4,000, and when the scourge was over a stricken and bruised city was left. Under some conditions dual disaster such as this would have discouraged the inhabitants and set back the progress of the city for many years; but the men who were building up St. Louis were of sterner stuff than this, and it has since turned out that the disasters were in many respects blessings in disguise. The new buildings which took the place of the old ones were much more substantial in character and much more metropolitan in appearance and far greater precautions were taken against loss by fire. Main street was widened, the levee was paved and sanitary regulations were adopted which have since proved of immense value to the city.

On October 15th of this year the second great railroad convention was held, and the building of the Pacific Railroad was assured. On the fourth of July, 1851, ground was broken for this road, and in 1852 work was commenced on the Ohio and Mississippi and on the Terre Haute and Alton roads. Thus was the foundation laid for the system of railroads which has made St. Louis the best railroad center in America. In 1855 the St. Louis Agricultural and Mechanical Association was incorporated with Mr. J.

Richard Barret its first president. The site still occupied by the Fair Grounds was purchased and in 1856 the first fair was held.

Early in the same year work was commenced on the Southern Hotel, but the progress made prior to 1861 was inconsiderable. Street railroads began to make their appearance at this period, and it is mentioned as quite an achievement that seven or eight thousand passengers were carried daily. In 1859 the old Post-office and Government building was erected on Third and Olive streets, and Mr. John Hogan appointed postmaster.

When the war broke out the population of St. Louis was a little more than 160,000. Progress was retarded by the " late unpleasantness," but not altogether checked. In 1862 the court house was finally completed, and in 1864 an act was passed by the Legislature incorporating the Illinois and St. Louis Bridge Company. In the following year the Missouri Legislature passed an amended act, and the necessary legislation was also obtained in the State of Illinois. In 1867 the Polytechnic building was finished, and in the same year Captain J. B. Eads completed his plans for the magnificent bridge which still bears his name, and which is regarded justly as one of the wonders of the world. In 1881 the Keystone Bridge Company of Pittsburg undertook the contract for the superstructure, and on the fourth of July, 1874, it was announced with great rejoicing that the magnificent bridge was completed. The tunnel was also constructed, connecting the bridge approach with the old Union Depot, and St. Louis at last was connected directly by means of railroads with the East.

This completes a brief outline of the history of Old St. Louis, from its first settlement by Laclede and Chouteau to the completion of the first bridge across the Father of Waters and the adoption of the Scheme and Charter. No attempt has been made to go into full details, but sufficient has been stated to indicate by what stages the little Indian trading point grew into a frontier village, a county town; an important river port, and finally a great metropolis.

The various events and happenings since the opening of the bridge will be found recorded in the various chapters dealing with the most important features of New St. Louis, a city which is destined to be at an early date the Metropolis of the Mid-Continent, and which is now the commercial and financial metropolis of the tier of prosperous and growing States which make up the great West, Southwest and South.

ANNALS OF OLD ST. LOUIS.

The following table of events of interest connected with Old St. Louis, will also be of value in tracing the growth of the city, and the building of great things out of small. It is not a complete historical index, but deals with points of importance with which every St. Louisan ought to be familiar:

February 15, 1764, Auguste Chouteau landed at site of St. Louis.

Louis St. Ange de Bellerive, French Commander, took possession July 17, 1765.

French supremacy supplanted by Spanish dominion, August 11, 1768.

Pontiac, the great Indian chief, visited St. Ange in 1769, and was murdered while visiting Cahokia.

Lieutenant Governor and Military Commandant Don Pedro Piernas assumed control for Spain, November 29, 1770.

St. Ange de Bellerive, who had accepted military services under Piernas, died in 1774, and was buried in the Catholic cemetery.

Pierre Laclede Liguest laid out and christened St. Louis, March, 1764.

First marriage, that of Toussaint Hanen and Marie Baugenon, solemnized April 20, 1766.

First Catholic church dedicated with solemn ceremonies, June 24, 1770.

First ferry established by Gamasche, June, 1776, forerunner of the Wiggins Ferry of to-day.

Les Petites Cotes, subsequently St. Andrews, now St. Charles, founded in 1769, and Florissant, then called St. Ferdinand, in 1776.

Pierre Laclede Liguest died June 20, 1778, while en route to New Orleans, and was buried somewhere near the mouth of the Arkansas.

Don Fernand de Leyba in 1778 succeeded Don

Francisco Cruyat, a wise and popular Governor in command of Upper Louisiana.

Monday, May 26, 1780, 1,000 Indians, incited by the English, attacked St. Louis and massacred forty citizens. This is known as *l'annee du coup*—the year of the blow.

Don Fernand de Leyba died June 28, 1780, and was succeeded by Lieut. Silvio Francisco Castabana.

The year 1785 was marked by disastrous floods, almost wiping out civilization in the valley. It was called by the French *l'annee des grandes eaux*—the year of great waters.

Boatmen on the Mississippi annoyed by pirates at Grand Tower, and in 1788 ten vessels united in an expedition from New Orleans, vanquished the robbers and reached St. Louis safely. This is known as *l'annee des dix bateaux*—the year of the ten boats.

The winter of 1799 was of extraordinary severity, and went into history as *l'annee du grand hiver*—the year of the hard winter.

Don Manuel Percy assumed gubernatorial control in 1788, the population of the St. Louis district then being 1,197, exclusive of Indians.

The beloved Zenan Trudeau was succeeded in 1798 by Charles Debault de Lassus de Lunerie, a native of France long in the Spanish service, and promoted to lieutenant-governor from military command.

May 15, 1801, marked the first appearance of small-pox, and the settlers commemorated the scourge by a peculiar title, *l'annee de la picotte* —the year of the small-pox.

The military fort of Belle Fontaine was established on the Missouri, near its mouth, by Gen. Wilkinson in 1806. Its site has long since been washed away.

Gen. Merriweather Lewis, the great explorer, and at the time Governor of the Territory, committed suicide in a moment of depression brought on by the hard times prevailing, while on a journey to Louisville, in October, 1809.

The Missouri Fur Company was formed by St. Louisans in 1808, and supplanted the Hudson Bay Company in what afterward became United States territory.

Charter granted St. Louis Lodge, No. 111, Masonic Order, September 15, 1808, to Gen. Merriweather Lewis, being the first lodge in the West.

First fire company organized January 27, 1810.

July 4, 1811, first public celebration of Independence Day.

Earthquake shook St. Louis and vicinity, December 16, 1811.

June 4, 1812, the name of Missouri was adopted for Territory, and first Territorial Legislature met, and the Post-office of St. Louis and departure of delegates to Washington.

First English school opened by Geo. Thompkins in room on Market street, near Second, in 1818.

August 2, 1815, first steamboat, the "Pike," Capt. Jacob Reed, reached the foot of Market street, and was greeted with holiday demonstration.

The Bank of St. Louis, first institution of its kind in the Territory, incorporated August, 1816; Samuel Hammond, president, and John B. N. Smith, cashier.

The Missouri Bank was incorporated February 1, 1817, with Auguste Chouteau, president, and Liburn W. Boggs, cashier.

First Board of School Trustees, formed in 1817, consisted of Wm. Clark, Wm. C. Carr, Thomas H. Benton, Bernard Pratte, Auguste Chouteau, Alexander McNair and John P. Cabanne.

A fine cathedral was built in 1818 on the site of the old log church. It was decorated with original paintings by Rubens, Raphael, Guido and Paul Veronese, but afterwards destroyed by fire, except the gift of Louis XVIII., now in Walnut Street Cathedral.

A duel between Thomas H. Benton and Charles Lucas, April 12, 1817, resulted in the wounding of Lucas. A second meeting on September 27, resulted in his death.

A duel between Joshua Barton, United States District Attorney, and Thomas C. Rector, brother of Gen. Wm. Rector, on Bloody Island, June 30, 1818, resulted in the death of Rector.

St. Louis was incorporated as a city by act of the Legislature December 9, 1822, and William Carr Lane elected mayor, with a board of nine aldermen.

May, 1819, the " Independence," first steamboat, left for up the Missouri, reaching Old Franklin in seven days.

Gen. Wm. H. Ashley's expedition from St. Louis, 1824, reached the great Utah Lake, and discovered the South Pass through the Rocky Mountains.

Marquis Lafayette visited St. Louis April 28, 1825, and was received with great honor and prolonged festivities.

The year 1825 was marked by the erection of the First Episcopal and the First Presbyterian churches. The commencement of the present court house and Jefferson Barracks and the establishment of the United States arsenal were in the next year, 1826.

Convent of the Sacred Heart founded at Broadway and Convent street, 1827, by will of John Mullanphy. It is now located at Marysville, in South St. Louis.

The St. Louis University, under Jesuit control, was permanently opened November 2, 1829, at Ninth and Washington avenue.

First jockey club organized and opened a three-day meeting Thursday, October 9, 1828. The St. Louis Jockey Club opened the Cote Brilliante track June 4, 1877.

In 1829, the first branch of the United States Bank, afterwards a bone of national contention, was established, with Col. John O'Fallon as president.

August, 1831, witnessed the bloodiest duel on record, Spencer Pettis and Major Biddle meeting on Bloody Island, firing at five paces, and both falling mortally wounded at the first fire.

The first water works, located at the foot of Bates street, were put in operation in 1832, and were a private enterprise, and purchased by the city in 1835. The Bissell's Point works were commenced in 1867 and delivered completed July 16, 1870.

The free public school system of St. Louis

under its present form was created by act of Legislature, February 13, 1833. Judge Marie P. Leduc was first president. The first free school was opened in 1837, four years later.

First lodge of Independent Order of Odd Fellows was established June 3, 1835, under the name of Travelers' Rest Lodge, No. 1, and had five members.

The year 1836 was marked by the burning alive by a mob of Francis McIntosh, a negro who had killed Deputy Constable Samuel Hammond, the atrocious event occurring on or about the present site of the old Polytechnic building.

The corner-stone of the St. Louis Theatre was laid in 1836 at Third and Olive, on the spot afterwards occupied by the custom house. N. M. Ludlow, chief of its founders, lived until three years ago. This was the first theatre in the West.

"The year the negroes were hung" was 1841, four men having murdered two young merchants, Jacob Weaver and Jesse Baker, for the purpose of robbery, and then set fire to the building in which the corpses lay. The criminals were early apprehended, and, being convicted, were executed upon Arsenal Island.

The first steamboat sent up the Yellowstone, the departure of the famous Bonneville expedition to the Far West, the exploration of Arkansas and establishment of Fort William, now Little Rock, were events of 1842.

The Bank of the State of Missouri was incorporated February 1, 1837, with a capital of $5,000,000, in time to meet the great panic of that year, during which it temporarily suspended. The Planters' House was commenced same year.

The great Daniel Webster visited St. Louis in the summer of 1837, was entertained at the St. Clair Hotel, and the next day he spoke for six hours to an audience of 5,000 which had gathered to a barbecue in the field which was afterward Lucas Market Square, and is now known as Grant Place.

Centenary M. E. Church corner-stone was laid May 10; Hon. J. B. C. Lucas died; the first steamboat was built in St. Louis; Judge Bryan

Mullanphy was impeached for oppression; July 3, the steamer' Edna blew up and killed fifty-five persons; General Atkinson died at Jefferson Barracks, all in the year 1842.

The Medical Society riots occurred February 25, 1844; the volunteer firemen's riot occurred July 29, 1849; the first of the Know-nothing riots April 5, 1852; a more serious Know-nothing riot August 7, 1854, in which ten persons were killed and thirty wounded, and the great railroad riots in 1877.

The "June rise" of 1844 eclipsed all previous high-water records, the crest being reached June 24, with the flood seven feet and seven inches above the city directrix. Steamboats landed at Second street and plied to the bluffs in Illinois. Over 500 people were rendered homeless. The city directrix was not reached in the abatement until July 14.

October 15, 1849, a mass convention was held at the court house to reconsider the building of a railroad to the Far West, which bore fruit, for on July 4, 1851, ground was broken in the practical commencement of the Pacific Railroad, the humble forerunner of the grand system of railroads now west of the Mississippi river. Thomas Allen was president of the first company.

Washington University was chartered in 1853 under the name of Eliot Seminary, which was, a year later, changed to Washington Institute. Smith Academy was added in 1856, and the University formally inaugurated April 22, 1857. The Law School was added in 1860, and the Manual Training School in 1880.

The old Lindell Hotel, on the site of the present hostelry, was commenced in 1857, and when completed, represented to the people of the country the astounding spectacle of a hotel beyond the Mississippi surpassing in magnitude any other in the United States. It was destroyed by fire in 1867, rebuilt and opened for business in 1874.

The first street car corporation in St. Louis was the Missouri Railroad Company, and the first car was driven by the president of the company, Hon. Erastus Wells, on July 4, 1859, who lived to see the development of the finest system of local transportation of passengers in the world.

In 1874 the Union depot was established and the Eads bridge opened for traffic. The Union depot has outlived its usefulness, but the bridge remains an honor to the city and to the man who designed it.

In 1876 the scheme and charter was adopted, and St. Louis became an independent city without either county government or taxation.

In 1878 the first Veiled Prophet's pageant was seen in the city, and crude attempts were made to illuminate the city.

The Mercantile and Commercial clubs were both organized in 1881.

In 1882 the Cotton Exchange building was opened; work was commenced on the Exposition building, and the first extensive illuminations were seen.

In 1882 the agitation in favor of granite paving on the down-town streets was commenced and took definite shape.

In 1883 and 1884 the Exposition building was constructed, and the first Exposition was held in the months of September and October of the latter year.

In 1884 work was commenced with a view to securing legislation for a rapid transit street railroad in St. Louis, and Old St. Louis ceased to have any practical existence.

CHAPTER II.

NEW ST. LOUIS.

SOME OF THE INFLUENCES WHICH BROUGHT ABOUT THE CITY'S SECOND BIRTH.—A SUCCESSION OF TRIUMPHS.

A WELL-KNOWN character in fiction is represented as expressing doubts as to her birth, and as hazarding an opinion that she was never born at all, but just "growed." So it is to a great extent with New St. Louis. We know to a day when Old St. Louis was born; we know how year after year it grew and flourished, and we know how and when it fulfilled and surpassed early expectations of greatness.

But just when New St. Louis commenced its existence cannot be determined by a reference to the calendar or a quotation from it. Old St. Louis is a thing of the past. The city in its magnificent maturity has "put away childish things" and ranks high among the foremost cities of the world. Its new Union Station is the grandest, largest railway passenger depot in the world, with track facilities and connec-

tions which are at once a marvel of intricacy and simplicity; the largest city on the largest river in the world, St. Louis has also unsurpassed railroad connections, with lines stretching out in every direction and running through every State in the Union; its manufacturing and commercial establishments are numerous and gigantic, and its manufacturing output is increasing more rapidly than that of any other city in the world. The little narrow thoroughfares of our grandparents have given place to some of the best paved and lighted streets in America. The street railway system of St. Louis has become the best in the country, and a veritable model even in these days of rapid transit and electric locomotion. Panics come and go, but the banks of St. Louis weather the storm with the ease of lifeboats, and emerge from it uninjured either in finance or reputation. The parks of St. Louis are exquisite oases of beauty and verdure in the midst of a profusion of commercial palaces and delightful homes, and New St. Louis is in a hundred other ways a model city, not perfect of course, but rapidly advancing towards the ideal of municipal excellence.

But this does not settle the question of the date of the birth of New St. Louis, always assuming that it was born and did not mysteriously grow. The preceding chapter contains a rough outline of events from the founding of the town to the establishment of the city on an entirely independent basis by the adoption of the scheme and charter, and it may be asked—does not New St. Louis date from the severance of the city from the county? Did not Old St. Louis come into existence in 1764 and pass out of it in 1876?

The answer to both questions is " No."

The difference between Old and New St. Louis is far greater than a mere matter of years. It is something infinitely more important than a question of area and boundaries. It involves something much more tangible than a mere increase in material wealth and influence. Old St. Louis clung to the traditions of the past long after it had become one of the largest cities of the Union. It followed where it ought to have led. It scented danger in every new project, and devoted too little energy to measures of aggressive advance. It ignored the rivalry of smaller cities, and allowed them to encroach upon its territory right up to its very gates, and it adopted a policy of ultra-conservatism with a motto, implied if not expressed, that what had made the city great would keep it so for all time and against all comers. In a word it stood still, resting upon its own strength, ignoring the changes which modern invention and enterprise were making around, and ridiculing the idea of a serious deviation from the old established lines. The commercial interests of the city were mostly in the hands of men of mature years, many of whom had come West and grown up with the country, before Horace Greeley had commenced to philosophize.

Some of these veterans heralded the New St. Louis idea with delight, and gave it the support and assistance of advice based upon half a century of hard work. But others, including some whose yeoman service certainly entitled them to rest and retirement, looked less favorably on the necessary rush and hurry of these latter days, in which every man who hopes to succeed must do at least the work of two men. They were literally astounded at the progress St. Louis had made during their sojourn in it, and instead of regarding that progress as evidence of unlimited possibilities, they were inclined to regard it as a magnificent achievement—as a battle valiantly fought and permanently won.

THE SENTIMENT IN 1878.

This feeling of finality, if the word may be used, was well expressed by a local writer in 1878: "Are St. Louis business men unprogressive? Some of our contemporaries out West are disposed to 'poke fun' at St. Louis because of the apparently unprogressive and unenterprising character of those who are rulers in her marts of trade and banks. Well, perhaps it is a truth that St. Louis is provokingly slow, but it would be well to remember that St. Louis is exceedingly sure, that she does not act for to-day only, but for all time. The truth is St. Louis is a very solid city; that the actual financial condition of her business men is a little too good for a very aggressive campaign for traffic. We do not say that the city is in danger of permanent injury from the prosperous condition of her citizens engaged in the business of merchandising, manufacturing, banking, building and other industries. St. Louis is a conservative city, that we readily admit; but the conservatism of our citizens does not lead them to neglect the great interests which center here, and which have thus far led to a great and substantial development. It is true, and we readily admit it, that the rather ultra-conservatism which prevails here sometimes delays the consummation of designs necessary to the continued prosperity of the city, and, to the extent of such delays, retards and injures its commerce. But the good people of St. Louis are neither blind nor destitute of ordinary intelligence.

They know their interests, and will be very certain to guard them with jealous care."

"Guarding with jealous care" is good, but it does not build up a city, nor is it either logical or progressive to speak of "the actual financial condition of business men" as "a little too good for a very aggressive campaign for traffic." Eternal vigilance is the price of a great many blessings besides liberty. A city can never be stationary in anything but location; in commerce, finance and influence it must either gain or lose —it must either achieve victories, or it must be content to suffer losses. Thus it was with Old St. Louis in the zenith of its glory. It ceased to be aggressive, and it lost ground. The census returns of 1880, the last it ever saw, were disappointing in the extreme, and the gains made by apparently insignificant rivals caused a general awaking to the fact that what the city had fought to obtain, it must fight to retain. "Poor old Missouri!" "Poor old St. Louis!" became every-day expressions, and an impression gained ground that St. Louis had seen its best days, that it was a great river town, but not in the race in the days of railroads, and that the western metropolis would not be on the western bank of the Mississippi, in the almost exact center of the great valley to which the Father of Waters gave its name.

New St. Louis is entirely different. Young, untiring men have assumed control of the city in every department, and where there was lethargy and content, there is now ceaseless energy and laudable ambition. People no longer say, "Good enough for St. Louis;" nothing is good enough which is not the very best. St. Louisans no longer hesitate when a new project of gigantic proportions is suggested; they are ready, to adopt a simile only partly applicable, to step in where angels fear to tread. In other words, the city leads where it used to follow; it insists where it used to yield; it frightens those it used to fear.

The change from the old regime to the new was in a measure gradual, and in a measure sudden. It did not take place when the Eads bridge was opened, nor was the extension of the city limits and the adoption of the scheme and charter celebrated by a ringing out of the old and a ringing in of the new. The last three or four years of the seventies belong distinctly to the Old St. Louis period, and we must look to the eighties for the day and hour of the birth of New St. Louis.

THE FIGHT FOR RAPID TRANSIT. And even here it is a case of doctors differing. According to one theory the death-knell to Old St. Louis was sounded when the ground was broken for the first rapid transit road in the city, the old Locust street cable, which in its twists and turns used to throw the passengers around with as little mercy as baggage handlers usually extend toward trunks and valises. Truly, the fight for a franchise was picturesque and emblematical. On the one side was the demand for rapid transit, with the unanswerable argument that time is money, and that there was no reason for St. Louis being content with mules and horses for street car traction, when smaller cities were building cable lines rapidly. The New St. Louis idea was well brought out, and there was a great deal of severe talk about old-fogyism, vested interests, Westinghouse air-brakes on progress, and the like.

As to the Old St. Louis theory, it was literally ridden to death. A good lawyer has been described as an advocate who knows when to stop; but the opponents to rapid transit helped on the good work of reform and progress by comical descents from the sublime to the ridiculous, and by riding their hobby to death. The street car powers that were naturally opposed the project because of its dangerous rivalry, and they succeeded in getting the ordinance so amended as to force upon the promoters what was described as "an impossible route." That is to say, they multiplied the curves and difficulties to such an extent that competent engineers expressed decided opinions to the effect that the road could never be operated even if built. This was fair fighting, but it was accompanied by considerable hitting below the belt. Worshipers of the old idea screamed with horror. Horses would be frightened, wheels would sink into the cable slot, children and even adults would be crushed out of existence by the threatened Juggernaut, and streets would be rendered absolutely impassable. These arguments were raised, not once or twice, but dozens of times, both before the committees of the City Council and House of Delegates, and in the columns of the newspapers. It was a cry of flee from the cars to come, and there was no dearth of prophets to foretell dire disaster as the immediate and certain effect of the proposed profanation of the streets.

Nor was this all. The old story of the man who objected to gas because his father had lived and prospered with no brighter illuminant than a rush-light, was retold in a new form and without the narrators noticing the humor of their argument. St. Louis, they said, had grown into a great city without rapid transit, and what had sufficed in the past would do in the future. It, or rather they, did not need any innovations, and the city's reputation for substantial solidity would be jeopardized by the change. People did not live far enough from their places of business to make rapid transit necessary, it was urged, the theorists calmly oblivious of the fact that they were mixing up cause and effect, and that the reason people lived in crowded homes was because the most attractive and healthy portions of the city were inaccessible to all but the favored few who could afford to keep carriages and horses. Public opinion was divided to a remarkable extent, but common sense finally triumphed, the necessary powers were granted and the road was built.

This was in the years 1884, 1885 and 1886, and, we are inclined to think, a little after the birth of New St. Louis. There was a pitched battle between the old and the new, and both forces organized with sufficient thoroughness to indicate the existence of the new idea which was gaining strength, as well as the old idea which was dying so painfully and so hard.

THE VEILED PROPHET'S INFLUENCE. Again, as evidence of the fact that the grand awakening took place prior to the building of the first rapid transit road, the erection of the Exposition

Building and the inauguration of autumnal illuminations may be recorded. That the Old St. Louis idea is not interred, although it is long past medical aid, is proved by the fact that there are still people to be found who doubt the good influence of hospitality, and who cry *cui bono?* every time St. Louis lays itself out to attract and entertain. But these are in a hopeless minority, for on every hand the opinion prevails that if the Veiled Prophet is not the actual creator of New St. Louis, he was present at the birth and assisted materially in bringing it about. It was the Prophet who taught the people of St. Louis to appreciate the beauties and resources of their own city, and it was the Prophet and his followers who downed cry after cry of the Old St. Louis order.

And if it was not the Prophet who suggested the building of a home for a permanent exposition, who was it? In the years 1883 and 1884, the suggestions took material shape, and it is probable that this event, more than any other, marked the change from the old to the new. The raising of the necessary funds to construct the building, and the general rallying around the standard, roused St. Louisans out of themselves and had an educational influence, the value of which it would be difficult, if indeed it were possible, to overrate. The change was not by any means completed while the work was in progress, because the air was full of prophesies of failure. No city had ever succeeded in making an annual exposition self-sustaining, and was it likely "poor Old St. Louis could"? It was not at all likely; but it was possible for New St. Louis to do what has since been so forcibly demonstrated. The millions of people who have come from east, west, north and south to see the Exposition, the illuminations and the other fall attractions, have carried back to their homes enthusiastic statements as to the grandeur of the city, and have concluded description after description with the qualification that the half had not been told.

In a search for the causes which led to an ignoring of the past and a determination to plan and construct a new future, it would be manifestly unjust to overlook the influence of two of the great clubs of St. Louis — the Mercantile and the Commercial. The Mercantile Club was established three or four years before the Exposition, and it has been the birthplace of nearly every important project which has since seen the light. The meeting at which it was proposed to construct an exposition building was held in the old building on Locust street, and many other projects of untold value to the city were plotted and schemed in one or the other of the rooms of the same building. It was almost an act of vandalism to tear down a club house which had so many pleasing and profitable memories; but it was erected in the reign of Old St. Louis, and was not in keeping with New St. Louis, either in capacity or elegance.

THE COMMERCIAL CLUB AND GRANITE STREETS. The Commercial Club differs from the Mercantile in one essential point. It is a debating society rather than a social club, and it also performs many of the duties which fall to the lot of boards of trade in smaller cities. Since the formation of the Autumnal Festivities Association, with its numerous committees, the Commercial Club has been less heard of than formerly. But in its earlier days it was an immense power for good, and its influence on improvements of the better kind has always been marked. Indeed, it competes with the rapid transit movement and the Veiled Prophet for the right to claim New St. Louis as its own particular offspring. The club was established in the year 1881, and its formation proved to no inconsiderable extent the existence of a spirit of dissatisfaction with the existing condition of affairs and a determination to strike out in fresh lines and pastures new. In March, 1882, Mr. George E. Leighton read a paper before the club in which he spoke strongly on the importance of an improvement in the streets and of better paving. The arguments were heartily appreciated, and if the paper did not result in the immediate repaving of the business streets, it at least opened the eyes of the public to the paramount importance of the work, which was commenced soon after its reading.

Again, the Old St. Louis ultra-conservatism was manifested; and the reform was fought bitterly. At that time, and, indeed, up to the year 1893, the cost of street reconstruction was charged against the property fronting on it, with a limit of charge fixed at one-fourth the assessed valuation, any excess being paid out of the municipal revenues. There is no limit now,* but even with the advantage given property owners under the old law, they protested bitterly, and the board room of the Board of Public Improvements, as well as the committee rooms of the two branches of the Municipal Assembly, and even the mayor's office itself, heard arguments which echoed in sentiment and purpose the still prevailing conservatism.

But the pavements which were good enough for Old St. Louis were not suitable in any respect for New St. Louis, and common sense won again. As the business streets were paved with granite, so did the standing of the city improve. History shows that, almost invariably, good roads and civilization have gone hand in hand; and the moral and commercial influence of good streets in St. Louis has been astounding. Whether the new era was the result of their being constructed, or whether their construction was an incident to the new era, this deponent sayeth not.

In the same line of thought it is difficult to distinguish cause and effect in regard to the phenomenal increase in the extent and importance of the city's manufactures. Certain it is that coincident with the commencement of work on the granite streets and with the building of Exposition Hall, the manufacturing interest had an awakening far too solid and lasting to be looked upon or spoken of as a "boom." New factories and office-buildings began to be erected, old ones were remodeled and enlarged, and "angels of commerce" were sent out to do missionary work in fields never before invaded by St. Louis houses. As rapid transit opened up new territory for homes, this good work con-

---

* The validity of the Stone Law, abolishing the 25 per cent limit, was being tried in the courts when this work went to press.

tinued, and New St. Louis is to-day one of the most important manufacturing and distributing points in the world, leading in many lines and a good second in many more.

So it will be seen that four distinct influences combined to bring New St. Louis into existence about ten years ago. Fortunately, there was an abundance of youthful talent and energy to pilot the old into the new and to take advantage of opportunities as they arose; and, hence, we have to-day a city old only in its history, its solidity and integrity, and new in every other feature—in its buildings, its streets, its manufactures, its commerce and its people.

TWO OUTSIDE OPINIONS ON THE CITY'S NEW GROWTH. Julian Ralph, who is perhaps the best authority of the decade on American cities, owing to the nature and extent of the special correspondence tours he has undertaken, has this to say of the transition or "new growth" of St. Louis:

"St. Louis is the one large western city in which a man from our eastern cities would feel at once at home. It seems to require no more explanation than Boston would to a New Yorker or Baltimore to a Bostonian. It speaks for itself in a familiar language of street scenes, architecture, and the faces and manners of the people. In saying this I make no comparison that is unfavorable to the other western cities, for it is not unfriendly to say that their most striking characteristic is their newness, or that this is lacking in St. Louis. And yet to-day St. Louis is new-born, and her appearance of age and of similarity to the eastern cities belies her. She is not in the least what she looks. Ten or a dozen years ago there began the operation of influences which were to rejuvenate her, to fill her old veins with new blood, to give her the momentum of the most vigorous western enterprise. Six or seven years ago these began to bear fruit, and the new metropolitan spirit commenced to throb in the veins of the old city. The change is not like the awakening of Rip Van Winkle, for the city never slept; it is rather the repetition of the case of that boy-god of

mythology, whose slender form grew sturdy when his brother was born. It was the new life around the old that spurred it to sudden growth." (*Harper's New Monthly*, November, 1892.)

A year later the Springfield *Democrat*, commenting editorially on a large real estate transaction, said: "St. Louis has never in any sense been a 'boom' town, but there is not to-day a city in the country in better repute as a solid, progressive, financial, commercial and manufacturing center, nor one which is making as rapid progress in expansion of trade, in architectural supremacy, or in increase of population. To within fifteen years ago it was regarded as an ultra-conservative town that compromised its future by the rejection of adventitious aids that were seized upon by its windy competitor by the lakes, and was the target of jibes and standing comparisons that were a dead-weight when the present generation took the helm and overthrew tradition by the utilization of every legitimate opportunity that gave the promise of a betterment.

"The New St. Louis is an object lesson for the careful, and, possibly, profitable, consideration of other communities with greater or less aspirations. It has demonstrated that while conservatism is advantageous as breakwater, it is a positive injury as dam to enterprise, and that the maxim, 'nothing venture, nothing gain,' has its application in the building of cities as in the determination of the fortunes of individuals."

FOREIGN CAPITAL AND ITS INFLUENCE. It was a favorite boast of the old regime that "St. Louis owns herself." In other words, the people gloried in the fact that local enterprises were supported exclusively by local capital. This fallacy has long since been exploded, and there is a realization of the fact that the more outside capital that is attracted to the city, the greater the advantage to its mercantile and manufacturing interests. Since the civilized world has begun to appreciate the fact that New St. Louis is one of its most progressive and prosperous cities, millions of outside capital have been attracted to it, and many of the most magnificent of the new buildings have been erected largely or in great part by eastern and even English money. The days of Chinese walls are over, and the city which earns for itself the confidence of the international financial world is the one that makes the most pronounced and prolonged improvement. Charity may begin at home, but it does not end there; and while the investment of local capital and accumulation is the first stepping-stone to municipal growth, the attraction of foreign capital for investment is indispensable in these days of competition and encroachment. Hence, while Old St. Louis was hampered by an excess of exclusiveness and an undue tendency to look with suspicion upon new enterprises from the outside, New St. Louis has sprung to the front and kept there, largely because it has attracted the attention, if not the envy, of the financial and mercantile world of two continents, and because of the impetus investment from the outside has given to almost every one of its industries.

When English gold was paid for a number of the breweries of which St. Louis had long been proud, there was considerable heartache in consequence. But the breweries remain where they were. They pay as large if not larger sums every week to St. Louis men to be spent at St. Louis stores, and for all practical purposes the city derives as much benefit from the industry as ever. True, the idea of the profits crossing the ocean in the shape of dividend warrants is the reverse of pleasant, but the local investment of the foreign purchase-money proved so advantageous in every way, and gave such an impetus to local building, that a great many dividends will have to be paid before St. Louis will lose one tithe of what it gained. And although there are not wanting those who regret the placing of municipal bonds in London during the current year, there are hundreds more who rejoice in the evidence furnished of the city's excellent credit abroad, and who also recognize the fact that had the bonds been subscribed for locally, just so much money must have been

withdrawn from the home loaning capital, to the probable curtailment of local enterprise and business. In short, it is not an unmixed blessing for a city to own itself, and the recognition of this fact has proved of incalculable benefit to New St. Louis in its fight for commercial supremacy—a fight which has been so overwhelmingly successful, and which is still being waged so gloriously and so well.

The preceding chapter closed with a brief chronological summary of events in Old St. Louis. This chapter cannot close more appropriately than with the record of some of the "footprints in the sands of time" made by New St. Louis. Each footprint marks a stride towards improvement and perfection; a casting aside of things that were, and a pressing forward to things that are to be. Reference is only made to distinct and absolute reforms, or movements in the direction of reform.

1881.

Commercial and Mercantile clubs established.

1882.

Agitation for granite streets commenced.

First extensive street illumination.

1883.

Exposition and Music Hall Association incorporated.

Active work commenced on repaving downtown streets with granite.

1884.

First franchise granted for rapid transit (Cable and Western).

Opening of Exposition Building, and first annual Exposition.

1885.

Ground broken for first lofty fire-proof office building.

1886.

First cable road operated.

Union Depot Company formed.

General activity commenced in building associations.

1887.

Streets first sprinkled by municipal contracts.

Charter obtained for second bridge across the Mississippi at St. Louis.

St. Louis made a central reserve city for national banks of other cities.

1888.

Work commenced on new Water-works, capacity 100,000,000 gallons daily.

General movement inaugurated to build freight depots on this side of river for eastern roads.

1889.

Merchants' Bridge constructed.

First electric cars successfully operated.

Largest electric arc light works in the world constructed.

1890.

Merchants' Bridge opened for traffic.

Foundation-stone of new City Hall laid.

Streets and alleys lighted by electricity.

1891.

First county electric road constructed.

New Mercantile Club Building commenced.

St. Louis Traffic Commission organized.

Work commenced on new Union Station.

Autumnal Festivities Association formed, and more than $500,000 subscribed.

1892.

Work commenced on New Planters' House, $2,000,000 hotel.

Sixteen million dollars appropriated by Congress for improvement of Mississippi river.

First postal street railroad car run in the United States on a St. Louis electric railroad.

New buildings erected with a total frontage of thirty-nine miles.

Grand Columbian street illumination.

Smoke Abatement Association formed.

1893.

Electric street car system completed, and last horse car run down-town.

Legislation against black and gray smoke, and first prosecutions under the ordinance.

National financial uneasiness. No bank or other failures in St. Louis.

City four per cent renewal bonds placed in London at par.

Largest Union Railroad Station in the world practically completed.

CHAPTER III.

MANUFACTURES.

A BRIEF SUMMARY OF THE IMMENSE IMPORTANCE OF THE MANUFACTURING INTERESTS OF NEW ST. LOUIS.

IT HAS BEEN asserted by political economists of every school, that production is the only actual and reliable source of wealth. Every nation that has attained eminence of a permanent character has done so by and with the aid of its manufactures; and every country which has gained temporary precedence by any other means has found its glories transitory and its supremacy short-lived. Statesmen and philosophers have differed as to the best means of encouraging home industries, but while the word "protection" has acquired a political meaning, and has become a party watch-word, every party in every country claims that its policy is designed to foster manufacturing in its own territory, and to encourage the production of commodities of every description at home. Especially is this the case in a comparatively new country like the United States. In the early struggles of colonists and exiles, every luxury—including in the term many articles which habit has made necessaries of every-day life—had to be imported from older countries, and the rise of the nation in wealth and influence has been the immediate and direct result of the increase in its manufactures which, although slow at times, has always been continuous. Adam Smith and Stuart Mill, and indeed all authorities on political economy, have proved that manufacturing and greatness go hand in hand, and although the majority of our statesmen during the last quarter of a century, have favored measures at variance in detail with the theories of these authorities, the policy has invariably been to expedite manufacturing supremacy.

And as it is with nations, so is it with cities. The "boom" towns of the West, which built up in a day, fell by the wayside almost as rapidly, because the growth was not the result of legitimate demand, and because the local manufacturing industry was not extensive enough to warrant or maintain the growth. The solid substantial cities of the East have, on the other hand, held their own because of the practical monopoly they have enjoyed in the production of commodities called for by the entire country. St. Louis owes its unique prosperity to the same cause—to the immenseness of its manufactures and the rapid increase in the amount of capital invested, wages paid, and goods produced. The influences alluded to in the preceding chapter made the manufacturing greatness of the city possible, and the greatness in turn has guaranteed the city a glorious future.

Up to the time when New St. Louis reared its head and asserted itself over Old St. Louis, very little encouragement was offered to outside capital or capitalists; and in a number of instances enterprises of great value were in consequence lost to the city. But as the manufacturing public found that a new order of things prevailed, immigration of the most advantageous character set in. Firms and corporations came from other cities and infused new life and energy into our institutions, encouraging a spirit of friendly rivalry and adding immensely to the capacity and output. St. Louis is pre-eminently the best adapted city on the continent for manufacturing. Situated a short distance west and

south of the center of population, it offers advantages in the way of distribution second to no other city, and its magnificent railroad and river connections enable these advantages to be made the most of. Raw material of every description is close at hand, and coal, the great source of mechanical power, is abundant and cheap. The southern Illinois coal fields yield an unlimited supply of excellent coal, which is delivered to factories at prices which excite the envy of manufacturers located elsewhere. The price varies according to the side-track facilities and the length of the haul, but contracts are now being executed at prices as low as $1.20, and even less, per ton. No other large manufacturing city can offer such inducements as this, and in most of them the cost of coal is at least twice as great. Only the manufacturer realizes what an important factor is the price of coal in his calculations, and the advantage which the cheap and good coal of St. Louis gives to the St. Louis producer over his competitors elsewhere.

The output of the coal fields, which are so close to St. Louis that they are part and parcel of its manufacturing greatness, is enormous, amounting to thirty million tons annually. The receipts of coal at St. Louis for the last ten years, or since the city's awakening to the New St. Louis idea, are worth placing on record, because they show what immense increase has been made in the consumption of the great power creating article without which manufacturing cannot successfully be carried on.

	Bituminous Coal. Bushels.	Anthracite Coal. Tons.	Coke. Bushels.
1883	56,687,225	52,000	6,956,500
1884	52,349,000	62,000	3,190,150
1885	53,387,064	80,000	3,500,000
1886	61,258,525	70,000	5,463,950
1887	66,524,925	131,000	9,584,350
1888	67,676,875	136,600	6,757,550
1889	65,403,025	121,500	8,646,200
1890	69,477,225	124,335	9,919,850
1891	72,078,225	139,050	6,924,250
1892	82,302,228	187,327	8,914,100

There are many other influences which have combined to force New St. Louis to the front in this all-important feature. These will be found enlarged upon in other portions of this work. It will suffice here to show briefly to what eminence St. Louis has already attained as a manufacturing city.

St. Louis has 6,000 factories.

It has the largest shot tower in America.

It has the largest iron jail factory in the world.

It has the largest stamping plant in the country.

It manufactures more tobacco than any other city.

It manufactures more chairs than any other city.

Its sugar refineries include the largest in the world.

It has the largest cracker factory in the world.

It is first in the production of stoves and ranges.

It has the largest woodenware factory in America.

It produces more boots and shoes than any other city.

It has the largest and best equipped brewery in America.

It easily leads in the manufacture of saddlery and harness.

The value of the product of 1890 was double that of 1880.

It is the fifth largest manufacturing city in the United States.

It has the largest terra cotta factory in the United States.

Its factory employes earn an average of about $200,000 a day.

It leads in the manufacture of street cars of every description.

It has the largest boot and shoe factory under one roof in the Union.

It is the only western city manufacturing silverware to any extent.

Its reclining chairs are in use in railroad cars in ten different countries.

It is the third largest furniture manufacturing city in the United States.

Its factories find employment for one-sixth of the city's total population.

It manufactures more coffins and caskets than any other city in the world.

It has recently executed the largest order for steam railroad cars ever placed.

It has the largest jeans factory in the United States, and probably in the world.

It manufactures one-fourth of the entire tobacco product of the United States.

It manufactured street cars which are in daily use in England, Australia and Japan.

Its monthly manufactured product is sold for sufficient to pay off the entire city debt.

It is the fourth largest producer of men's clothing, and leads in the higher grades.

It has the largest press brick, fire brick and sewer pipe factories in the United States.

It is first in the manufacture of white lead, with the largest white lead factory in the world.

It has a tobacco factory which has paid more government tax than any other factory in the Union.

It is the home of the largest electric arc light plant and the largest incandescent station in America.

Its millers manufacture more flour than those of any other city in the world, with but one exception.

It manufactured more of the glass used in the World's Fair buildings than any other three cities combined.

Its manufactures are more extensive than those of Kansas City, Omaha, Denver and San Francisco combined.

Its annual manufactured product, on a cash valuation, is twelve times as great as the city's bonded indebtedness.

Its manufactured product is equal in value to over $400 per annum per inhabitant, including men, women and children.

It is the greatest distributing point for agricultural machinery, and ranks among the largest manufacturing cities in this specialty.

Its factory employes are 25 per cent more numerous than when the census was taken in 1890, as proved by the State Labor Commissioner's report, published early in the winter of 1893.

THE GAIN IN EASTERN CITIES DURING THE EIGHTIES. This list does not include every industry or factory which is a record-breaker. It is rather typical than complete, and is given for the purpose of showing that when the statement is made that St. Louis is a manufacturing monarch, there is not even a suspicion of exaggeration. No other city in the world can claim such cosmopolitanism in its manufactures, and no other city can produce such a showing of excellence in such a vast number of varying lines and branches. Nor are the claims a mere matter of surmise. They are based upon actual facts and figures recorded in the census of 1890 (Bulletin 170), and have hence the stamp of official confirmation. The progress made since the war has been both rapid and continuous. In 1860, St. Louis ranked ninth in the list of manufacturing cities. The returns for 1870 were so notoriously inaccurate that they are worthless for purposes of comparison; but the year 1880 found St. Louis in the sixth place, with an annual product of $404,000,000. It was still led by New York, Philadelphia, Brooklyn and Boston, in addition to which Chicago had risen to third place. Pittsburgh was entirely distanced and Providence, Newark, Cincinnati and Baltimore were left far in the rear, St. Louis having made a growth of about 400 per cent for the twenty years as against their comparatively small increases.

During the eighties the influence of New St. Louis made itself felt in a most decisive manner in its manufactures, and during the decade it made a greater increase than any of the great Eastern centers of manufacture. Thus the manufactured product doubled itself during the ten years, while the increase in New York was but fifty-six per cent, in Philadelphia seventy-two per cent, in Cincinnati sixty-seven per cent, and in Baltimore sixty-nine per cent. In the amount of capital invested a comparison is still more favorable to St. Louis, which made a gain of 180 per cent during the decade while the increase in New York, Philadelphia and Baltimore averaged 100 per cent, and the gain

in Cincinnati was about seventy-seven per cent. These phenomenal gains easily placed St. Louis in the fifth place, Boston being overtaken in the race and only New York, Chicago, Philadelphia and Brooklyn left in front of New St. Louis in the race for manufacturing supremacy.

Chicago still leads St. Louis in manufactures. It is not proposed in this work to go into details over the battle royal between the metropolis of the Northwest and the metropolis of the West and Southwest. The contest has been of so long duration and its discussion has become so tiresome in consequence of the almost innumerable charges and counter-charges made, that the subject can profitably be ignored. The territory of each city is so different that there is ample room for both and while Chicago has derived immense advantage from the enormous growth of the new States in the Northwest, St. Louis has the benefit of the almost exclusive trade of the equally important and even more promising States of the West, Southwest and South. Omitting Chicago from the calculation, we find St. Louis by all odds the great manufacturing head of the West. The value if its product is almost twice as great as that of San Francisco, three times as large as that of Minneapolis, six times as large as that of Omaha, seven times as great as either St. Paul or Kansas City, eight times as large as Denver, twenty times as great as St. Joseph, and so much larger than that of any other Western manufacturing point as to make calculations and comparisons impossible and percentage tedious. The value of the manufactured product of St. Louis is equal to the combined output of San Francisco, Denver, Omaha, Kansas City, St. Joseph and all other strictly Western cities.

THE RECORD OF THE ELEVENTH CENSUS. It is not desired to occupy space with a multiplicity of tables or comparisons, but the census of 1890 being necessarily the basis upon which a treatise on the city's manufactures has to be based it is necessary to give a table showing the totals in the most important lines of industry. This is given on the following page:

MANUFACTURING INDUSTRIES IN ST. LOUIS,
CENSUS OF 1890.

INDUSTRIES.	No. of Establishments.	Capital Employed.	Value of Product.
Agricultural Impl'mts	1	$ 686,484	$ 1,107,454
Bags, Paper	3	174,425	431,228
Bak'g and Yeast Powdr	14	373,181	403,772
Blacksmithing a n d Wheelwrighting	219	406,121	898,177
Bookbinding and Bl'nk Book Making	14	196,618	336,227
Boots and Shoes	24	4,170,027	4,250,061
Bread and other Bakery Products	291	1,244,167	3,597,392
Brick and Tile	38	2,531,128	1,691,692
Carpentering	407	4,364 659	10,364,922
Carriages and Wagons	114	2,523,448	3,003,735
Cars (Railroad, Street and Repairs)	24	2,453,443	5,641,252
Chemicals	16	1,500,068	2,672,749
Clay and Pottery Products	13	939,906	899,855
Clothing, Men's	348	5,765,150	9,630,688
Coffee and Spices, Roast'g and Grind'g	9	816,688	2,466,392
Confectionery	48	1,078,426	2,462,037
Cooperage	71	1,042,643	1,912,779
Flouring and Grist Mill Products	21	4,320,955	12,641,000
Foundry and Machine Shop Products	103	10,184,926	11,945,493
Furniture, Upholstering and Chairs	121	3,108,211	4,658,546
Glass	5	842,354	838,930
Iron and Steel	6	2,655,199	2,513,761
Iron Works, Architectural and Ornamental	23	1,732,748	2,023,526
Leather, Tanned and Curried	15	682,753	1,502,680
Liquors, Malt	8	15,910,417	16,185,560
Lumber and other Mill Products and Logs	7	2,766,012	1,689,832
Lumber, Planing Mill Products	23	1,860,036	3,061,178
Masonry, Brick and Stone	160	4,436,578	9,122,952
Oil, Linseed	3	1,018,562	1,438,201
Painting and Paper Hanging	331	867,194	2,841,041
Paints	14	3,498,107	3,163,818
Patent Medicines and Compounds	58	1,601,999	2,196,416
Plumbers' Materials	4	1,280,466	1,465,371
Plumb'g and Gasfit'g	124	581,067	1,651,169
Print'g and Publish'g	213	5,192,065	8,551,349
Saddlery and Harness	110	2,160,963	2,803,961
Slaughtering and Meat Packing	60	3,274,671	12,047,316
Soap and Candles	10	806,301	1,203,406
Tin smithing, Copper smithing and Sheet Iron Working	132	1,132,588	2,369,540
Tobacco, Chewing, Smoking and Snuff	12	3,894,320	14,354,165
Tobacco, Cigars and Cigarettes	296	787,520	1,558,401
All other Industries	2,632	35,915,588	54,515,383
Total, 1890	6,148	$140,775,392	$228,714,317
Total, 1880	2,924	$ 50,832,885	$114,333,375

The exact percentage of increase in the various features is best ascertained by deducting several minor industries not included in the returns for 1880, which leaves the figures as follows:

	1890.	1880.	Per cent of increase
Number of establishments reported	5,453	2,924	86.49
Number of hands employed	90,966	41,825	117.49
Capital invested	$133,292,606	$50,832,885	162.22
Miscellaneous expenses	17,381,271		
Wages paid	52,170,536	17,743,532	194.03
Cost of materials used	120,887,355	75,379,867	60.37
Value at factory of goods manufactured	225,500,657	114,333,375	97.23

The great reduction of prices in almost every line accounts for the fact that although capital and wages show an increase of 162 and 194 per cent, the value of the product only increased 97 per cent. In actual weight and bulk the increase was far greater.

The way in which St. Louis has gained on the largest eastern manufacturing cities during the last thirty years, is shown by the following comparisons of the value of annual product:

New York ... { 1860 $160,000,000
{ 1890 770,000,000

Philadelphia . { 1860 135,000,000
{ 1890 577,000,000

Cincinnati ... { 1860 47,000,000
{ 1890 196,000,000

Boston .... { 1860 37,000,000
{ 1890 210,000,000

Brooklyn .... { 1860 34,000,000
{ 1890 269,000,000

Baltimore.... { 1860 29,000,000
{ 1890 141,000,000

Pittsburgh... { 1860 26,000,000
{ 1890 126,000,000

St. Louis.... { 1860 27,000,000
{ 1890 228,000,000

In 1860 the seven large eastern cities manufactured seventeen times as much as St. Louis; in 1890 St. Louis products equaled one-tenth the total for the seven cities combined.

Since 1860 the manufacturing output of the

seven eastern cities has increased less than 500 per cent; during the same period the increase in St. Louis *has been nearly one thousand per cent.*

A glance at these figures shows how imposible it is to exaggerate the greatness of the city in the important detail of manufactures. It will be observed that the percentage of increase in the number of establishments reported, the number of hands employed, the capital invested, the wages paid, the cost of material used, and the value of the product varied from sixty to nearly two hundred per cent, with an average of over 150 per cent. It will also be noted that the greatest increase was in wages paid, a fact which has a great deal to do with the popularity of St. Louis manufactures. St. Louis has always been noted for the high grade of workmanship its products display, and this is the result in large measure of the care exercised in its selection of mechanics, and the inducements offered them over and above those held forth in other cities. The sweating system is practically unknown in St. Louis, which is also noted throughout the entire country for the excellence of its manufacturing plants and the modernness of its machinery.

It would be interesting, if space permitted, to trace in detail the causes which have led to the center of American manufacturing leaving the Atlantic States, but this would hardly come within the province of an article of this character. One great reason for the growth of manufactures of every kind is the marvelous increase in population and wealth of the district of which St. Louis is the commercial and financial metropolis. This will be found more fully enlarged upon in the chapter relating to St. Louis as a commercial metropolis and distributing point, and it need only be said here that rapid as has been the increase of the city's manufactures, it has continued to act as a distributing point for other manufacturing centers, and that in many lines its jobbers actually import more goods from other centers than in the days when our manufacturing output was comparatively insignificant.

TWO WAYS OF LOOKING AT PLAIN FIGURES. A writer in the *New England Magazine* in January, 1892, speaking of the marvelous showing made by St. Louis in the census returns which had just been made public, says, with a lingering remembrance of the Old St. Louis idea, and with evident danger of being classed as a town boomer or an extravagant writer:

" I now come to speak of the great activity which absorbed the working strength and energies of our people. The situation of St. Louis, at the junction or two great rivers and at the head of deep-water navigation, naturally suggests trade rather than manufacture, yet, even now, it is pre-eminently a manufacturing city. The reports of the tenth and eleventh censuses furnish figures which indicate in a most emphatic manner the growth and tendency of the city in the direction of manufacture during the past ten years. I dare not quote those figures here—they make a showing so extravagantly favorable as to suggest criticism. It is probable that the business statistics for 1880 and those for 1890 were compiled in very different ways, and that comparison should be made with caution."

This rather reminds one of the story of the boy, who, coming home from school with a very favorable report of his year's work, handed it to his father with an apology for being at the head of his class, explaining that the remainder of the boys were inclined to be indifferent, and that it was doubtful whether the system of marking and awarding prizes was good enough to be accepted as final proof of the superiority of those at the top of the class, or the intellectual inferiority or indifference of those at the bottom. In striking contrast to this self-abnegation and pessimism is the explanation which Mr. Robert P. Porter, Superintendent of the Eleventh Census, thought proper to add to the first information ever given out concerning the results of the industrial census of 1890. In an address before the Commercial Club, on November 21st, 1891, Mr. Porter went very fully into the returns, a synopsis of which he had brought with him from Washington, and concluded a thoroughly conservative and logical argument with this peroration:

"Have we not here in the tables which indicate the story of ten years of municipal industrial and commercial progress of a great center of population many things which an organization such as the Commercial Club of St. Louis can rejoice and feel proud over? In ten years you have added over a hundred thousand to your city population, an increase of nearly thirty per cent! The mileage of railroads tributary to your city has gone from 35,000 to 57,000 miles, an increase of sixty-one per cent, while the mileage centering in the city has increased over 10,000 miles, and is now more than 25,000 miles. You received in 1890 15,000,000 tons of freight, an increase of 6,400,000 tons over 1880. In spite of the change from water to rail, your waterways are still a source of profit and can be made still more so. Over $70,000,000 has sought investment in new industry since 1880. Over 44,000 additional artisans have been given employment, making a total of about 86,000 engaged in manufacturing occupations. You are distributing annually nearly $50,000,000 in wages, and have increased your pay-rolls $30,000,000 since 1880. The value of the manufactured product has grown from about $114,000,000 to nearly $214,000,000, a gain of a cool hundred million dollars. And in the fact that the number of children employed in your industry has decreased can be discerned humane sentiment with this increased prosperity. Your municipal finance is sound; your debt is decreasing, and your wealth is $141,000,000 greater than when the last national inventory was taken.

"These are the simple official facts. They are not presented with local coloring, but the data had been collected by government agents under the strict rules which apply to all other communities, and for comparison with all other cities under a system, the tendency of which must necessarily be to understatement rather than overstatement. Within a few days you, as citizens of this fair and progressive city and

of the United States, will be called upon to give thanks for the numerous blessings which Almighty God has bestowed upon the people of this country. Is it presuming too much to venture the suggestion that the continued prosperity of your own city, as shown by the eleventh census, should come in for at least a share of your gratitude, and that you may view with a spirit of fairness a census that has announced to the world such gratifying facts about the great Southwestern river city of the American Continent?" *

This quotation, from what may be described as an official speech by a thoroughly impartial government official, should surely be accepted as proof positive that the figures relating to the manufactures of St. Louis, as published in the eleventh census, may be relied upon. If anything, they understate rather than overstate the increase in the manufacturing importance of St. Louis, because it is a notorious fact that a higher standard was adopted in deciding what was and was not a manufacturing establishment. Thus while many small workshops and factories were omitted from the calculations of 1890, in 1880 very little discrimination was used, and the 2,924 establishments then reported included some far below the standard adopted ten years later. But the census returns for 1890 show how marvelously the New St. Louis idea had taken hold of the city, and how success already achieved was acting as an inducement for further effort. The *St. Louis Globe-Democrat*, commenting editorially on Mr. Porter's speech, said:

"The truth is, St Louis has only just begun to improve her opportunities and to realize upon the profits that logically belong to her. She possesses certain advantages that cannot be taken away from her by any act of hostility, and she is learning how to make the best practical use of them. There are no lurking dan-

* Mr. Porter spoke from the draft returns, several weeks before their final revision and publication. Hence his figures differ slightly from those in the official bulletin, the latter being more favorable to St. Louis than those quoted by the Superintendent and upon which he calculated his percentages.

gers in her financial and commercial system. It is entirely sound and equal to all emergencies. There will be a continuance of past success, with new triumphs of skill and energy. The progress of St. Louis, in short, is one of the fixed facts of American civilization, and her citizens have every reason to be satisfied and grateful."

ST. LOUIS BOOT AND SHOE FACTORIES. Passing from St. Louis manufactures generally to the various lines in which the most remarkable progress has been made, and in which St. Louis most particularly excels, it is natural to deal first with shoes, because in this line the gain has been phenomenal. Old St. Louis made very few shoes, and during the seventies little advance was made in this industry. At that time New England had a practical monopoly in shoe manufacturing, and the idea of the west producing a rival to Boston and Lynn had never been thought of. Now, however, St. Louis has the largest shoe factory under one roof in the country, with others almost as large and as well equipped, and it manufactures more shoes than any other single city in the Union. The accuracy of this assertion has been challenged, and it is undoubtedly true that Boston is still the greatest distributing point for boots and shoes in America, and probably in the world. But Boston is situated in the midst of a shoe manufacturing district, and by actual count it does not produce within its city limits as many shoes as its once despised but now powerful western rival.

In 1880 there were 184 establishments in St. Louis devoted to the manufacture of boots and shoes. The capital invested was less than $700,000, and the number of men employed was only 658, with 217 girls and 197 children. The aggregate product was about $1,600,000. It will thus be seen that the average number of men per factory was less than four, and that the annual value of the product was less than $10,000 per establishment. It is evident from these figures that the bulk of the establishments reported were practically retail stores with a custom-made connection, and, indeed, there were not in St. Louis at that time any large factories in the 1893 sense of the term. To-day we have one factory selling three times as many shoes as the total product for the year 1880, and at least ten which will each exceed that total within a very short period. In 1882 St. Louis manufactured less than half a million pair of shoes, but about this period there was a distinct awakening, and in 1886 about a million and a quarter pairs were made, valued at about $2,000,000. For the next four years the increase was rapid, and when the census was taken again in 1890 the value of the product was found to have increased to $4,250,961, an increase over the figures of 1880 so enormous as to make the most indifferent wonder.

We have seen that 1880 the average number of men per factory was less than four, and that the annual value of the product averaged less than ten thousand dollars to each establishment. In 1890 the average number of hands per factory was one hundred, and the average product of each factory was nearly $140,000. The custom work and repairing shops, which were classed as factories in 1880, were returned separately in 1890 and numbered 477. It will be seen from these figures that the census enumerators in 1880 were much more lenient and less exacting than those of 1890, and that during the ten years St. Louis practically established what may be termed a wholesale shoe manufacturing industry, and brought it into the first rank. Since the census was taken in 1890 the output has more than doubled. New factories, magnificent in elevation and marvelous in internal arrangement and equipment, have been erected every year, and these have enabled the city to outstrip more competitors. To-day the monthly output is larger than the annual output twelve, if not ten, years ago. In other words St. Louis is manufacturing boots and shoes worth a million dollars every month in the year, and is adding to its capacity with a regularity and persistency which indicates that before the end of the present century it will have attained an eminence in this line which will make it the great manufacturing and distributing point of the bulk of the American continent. Its factories are a subject of general admiration, and are to be classed among the attractions which excite the admiration and surprise of visitors from every section of the Union.

St. Louis-made boots and shoes are in demand all over the western and southwestern territory, and they are shipped in very large numbers to all points, quite a large number of cases going east and north every month. The shoes have a reputation for durability and style. Competing cities have sometimes stated that St. Louis shoes are of a heavy type, and that only the agricultural and laboring demand is catered for. This is entirely erroneous. Boots and shoes suitable for out-of-door work are made in St. Louis and are of the highest grade, but lighter and more elegant kinds are also produced in immense quantities. St. Louis-made shoes obtained the highest awards at the World's Fair, and orders are received from connoisseurs as far away as San Francisco and Montreal. Strange to say a comparatively small percentage of the local retail trade is supplied from St. Louis factories. There are various trade reasons for this which time only can overcome. The president of one of the largest shoe manufacturing corporations in the city, on being asked why it is so difficult to obtain a single pair of the remarkably fine shoes his house was producing in such large quantities, said:

"This is a characteristic of the shoe trade all over the world. Shoe dealers carry more coals to Newcastle, to quote the favorite English expression, than any other trade. We ship immense quantities of shoes to cities which have large factories of their own, and while we are sending out cases by the thousand, we still handle large shipments from New England. We have never encouraged a local trade for our manufactured product, because we have found outside trade pays the best. If we were to supply the retail stores direct, we would have errand boys and clerks, at all hours of the day, asking for individual pairs of shoes of special size and grade. As it is, our orders are much more wholesale in character and suit the exigencies of our trade much better."

MEN'S CLOTHING. The men's clothing manufacture of St. Louis is, at least, ten times as extensive as is generally supposed. Centralization is the policy in the shoe trade and it is quite easy to appreciate the work that is done by the magnificent factories which greet the eye on every side; decentralization is the invariable policy of the clothing manufacturer, who, instead of having all his departments under one roof and close at hand, finds it more profitable to give out his work in sections to smaller factories or shops, which make specialties of various lines of work. This plan prevails in St. Louis, as elsewhere, and hence there is very little to indicate that the value of the product is already largely in excess of ten millions per annum and increasing rapidly. It is to the credit of the St. Louis clothing trade that little or no shoddy goods are made in the Southwestern metropolis. Woolen goods of varying grades are chiefly made, large quantities of cloth being imported from the European markets, mostly coming direct in bond to the port of St. Louis. Special attention is paid to cut and finish, and St. Louis clothes are shipped to those markets which appreciate a high grade of goods.

Mention has already been made of the fact that the sweating system is discountenanced in St. Louis. In no other line of industry is this fact so apparent as in men's clothing. From time to time exposures have been made of the disease-breeding hovels in which home work in the clothing trade is performed in the large cities of the East and of Europe. Careful investigations by labor commissioners, philanthropists and others have failed to reveal a single instance in St. Louis where this dangerous system prevails. The business is in the hands of men of exceptional intelligence and integrity, and it is their special care that every garment given out by them shall be made and completed in a properly constructed and ventilated room. The clothing trade generally appreciates this policy, which is in a large measure

responsible for the ever-increasing popularity of
St. Louis-made clothes.

In further evidence of the high grade of the
product in this line, it may be stated that shipments are made to States as far removed from
St. Louis as Georgia, California and Washington. An interesting contest has been going on
for years between New York and St. Louis for
the trade of Texas. It is now practically over,
St. Louis having well-nigh driven its eastern
competitor from the field. The increase in the
orders from this and other Southwestern States
are causing phenomenal growth in the St. Louis
clothing trade. Already the city has the largest
jeans factory in America, and projects are in
contemplation which will give it equal prominence in other branches of this industry.

FURNITURE AND CHAIRS. Among the other industries which may be classed
as domestic in character,
the furniture manufacture of St. Louis must be
specially mentioned as typifying the exceptional
growth of the city's commercial interests. Its
steady and continuous growth is due largely to
the excellent work done by the St. Louis Furniture Board of Trade, one of the most useful
trade organizations in the city. Mr. George T.
Parker, Secretary of the Board, expresses the
situation very accurately when he says: "Up to
ten years ago St. Louis was not known as much
of a furniture manufacturing city; now it is one
of the foremost. Within ten years this industry has increased over a hundred per cent. The
advance of the city in all lines during the last
decade has been partly responsible for this; but
to the aggressive and progressive nature of the
men who managed this branch of industry is due
the present business of fully twenty millions."

It is only necessary to glance at the census
returns of 1880 to see how phenomenal has been
the growth of this business. There were in that
year but seventy-two establishments, employing
about one thousand hands, to whom were paid
about half a million dollars a year in wages.
Now the number of establishments is at least
one hundred and fifty, the number of men employed is considerably in excess of three thou-

sand, and the annual disbursement in wages is
more than two millions. These figures include
the chair factories, which are even more remarkable in their growth and individuality than the
establishments devoted to the production of furniture of various kinds. Especially in reclining
chairs for railroads has St. Louis made itself
famous; and contracts involving thousands of
dollars in this line alone are constantly being
placed in the city, in which several valuable
patents are owned.

The exceptional advantages of St. Louis as
a lumber—especially hardwood—market, have
helped to bring the city from obscurity to prominence in the matter of furniture manufacture, and
its central location also helps it to gain on
its competitors. It now occupies at least third
rank in manufacturing cities, and if the present rate of progress is maintained it will soon
lead the entire country. Car loads of furniture are shipped in every direction, and the
high reputation which the product of the city
has made for itself throughout the entire United
States, and also in Mexico, makes it comparatively easy to obtain orders even in districts upon
which other manufacturing cities claim an iron-
clad mortgage.

The Furniture Board of Trade is entitled to
more than a passing notice. Its work has been
of a most valuable character, and one of its
latest achievements was the securing of the
National Furniture Convention for St. Louis in
1893. It maintains a credit department, which
has proved of immense value, and it has made its
influence felt in national legislation on more occasions than one. From reports issued by this
body it is shown that more chairs are made by
three St. Louis factories than by all the factories
combined in any other city in the country.
In kitchen safes it makes more than all the
rest of the United States; and the spring bed
industry is remarkably large. The railroad
car chairs already referred to are being used in
cars and "coaches" in India, Russia, England,
Australia and South America, and the Board of
Trade is now in negotiation with other countries
not generally looked upon as accessible, but

which offer a magnificent market. Among the
accessories to the furniture trade which are
specially prominent, may be mentioned the manufacture of coffins and caskets, in which St. Louis
easily leads the entire country.

IRON AND KINDRED INDUSTRIES. It is difficult to estimate
the actual extent of the
iron and kindred indus-
tries of St. Louis, owing to the fact that the
number of branches is so great that the figures
are necessarily freely subdivided. Under the
head of "Iron and Steel" the census returns six
large establishments, with a total capital employed of a little over $2,500,000, and with an
output about as large. This, however, does not
begin to cover the local trade, for under the
head of "Architectural and Ornamental Iron
Work," there is found the record for 1890 of
twenty-three establishments, employing a capital of $1,700,000, and with a total output of
about $2,000,000. Under "Foundry and Ma-
chine Shop Products," the record is still greater,
the figures for 1890 showing that there were 103
establishments in operation, with a capital of
upwards of $10,000,000, and with a total pro-
duct of about $12,000,000. To produce this,
over 6,000 men were employed, and their earn-
ings for the one year approximated $4,000,000.

Even under the head of "Bolts, Nuts, Wash-
ers and Rivets," four establishments are recorded, with a capital of more than a quarter of
a million, and an output of similar value; and it
would appear as though $20,000,000 would be a
small estimate of the total product in the iron
and steel and kindred industries, which find
employment for millions of dollars of capital
and for an almost unlimited amount of labor.
In 1880, Governor Johnson, in an address before
the State Immigration Convention, spoke of St.
Louis as the "Center of the World's trade, the
future metropolis of the World's Empire, the
favored child of the mighty Valley of the Mississippi, the City of the Iron Crown." Since
that time great progress has been made in the
iron and steel industry throughout the country,
and although, perhaps, the gain has not been
so phenomenal as the eloquent speaker desired

or anticipated, yet it has been great enough to
more than justify his remarks. Certain it is,
that within easy distance of St. Louis there is
an abundance of iron ore sufficient to supply the
requirements of the world for generations to
come, with every indication of still greater un-
discovered supplies. The unlimited supplies of
coal, timber and water-power, and other similar
aids to manufactures of this character, make it
appear probable that St. Louis will eventually
outpace all competitors in the race and become
the leader in iron, as in other industries.

St. Louis commenced the manufacture of iron
nearly eighty years ago, and although the production was on a very limited scale it had the
effect of introducing other work of a similar
character. Foundries came to be erected, and
many thousands of wagon-boxes and tires were
manufactured here during the first quarter of
the present century. Foundries on a larger
scale were established about the year 1830, and
long before the middle of the century the city
had assumed quite an activity in the iron trade.
Agricultural implements, and everything in
which iron was used to any large extent, began
to be manufactured in large quantities, and
about the year 1850 the magnificent resources
of the Iron Mountain began to be appreciated.
The splendid furnaces and rolling mills belonging to the Chouteau family began to exert an
influence over the city's trade, and in 1856 a
careful estimate showed the existence in the
city of as many as thirty iron works, with a
total output of about $5,000,000. The amount
of pig metal mined and produced at this early
period exceeded 100,000 tons a year, and all
through the sixties and seventies the business
was pressed to full advantage.

In agricultural machinery St. Louis is well to
the front, and many of its specialties are in demand
in very remote centers. Some of the largest factories in this line to be found in the entire
country are situated in St. Louis, and the high
standard of work, in every detail, keeps up
the demand. Travelers through Mexico have
been struck with the very general use in that
country of agricultural machinery made in

St. Louis; and in all parts of the rich agricultural country in St. Louis territory, the products of our local factories are appreciated at their full worth. As soon as more intimate trade relations with Mexico and the Spanish-American republics are encouraged by a mutual reduction of tariffs, a further immense impetus will be given to this business, and St. Louis will easily maintain its position as a manufacturing point for agricultural machinery of every kind. In carriages and wagons, which are in a measure connected with this industry, St. Louis has been prominent and famous for years, and the increase in its output since the census of 1880 has been a subject of general comment in trade circles everywhere.

RAILROAD SUPPLIES AND STREET CARS. In cars of every description, the city is a producer on a thoroughly wholesale plan. Its railroad supply houses execute orders from railroads with headquarters in cities many miles distant, and the output of cars, both freight and passenger, is very large. It is an interesting fact to record that, within the last two years, one of the prominent factories has executed a larger order for cars than was ever given, at one time, to any other factory in America. The growth in this industry has been stupendous. It is estimated that the value of the output during the year 1892 exceeded $8,000,000, and this is probably correct, although, if accessories were added, the total would be much larger. The census of 1880 only recorded the existence of seven establishments in this line, which were credited with employing a capital of some $314,000, and with having 601 men on their pay-rolls. The value of the output was placed at a little over a million dollars. In 1890 twenty-four firms were returned in the government census, their combined capital was stated at $2,500,000, and the number of men and boys on their pay-rolls approximated 3,000. They paid, in wages alone, nearly twice the sum total of the product of 1880, and the total result of the year's work was placed at a trifle less than $6,000,000. These figures are very conserva-

tive, and the estimate for 1892 is much more nearly accurate than the official record for 1890.

In the manufacture of street cars St. Louis easily leads the world. Prior to the war the city turned out large numbers of passenger-carrying vehicles, and even during the war a very extensive stage-coach, omnibus and transfer business was done here. At the close of the war a fresh impetus was given to the business, and for the first time St. Louis vehicles began to acquire prominence in the country. Other large western cities commenced to manufacture omnibuses and similar vehicles, but they did not possess either equal advantages or similar enterprise, and St. Louis soon forged to the front and secured a foremost position, which it has held ever since. Mechanics of ability were attracted here, and, when late in the sixties an improved type of street cars was produced, attention was attracted from all parts, and the new type of vehicle came to be regarded as a standard one. During the fifteen or twenty years which followed, street cars of every description were manufactured here, and improvements of every character were introduced. The demand for bobtail cars was met by the manufacture of these somewhat unsatisfactory vehicles, and so many St. Louis improvements were introduced that they lost much of their original unpopularity.

The introduction into St. Louis of rapid transit, some six or eight years ago, led to another marked revival in this industry, and the resources of the establishments were soon taxed to their utmost to meet the demands of the energetic street railway presidents, who insisted on getting the best of everything, regardless of price. Some of the cars in use on local street railroads at the present time are unequaled, and, indeed, scarcely imitated in any other city, and so many patents have been produced here that the name of St. Louis is identified with nearly all of the best types of street railroad cars to be found in any city in the Union.

Very large shipments are made from time to time to Chicago, some of the roads in that city having been equipped exclusively by St. Louis houses. The awakening in New York in favor of surface rapid transit has also been felt in an advantageous manner in St. Louis, orders of a very large character having been placed here during the last two or three years. Boston, Baltimore, Washington, Columbus, Cleveland, Kansas City, Denver, Salt Lake City, Milwaukee, Detroit, Minneapolis and St. Paul have all looked to this city for street railroad supplies, and extensive shipments have also been made frequently to extreme southern points, such as New Orleans and Galveston, to say nothing of such distant cities as Los Angeles, Portland and Tacoma.

Nor is the popularity of St. Louis street cars confined to the United States. A good lesson in geography can be learned by a glance over the shipping books of any one of the gigantic street car factories of this city. England buys from St. Louis freely, while there are now running on Australian streets, cars made in the northern portion of St. Louis. A year or two ago an order was received and executed whereby the subjects of the Mikado of Japan were given an insight into the progress made by the street car builders of America in general, and of St. Louis in particular.

SADDLERY AND HARNESS. St. Louis is by far the best saddlery and harness center in the United States. When it was merely a frontier town it commenced the manufacture of saddles and harness for the use of immigrants and pioneers, and when the war broke out the number of people engaged in the business was considerable. During the war immense orders were placed in St. Louis for army saddles and harness, and this is one of the few industries which in consequence did not suffer materially from the national disaster. During the last quarter of a century the business has assumed immense proportions, and a careful review of the transactions of the twelve exceptionally large factories of St. Louis, and of the many smaller ones, indicates that the annual value of the output is now a little more than $5,000,000. The trade is very varying in character. St. Louis has a practical monopoly of the business in the Western and Southwestern States, and to these it ships saddles of the Texan or Mexican type of the most elaborate character, some of them heavy enough in themselves to provide what would appear to be quite a considerable load for the little animals on which they are usually fitted. But the trade is not by any means restricted to heavy saddles for cowboys and farmers. Some of the best retail establishments in New York obtain their supplies from St. Louis, which also ships to points as far distant as British Columbia and even Europe. Light racing saddles of great popularity are made in the city, and harness of every description is also produced. One of the largest whip factories is to be found here, and in every department activity prevails. During the last eight or ten years the practice of sending out of the city for supplies needed in these kindred trades has entirely died out, and now nearly everything required is made at home, and an additional impetus thus given to other branches of the leather industry.

STOVES AND RANGES. For its stoves, ranges and furnaces St. Louis was famous long before it took first rank among manufacturing cities, and it has maintained its supremacy to this day. The history of the industry is the history of the lives of some of its best-known citizens, and it is full of facts which are far stranger than fiction. The value of its output in these lines is considerably in excess of two millions per annum, and is increasing, not every year, but every month. The largest factory in the world devoted to this class of manufacture is situated in St. Louis, and the name of the city is a by-word with all who handle stoves or ranges of any description. There are no geographical limits to this trade. St. Louis ships to every State in the Union, and to all parts of the American continent. Europe has been slow in appreciating the value and convenience of American stoves and ranges, but of late years St. Louis has shipped many of its best products in this line to London and other trans-Atlantic markets. St. Louis ranges swept everything before them at the World's Fair, and came back loaded down with blue ribbons.

THE LEAD INDUSTRY IN DIFFERENT BRANCHES. St. Louis is the largest white lead manufacturing city in the world, and it continues to increase its output every year. The annual yield now exceeds 30,000 tons in weight and $1,000,000 in value. The three largest factories in the country are in the city, and their capacity appears to be unlimited. The figures would be even more astounding but for trade combinations which have had an effect on prices and restricted the output throughout the entire country. Pig lead had been held for too great an advance, and this had the effect of putting up the price of white lead too high, giving the dealers in mixed paints an opportunity to compete more bitterly than ever. The heavy floods in the Mississippi Valley of two or three years ago also had a depressing effect on this industry, which however has nearly regained lost ground and is now in a very flourishing condition, with annual shipments of white lead amounting to something like forty million pounds, as compared with fourteen millions in 1880 and twenty-one millions in 1886. The trade is one in which great variation in the annual output is unavoidable, but the general tendency in St. Louis is decidedly in the right direction, and there is no fear of the city's claim to supremacy being challenged in the long run.

Another branch of the lead business which has shown even more remarkable and satisfactory increase is lead pipe and sanitary supplies generally. One of the largest plumbers' supplies establishments in the world is located in St. Louis, with a large branch in an Illinois city. It has advertised St. Louis throughout the entire labor world by the successful efforts of its controllers to introduce the profit-sharing system into its pay-rolls. One effect of this act of genuine philanthropy has been to so popularize and strengthen the local trade that it is very unusual for any supplies to be obtained from out of the city, in spite of the fact that some of the eastern factories boast themselves of being the best in the world; and besides establishing a practically local monopoly, the enterprise of the establishments has enabled them to make vigorous inroads into the territory of New York and Boston manufacturers, shipments in this line of business going daily to the Atlantic and Pacific Coasts and even to foreign countries.

In the South and Southwest St. Louis is known as a great sanitary plumbing center, and in many lines of business the factories can hardly keep up with the heavy orders their own enterprise has called forth. The more general incorporation of bath-room accommodations in private houses, together with the enormous quantity of plumbing called for in the commercial palaces which are being erected in every part of St. Louis, have also combined to keep the factories busy and to drive away any possible fear that might exist as to the future of the city in this regard. Improved methods in building, which have enabled contractors to keep up their work for the entire year instead of limiting their operations to six or eight months in the spring, summer and fall, have abolished the quiet time which used to be looked for in the plumbers' supplies industry in winter, and taken away the possibility of catching up with orders in arrear during the winter months. The capacity of the factories has been steadily increased, and although the sales of sanitary plumbing materials now exceed four millions per annum, the supply is ample without going out of the city for assistance.

St. Louis is the largest shot manufacturing and distributing center in the world. Nearly a million dollars are invested in the shot towers, and these convert into shot 6,000 to 10,000 tons of pig lead every year. The competition in this line of business is heavy, but the local manufacturers succeed in holding their own and in doing a profitable business in spite of drawbacks. The census of 1890 gave some interesting information as to the capital employed and the number of men engaged in the various industries connected directly with lead. This shows that upwards of 4,000 men find employment in this line, to say nothing of an immense number of others who are engaged in kindred industries returned under other heads.

BRICK AND SEWER PIPE. St. Louis bricks are in demand as far east as New York, as far west as the towns on the Pacific Coast, and as far north as Canada. The clay found in the neighborhood of St. Louis is the finest in the country, and nearly 100,000 tons of it are shipped out of the city yearly, though enough is kept at home to make St. Louis one of the largest brick manufacturing cities in the world. The clay is free from gravel, and can be made into brick with the aid of water and shovel alone. Such primitive modes of construction have, however, been long since superseded by machinery. One company alone makes over 100,000,000 bricks in St. Louis every year, and it is almost impossible to ascertain the actual total output, though it far exceeds 200,000,000 annually. Hydraulic press bricks are a specialty of St. Louis, and their popularity throughout the entire country is generally known. These, together with the other most popular St. Louis-made bricks, are in growing demand in all sections, and during the year 1893 the capacity for manufacture was increased to a most remarkable extent.

Other clay manufactures show almost equally astounding totals for St. Louis. There is an abundance of good fire clay to be found near the city and, indeed, within its corporate limits. Sewer pipe is also produced in immense quantities, the output exceeding fifty tons every year. The local demand, which is always heavy, is augmented by large orders constantly received from all the central and Western States, and there are, in addition, sales every year in New England and on the Pacific Coast. This is an industry which has made enormous strides during the last few years. The exceptional value of the trade is now generally admitted, and inquiries are being received from manufacturers in all sections who are looking out for suitable territory in which to carry on their business.

The *Clay Record*, published at Chicago, in a recent review of the brick industry of the United States, said:

"The increasing use of pressed brick in this country is due more largely to the growth of the St. Louis manufacture of pressed brick than any other cause. St. Louis ships pressed brick to New York, New Orleans, San Antonio, Duluth and Seattle. It is the head and front of the pressed brick industry. Its product last year was 220,000,000 brick. Fifteen years ago the product was not 30,000,000, and these latter figures include brick made by the old-time process. One St. Louis company is the biggest manufacturer of pressed brick in the world, and has branch yards in several cities. It began operations twenty-five years ago, with every architect in the country opposed to pressed brick. Now nearly all of the tallest buildings in America are made of this material. The St. Louis brickmaking capacity has increased within fifteen years from 240,000 a week to 2,000,000. Nineteen hundred workmen are employed, and even in the East, where brickmaking has at least reached something like the proficiency of the West, St. Louis brick is preferred, though it must be purchased at an advance over the price paid for native brick. There is some virtue in the St. Louis clay, which also adds to the quality of the brick.

"The fancy and ornamental brick trade was not known there fifteen years ago. It is now a great business. Over 250 different shapes and designs are kept in stock. Gravel brick, unknown, save in England, fifteen years ago, are now made in St. Louis with as good success as in England. The only terra cotta works in St. Louis began in a small wooden building in 1882. Now they are shipping their product East, West, North and South. A quarter of a million represents their annual output.

"St. Louis leads in fire brick and fire clay products. Fifteen years have shown wonderful growth. The Cheltenham district produces more fire clay sewer pipe than any other district in the United States. The St. Louis output of brick is but little behind the entire output of the State of Ohio, and fire brick, gas retorts, chimney tops, fire-proofing, crucibles, and sewer pipe are the Cheltenham goods. The City of Mexico, Monterey, and all the eastern cities use its fire brick. It turns out, at full capacity, three miles of clay sewer pipe a day. One concern ships thirty-five to forty tons of fire brick. St. Louis has the best fire clay out of England. Near Rolla, Missouri, is another great deposit, even more refractory than that found here in such inexhaustible quantities. There are eleven fire brick firms. The shipments last year were 9,329 cars of fire brick at $90 a car, 747 cars of fire clay at $35 a car, and 2,211 cars of tile at $195 a car. The industry employs 1,172 hands."

THE BREWERIES OF ST. LOUIS. The beer brewing industry of St. Louis ranks among the most important of its manufactures. The city is one of the first beer manufacturing cities in the world, and it boasts proudly of the largest brewery in the United States and the most magnificent brewery in the world. At the world's competition at Chicago, this year (1893), St. Louis beer won the highest award, scoring more points than the products of any other city. This is an industry which has more than kept pace with the growth of the city, a fact which a perusal of the following extract from the *Missouri Republican*, of September 20, 1854, clearly indicates:

"St. Louis has about twenty-four breweries, and every one of them has stored nearly twice the quantity of ale, for this summer, that has been made in any preceding one. As we are informed by one of the largest dealers of this article, the quantity may safely be reckoned at forty thousand barrels of lager beer and, perhaps, twenty thousand barrels of common beer. By an average count, one barrel of about thirty gallons gives about three hundred glasses. Thus we have about twelve million glasses of lager beer and about six million glasses of common beer. Common beer is sold at five dollars per barrel and lager beer at seven dollars, that is at wholesale. This will make the amount received by the brewers: for lager beer, $290,000, and for common, $100,000. The retailers, at five cents a glass, took in $600,000 for lager beer, and $300,000 for the common article. Just think of it, nearly a million dollars spent in St. Louis, during one summer, for beer."

In 1860, 122,400 barrels of lager beer, 85,500 of common beer, and 4,400 barrels of ale were manufactured, worth at wholesale $1,500,000, so that during the six years preceding the war the brewing industry of St. Louis increased with remarkable activity. Between 1860 and 1870 the production of beer more than doubled itself, and during the next seventeen years the increase was nearly five hundred per cent, for at the present time the breweries of St. Louis are producing fully 2,000,000 barrels, or more than 60,000,000 gallons yearly. The following table shows the increase, year by year, since 1877, with but one fractional decrease during the entire period:

Year.	Barrels.	Gallons.
1877	471,232	14,608,192
1878	521,684	16,172,204
1879	613,667	19,023,677
1880	828,072	25,670,232
1881	959,236	29,739,313
1882	1,069,715	33,661,165
1883	1,100,000	34,100,000
1884	1,122,265	34,790,215
1885	1,086,032	33,666,992
1886	1,280,091	39,682,821
1887	1,383,361	43,557,872
1888	1,482,883	46,710,815
1889	1,546,587	48,717,490
1890	1,856,883	58,498,114
1891	1,810,812	56,135,172
1892	1,961,449	60,814,919*

The census returns for 1890 go more fully into the growth during the eighties. Thus, in 1880 the capital invested in this industry was returned at $4,000,000, just one-fourth the total for 1890. During the ten years the army of employes increased from 1,200 to 2,800, and the annual wages from a little more than half a million to two millions and a quarter. The value of the product annually appears to be almost identical with the capital invested, and the increase during the ten years was hence about four hundred per cent. Several new breweries have been started since the census was taken, and at the present time the number of men employed ex-

---

*The returns for 1893 could not be included in this work. Taking the actual figures for November and estimating for December, the number of gallons would be about 63,000,000.

ceeds 3,700,* to whom there are paid in wages at least two and a half million dollars.

There are about twenty-five large breweries in St. Louis, in addition to several others which are small only by comparison. Reference has been made in the preceding chapter to the purchase by the English syndicate of some fifteen of our most prominent breweries. This transaction was completed some five years ago, and the syndicate has so increased the capacity of its enormous plants that it now produces three-quarters of a million barrels of beer annually, and can increase its output to a million and a half barrels when the demand makes it necessary. The purchase of the breweries by these capitalists created quite a sensation, and called attention to St. Louis in a variety of ways. The two largest breweries held aloof from the transaction, and could not be tempted by English gold. These breweries are visited every year by thousands of tourists, and a regular system of guides to pilot the strangers over the immense plants is maintained. The largest of them is in itself a small town, in addition to which it maintains branches in New York, Boston, Philadelphia, Pittsburgh and other cities, and the actual number of its employes exceeds 4,000. Shipments are made to Mexico, to West Indies, Central America, Brazil, the Sandwich Islands, Australia, Japan, China and other equally distant points. Quite recently another attempt has been made by wealthy London bankers to obtain control of the two mammoth breweries of St. Louis which have so far reserved their individuality. The effort was not successful, but the persistency of those making the offer cannot be regarded as other than a well-merited compliment to a city which is just beginning to be appreciated at its full worth in the old world. During the years 1890, 1891 and 1892 new establishments have been erected in St. Louis, and increased competition has been

*State Labor Commissioner's Report, 1893. These calculations exclude resident agents and salesmen, traveling men, clerical help, etc. The Anheuser-Busch Brewery, alone, finds employment for more men than are returned for all the breweries combined, but its vast army of employes includes many hundred men who are not brewers or actual producers.

created. St. Louis is not quite the greatest beer producing city in America, but it does not fall far below the leaders in this respect, and before the century expires it will pass at least two of the three cities which now lead it.

TOBACCO AND CIGARS.

In tobacco St. Louis leads the entire country, a fact which can be easily proved by reference to the returns made yearly to the government officers and to the amount of revenue paid. Our largest tobacco house has the record of paying a larger tax in a given period than any other establishment, and it is certainly the best equipped establishment of its kind in the world. As long ago as 1850 the city claimed the largest tobacco manufacturing house in the West, and from that time to this it has easily maintained its supremacy, not only over the West, but also the entire country. In 1880 there were in the city 222 establishments engaged in the manufacture of tobacco or cigars, with a capital of about one and a half million. The number of hands employed was 2,627, and the value of the product was less than $6,000,000. The census for 1890 revealed the existence in the city of 12 tobacco factories and 296 cigar factories, with a total product valued at about $16,000,000. The way in which the government revenue is collected makes it easy to ascertain at any period the condition of the tobacco industry. From the government returns it is evident that St. Louis manufactures about one-fourth the tobacco product of the United States. The number of pounds now manufactured yearly is about 60,000,000, worth nearly $20,000,000. About 6,000 people are kept constantly employed, and the popularity of St. Louis brands is so great that they sell practically in every part of the civilized world, and certainly in every city of the United States. The annual increase in the product varies from ten to fifteen per cent, and, although the output was reduced in 1892 by a disastrous fire, the returns for that year showed a gain of upwards of 2,000,000 pounds. The New Jersey district, which comes second to St. Louis in the returns, had for many years a very valuable trade in the far West, but

St. Louis factories have now secured a practical monopoly of this trade, and, in addition, the demand from Mexico and other Spanish-American countries is largely on the increase.

The city is, of course, exceptionally well located for a cigar jobbing center, and one house in it handles more cigars than any one house in any other city. From $3,000 to $5,000 is paid weekly by manufacturers in the way of duty, and there are now more than a million cigars manufactured every week. About 30,000 pounds of snuff are placed on the market by St. Louis houses every year.

Passing to a more indispensable article of every-day life, it may be stated that St. Louis is the third largest flour manufacturing city in America, its output being exceeded only by Minneapolis and Milwaukee. If the returns from factories situated outside of the city limits, but owned and operated by St. Louis millers, are included, the city is second in the order. The annual output of mills within the city limits exceeds 1,600,000 barrels, to which should be added 1,800,000 manufactured annually at mills situated at Alton, Litchfield, Belleville, Red Bud, Nashville, Clinton, St. Mary's and other points, but which are owned and operated by St. Louis firms. The amount of flour handled by millers and dealers has increased more than fifty per cent since 1886, and the industry is in as healthy a condition as is possible with wheat at the phenomenally low prices which have prevailed for over a year. Even this low price has its advantages, for it has enabled millers to place flour in eastern and other markets hitherto closed against them. About half a million barrels are shipped yearly to Europe, about 38,000 to Canada, about twice that quantity to Havana, by rail to Gulf points, in addition to over 80,000 barrels sent down the river to New Orleans and thence to Havana. About 80,000 barrels are shipped to eastern points, and about 1,500,000 barrels to the Southern States.

"OTHER INDUSTRIES" $54,514,383. It is impossible to deal at length with the immense manufacturing interests grouped in the table on a preceding page as "other industries," with an aggregate annual product valued at $54,514,383. Indeed, if each industry were to be handled in detail an entire work would be occupied. But there are some points of especial interest in connection with some of the trades not mentioned specifically, which ought to be recorded. Thus, St. Louis is one of the largest publishing centers in the world, producing and binding an immense number of books. Its planing mill industry is one of immense importance, gaining in magnitude every year. It is one of the largest candy and cracker manufacturing cities in the world, besides having within its corporate limits the largest cracker factory in America. The first city to have its streets lighted from end to end by aid of electricity, the business in electric supplies of every description has naturally grown until to-day it has assumed a magnitude far beyond general acknowledgment. The value of the output is $6,000,000 per annum, and shipments are made regularly to New York and London.

Enough patent medicines are manufactured in the city every year to either kill or cure the entire population of a good-sized nation, and the product of St. Louis chemical manufactories is also enormous. The census returns show that these two industries together have a product in excess of $5,000,000 per annum, and this calculation is probably an under-statement rather than otherwise. In paints and oils its business is constantly increasing, and in bags and bagging it defies competition. Glass manufactured in St. Louis was used almost exclusively in the World's Fair buildings, a striking tribute to the manufacturing greatness of St. Louis by its old-time rival. One of the largest contracts for glass ever issued was the one for the lights in the enormous roof of the new Union Station, and this contract was executed by a St. Louis house. St. Louis was the first city to manufacture silverware west of the Alleghany mountains, and in a hundred other ways it has established its right to be regarded as the greatest manufacturing center of the West, and as one of the greatest manufacturing cities in the world.

CHAPTER IV.

TRADE AND COMMERCE.

ST. LOUIS TERRITORY, AND THE WAY IN WHICH ITS ORDERS FOR MERCHANDISE ARE EXECUTED.

TAKE A MAP of the United States and draw a circle with a 500-mile radius round New York, Chicago and St. Louis. The result will astonish you, unless you are already acquainted with the fact that a larger number of people reside in or within 500 miles of St. Louis than in or within 500 miles of any other city in the United States. At least two-fifths of the New York circle extends into the Atlantic Ocean, and more than another fifth is taken up by Lakes Erie and Ontario and the southern section of Canada. Of the Chicago circle, the lakes occupy at least a third.

St. Louis is much more fortunate, for nearly the entire circle covers rich land in a district the growth of which has surprised the world. It includes the whole of Missouri, Illinois, Indiana, Kentucky, Tennessee, Mississippi, Arkansas and Iowa, with portions of Nebraska, Minnesota, Wisconsin, Michigan, Ohio, West Virginia, Virginia, North and South Carolina, Georgia, Alabama, the Indian Territory, Oklahoma and Kansas—truly, a magnificent territory, and one whose possibilities are unlimited In a few short years we shall be called upon to celebrate the centennial of the Louisiana purchase. When the treaty of Paris was signed, the American minister, Mr. Robert R. Livingston, said to M. Marbois, with whom he had been treating: "We have lived long, but this is the noblest work of our lives. The treaty which we have just signed will change vast solitudes into flourishing districts." This prophetic utterance has

been amply justified by results; and as that portion of the old Territory of Louisiana which is tributary to St. Louis has emerged from darkness into light and from wilderness to fertility, so has the city which is its commercial metropolis risen head and shoulders above all competitors, and become literally the best distributing point for merchandise in the United States.

"St. Louis," says Julian Ralph, in the exceptionally able article from which an abstract has already been taken, "is commonly spoken of as the capital of the Mississippi Valley, but her field is larger. It is true that there is no other large city between her and New Orleans— a distance of 800 miles—but there is no other on the way to Kansas City, 283 miles; or to Chicago, 280 miles; or for a long way east or southwest. Her tributary territory is every State and city south of her; east of her, to the distance of 150 miles; north for a distance of 250 miles; and in the west and southwest as far as the Rocky mountains. Between 1880 and 1890, the State of Missouri gained more than half a million inhabitants; Arkansas gained 326,000; Colorado, 300,000; Kansas, 430,000; Kentucky, 200,000; Nebraska, 600,000; Texas, 640,000; Utah, 64,000; New Mexico, Arizona and Oklahoma, 114,000. Here, then, was a gain of 3,171,000 in population in St. Louis' tributary country, and this has not only been greatly added to in the last two and a half years, but it leaves out of account the growth in population of the States of Illinois, Iowa, Indiana, Mississippi and Louisiana."

A ST. LOUIS COMMERCIAL SUBURB. We have said that the section of country within a 500-mile radius of St. Louis is rich, and that its possibilities are prodigious. The States named as coming within the circle have made themselves famous by their achievements in agricultural and other directions, and their greatness need not be dilated upon. But there has arisen during the last four or five years a new territory whose growth has been phenomenal. Reference is made to Oklahoma, a commercial suburb of St. Louis, and a country which was unknown to civilization until the three "openings," the first in 1889, and the third in 1893. In 1890, the original Oklahoma had a population of 62,000, and now it is 150,-000, a gain of 250 per cent in less than three years. The Cherokee Strip, recently opened, adds, it is computed, 100,000 to the population, bringing the total number of inhabitants in the Territory up to 251,000. This gives Oklahoma a larger number of inhabitants than any other of the Territories, for Utah, the most populous of all of them in 1890, had only 208,000 in that year, which number must still be considerably below the 250,000 mark. New Mexico's population in 1890 was 154,000, and Arizona's 60,000. In general business development and wealth, the growth of Oklahoma has been equally wonderful. The six national banks and twenty-four private banks in the Territory show that the industrial, commercial and financial interests of that region are well taken care of. The railroads running through it are well patronized, and new lines are projected to meet the requirements of a steadily and rapidly expanding community. It was less injuriously affected by the financial disturbance than were the other Territories and some of the States, and, as a consequence, it has rallied quicker from the effects of the panic. Agriculture, of course, is far ahead of all other interests in the Territory, but factories are being established and mines opened. Within a few years its activities will be fairly well diversified, and a well developed and symmetrical growth will be had.

St. Louis is especially interested in the growth and fortunes of the Territory. Her business relations with this city have been close and extensive from the beginning, and they are being diversified and expanded rapidly. This city is the chief distributing point for the entire Southwest, and Oklahoma is a growing, prosperous and progressive portion of that section. The creation of a prosperous territory with a population of a quarter of a million inhabitants in three years, shows how limitless are the possibilities of the country in which it is situated. There are yet countless acres to be opened for settlement in the Indian Territory, and there is also room for millions of people in the great States that surround it. St. Louis is not exactly the center of population of the United States, which on June 1, 1890, was situated about twenty miles west of Columbus, Indiana. The center moved nearly fifty miles west during the eighties, and will reach St. Louis in its westward course within ten or twenty years. But it is unnecessary to wait for this event to happen, for St. Louis is to-day practically the center of commerce of the North American continent. It is too far east to be western, too far west to be eastern, too far north to be southern, and too far south to be northern. It is, in short, all things to all men and to all States — the great commercial and financial center of the most prosperous nation in the world, and within comparatively easy access by rail or river of all points.

Thus, in addition to being the great distributing point for the West and the great wholesale supply point from which the leading cities of Kansas and Colorado obtain merchandise of every description, it is also in every sense of the word the metropolis of the South. The New South and New St. Louis may be spoken of as twin sisters, for their birth and growth has been practically simultaneous. Cincinnati alone competes with St. Louis for the southern trade, but during the last twenty years the latter has so completely outstripped the former that the competition can scarcely be said to exist at this time. The rapid development of new and practically unsettled sections of the Southern States has caused an immense increase in the demand from those sections, and in view of the popularity which immigration southward has attained, a still further growth in this direction is a certainty.

TRADE WITH MEXICO AND SOUTH AMERICA. Nor is the trade of St. Louis limited by the boundaries of the United States. It is the nearest large city to Mexico, and is rapidly becoming the great center of distribution for all points in the Mexican republic as well as in Spanish-American countries generally. European exporters up to a few years ago enjoyed a monopoly of this trade, to which they catered so carefully that they popularized their goods and also their methods of doing business to an extent which practically shut out trade from this country. The Spanish Club of St. Louis deserves credit for having done more to get rid of this anomally than any other trade organization in the United States. Mexican merchants, as a rule, are well situated financially, but a system of long credits prevails, and this makes it absolutely necessary for the wholesaler to keep himself acquainted with the financial standing of those from whom orders are solicited. The Spanish Club, with the co-operation of the Autumnal Festivities Association, has made this easy by the collection of data of every description, and by placing these data at the disposal of merchants. The city is now supplying Mexico with goods of almost every description, but more notably with agricultural and other machinery, mill and mining supplies, steam and traction engines, shovels, hardware, sewing machines, belting, smoked and dried meats, groceries and provisions, wooden and willowware, glassware, fire brick, fire clay, cement, drugs and chemicals, paints and oils, cordage, rubber goods, dressed lumber, street and railway cars and supplies, blank-books and stationery and printing presses, importing in return large quantities of coffee, sugar, rice and fruit. During the year 1892 nearly a million pounds of hardware were shipped from St. Louis on through bills of lading to Mexico, Cuba and Central and South America. Groceries and chemicals of equal weight

were sent, in addition to which 157,000 barrels of flour were shipped to Cuba. These totals merely represent the direct shipments from St. Louis which the work of improvement on the Mississippi river, now in progress, will make both easier and cheaper. A large quantity of merchandise is still shipped to Spanish-American countries via New York houses, but the adjustment of freights and the improved railroad communications between St. Louis and Mexico favor direct shipment only.

Before passing to a consideration of some of the principal articles included in the wholesale and jobbing business of St. Louis, it is interesting to note that during the eighties the tonnage of freight received at St. Louis increased from 6,000,000 to nearly 10,000,000, while the quantity of freight forwarded by railroads out of St. Louis increased from 2,756,000 tons in 1880 to nearly double that total in 1890. The freight tonnage of the railroads tributary to St. Louis increased from about 35,000,000 in 1880 to nearly 49,000,000 in 1890, an increase during the ten years of nearly 14,000,000 tons. Since these figures were published in connection with the census of 1890, there has been a marked increase in shipments of goods from St. Louis, and in 1892 nearly 9,000,000 tons of merchandise crossed the Mississippi river at St. Louis, an increase of fifty per cent since 1887. The total receipts of merchandise of St. Louis by river and rail were almost 12,000,000, as compared with 10,600,000 in 1890. The shipments also show a very large increase and point to prosperity of a most pronounced type.

DRY GOODS, BOOTS AND SHOES, GROCERIES AND DRUGS. The wholesale and jobbing dry goods business of St. Louis shows an increase in the cash receipts of from ten to fifteen per cent per annum. The total sales now exceed $40,000,000 per annum, and they extend to points west of the Rocky mountains, as well as to cities in Indiana and over the entire South. In addition to the immense jobbing trade, the retail dry goods trade of St. Louis has assumed immense importance, and the business trans-

acted in response to mail orders is very large.
The hat and cap trade has developed from practically nothing ten years ago, to about $5,000,000
per annum at this time, and is growing with
great rapidity. As a boot and shoe distributing
city St. Louis is second only to Boston. Enormous as is the manufacturing output of the St.
Louis factories, and rapid as has been the increase during the last ten years, the jobbing
business in boots and shoes has shown an even
more astonishing growth. The exceptional
causes which made trade dull throughout the
entire country during at least six months of the
current year had less effect on the shoe trade of
St. Louis than on any other city in the country.
In 1892 St. Louis received 828,071 cases of
shoes, a gain over 1891 of about forty per cent.
Ten years ago the receipts were less than
300,000 cases, so that the gain has been exceptionally pronounced, though it has chiefly taken
place during the last four years. The shipments from Boston to various trade centers are
usually considered as criterions, and it is interesting to note that while St. Louis received
13,500 more cases from Boston than in the preceding year, there was a falling off in the receipts of New York of 13,000, at Chicago of
86,000 and at Baltimore of 44,000, showing
that the immense gain of St. Louis meant a
great deal more than an increased demand in
keeping with the natural increase in population.

The wholesale grocery trade of St. Louis is
so large that the sales are now nearly $90,000,000
a year. The increase for the year 1892 over
the preceding year was twelve and a half per
cent, largely due to increased orders from Missouri, Arkansas, Illinois, the Indian Territory
and the Southeastern States, and to the opening
up of new trade in the Iowa district. In
branches of the grocery trade, such as sugar,
syrups and rice, very healthy gains are reported
every year; and in coffee, which is one of the
city's specialties, the gain in 1892 was enormous, the shipments increasing from 232,000
sacks to 367,000.

St. Louis is either the first or the second
largest distributing point for drugs and chemicals, and the volume of the business in these
specialties now exceeds a million dollars a
month. The largest drug house in the world
has its home in St. Louis, and there are other
establishments of enormous proportions. The
trade depression of 1893 checked the increase
of eight or ten per cent in business which had
been reported annually, but did not cause any
marked falling off. The wholesale drug business is one which is not generally understood
by the outside public, to many of whom it will
be news that it is quite a common practice for a
new proprietary article to be placed in the hands
of St. Louis jobbers, irrespective of the home of
the inventor, simply because it has been ascertained by experience that St. Louis possesses
unrivaled facilities for introducing into the
market any novelty in the drug trade. The
volume of business transacted is amazing in its
extent and variety, and is a source of general
surprise to those who have made themselves
acquainted with the details.

**HARDWARE
AND HARDWOOD.**
St. Louis has the largest
hardware house in the world,
and the city has few equals
as a distributing point for this commodity. The
year 1892 was an exceptionally favorable one
for this trade. The actual receipts showed an
increase of fifteen per cent and, as there was a
general reduction in prices, the actual increase
in the volume of trade was little, if any, less
than twenty-five per cent. The foreign trade is
exceptionally good, in addition to which the entire country west of the Alleghany mountains is
supplied. Indeed, shipments are made into
many States which cannot, by any species of
reasoning, be regarded as St. Louis territory. Shipments are also made frequently to
points within half an hour's ride of Chicago,
and, what is even more remarkable, quite an
extensive business is done with strictly eastern
sections. The old craze for sending East for
high-class decorations for homes is rapidly dying
out in face of the progress made by St. Louis,
which now sends more high-class hardware
to the East than it receives from it. The

annual sales amount to about $18,000,000, and are increasing with great rapidity. In wooden and willowware St. Louis does such an enormous trade that the sales are equal to those of all the other American cities combined—a statement which may seem extravagant, but which is easily borne out by an examination of tables.

St. Louis is the best hardwood market in the world, and its lumber interests are enormous. It is so situated that the very best lumber regions are within easy access; and the reputation the city has obtained as a lumber market has led to the choicest products coming to it. The receipts of lumber are so large that the figures are a trifle bewildering. Thus, in 1892 the number of feet received was 883,943,163, an increase of fully twenty-five per cent on those of two years previously. The shipments were less than half the receipts, showing that during the year 460,000,000 feet of lumber were consumed in the local planing mills, wagon and carriage factories, and other establishments, a marked tribute to the city's manufacturing activity. The planing mill products alone realized at least $4,000,000 during the year, and are steadily increasing.

COTTON AND WOOL. The general depression in the cotton trade during the last few years has been so great that much activity is impossible, but St. Louis is rapidly increasing its importance as a receiving and distributing point. It draws most of its supplies from Arkansas, the other States which ship largely to St. Louis being Texas, Mississippi, Tennessee, Alabama, Missouri, Louisiana and Kentucky. During the year 1891 the city built up a very valuable export trade, shipping 185,000,000 bales to England, and smaller quantities to Germany, France, Belgium, Ireland, Saxony, Austria, Italy, Holland and Switzerland, the shipments to Ireland, Saxony and Holland opening up an entirely new trade. The total shipments during the year ending August 31, 1892, were 685,000 bales, of which nearly a third went direct to Europe, and 176,000 bales to England. A great gain in this business cannot be looked for until condi-

tions over which the city has no control are changed.

At one time there existed a prejudice against St. Louis as a wool market, but this fortunately has entirely died out. The receipts in wool in St. Louis in 1892 were about 26,000,000 pounds, 4,000,000 greater than in 1891, and larger than any year's in the city's history. The years 1888 to 1891 showed a satisfactory business, increasing during the four years a little over 2,000,000 pounds. The early eighties showed unfavorable returns, none of them exceeding or even approaching the business of 1879. A great jump was made in the forward direction in the year 1885, and now the strength of the St. Louis wool market is so great that there can be no possible anxiety as to the future. St. Louis is now a very much stronger wool market than Chicago, and for domestic wools it is now the greatest market in the country, with the single exception of Boston. The great gain has been brought about mainly by the energy of the wool merchants, who have established for the city a great reputation for promptness in handling consignments and making remittances. This fact, coupled with the improved railroad facilities and reduced freight rates, has brought the St. Louis wool market in touch with the large wool producing areas in Montana, Wyoming and Colorado. Two of these States are within what is regarded as Chicago territory, which city formerly secured the bulk of the Colorado trade. Now, however, these three States send nearly the whole of their product to St. Louis, and the indications are that other extreme Western States will soon follow the good example set them.

In shipments, St. Louis was even more active in 1892 than in receipts, the splendid total of 27,000,000 being reached, showing an increase of considerably over 5,000,000 pounds. The stock on hand on January 1, 1892, exceeded 7,000,000 pounds, but the transactions for the year were so heavy that in spite of the great increase in receipts, the stock carried over to 1893 showed a very gratifying decrease. It is probable that the increased demand from

4

Northern and Northwestern areas is mainly responsible for this increase in shipments. Formerly these mills relied upon Chicago for their supplies, and it is only in recent years that they have found out that they can get better treatment in St. Louis than in any other city in the country. Wisconsin is taking more and more of our wool every month, and mills within the city boundaries of Chicago send their orders in here with gratifying regularity.

Strange buyers are seen in the city constantly, and are more than welcome. They are attracted here by reports of friends in the same line of business who have commenced drawing their supplies from St. Louis, and who have found it to their advantage to do so. The superiority of the St. Louis wool market in the matter of selections is its guarantee for future success, and the great increase in wool manufacturing in the West and Northwest renders any anxiety unnecessary as to the maintenance of the demand in the sections which the city rightfully looks upon as its own.

While the receipts of wool have doubled themselves during the last twelve years, the gain in hides and leather has been even more pronounced. The weight of the hides received has increased from 18,000,000 pounds in 1880 to nearly 40,000,000 pounds per annum now, while the shipments have about doubled during the same period. In the early days of St. Louis it was noted for its transactions in peltries and furs, which increased steadily up to about the year 1870. For the next fifteen or sixteen years comparatively little progress was made, owing to causes which affected the wool industry of the entire country, but the business has increased six-fold during the last six years, and has now assumed enormous proportions.

WHEAT AND OTHER GRAIN. St. Louis is known as the best winter wheat flour market in the world, and it is the second in the list of primary grain markets in the United States. Its receipts in grain have increased more than sixty per cent in the last five years, as will be seen by the following condensed table:

Bush'ls	1892.	1891.	1890.	1889.	1888.
Wheat	27,483,855	25,523,183	11,730,774	13,810,591	13,010,108
Corn	32,030,030	21,530,940	45,003,681	34,299,781	20,269,499
Oats	10,604,810	12,432,215	12,259,955	11,347,340	10,456,760
Rye	1,189,153	1,149,490	501,054	679,364	421,514
Barley	2,691,249	2,108,546	2,794,880	3,070,807	3,044,961
Total.	73,999,097	62,744,374	72,260,344	63,207,883	47,202,842

The export trade has increased with great rapidity, the European shipments being six times as large in 1892 as in 1890 in wheat alone. The popularity of St. Louis as a grain market is also proved by the increased receipts in wheat since 1886, when they were 8,400,000 bushels, as compared with 27,000,000 in 1892. The transactions in hay have increased very rapidly during the last ten years, though, owing to the increased home consumption, the shipments have remained nearly stationary. During the current year, hay has been shipped from St. Louis to France, and although the transaction was a comparatively insignificant one, it is of importance as showing what an immense field is open for St. Louis in exporting, and how easily these opportunities can be taken advantage of.

HORSES, MULES AND LIVE STOCK. St. Louis is the best horse and mule market in the United States; and so far as mules are concerned, its transactions are larger than those of all the other markets in the country combined. The trade is confined to a comparatively small area on Broadway, a few blocks north of the Eads bridge. About 50,000 mules are sold every year in this section, and the receipts from sales exceed $5,000,000. The government purchases between 1,000 and 2,000 mules every year from St. Louis, and the southern planters rely on the city entirely for their supply. Shipments are made to Cuba in large numbers, one firm alone selling as many as 5,000 head a year to Cuban planters. To such a perfect system has the trade been brought that telegraphic orders are often received and executed for from twelve to a hundred mules wanted at distant points. The animals are graded very carefully, and there is hence little difficulty in fixing values or completing trades. In horses, St. Louis also does a very large trade, as many as 20,000 being sold every year. It is quite an every-day occurrence for high-grade carriage horses to be ordered from St. Louis by New York and Chicago dealers. This is because St. Louis has the reputation of paying a higher price for stock than any other market, while the rapidity with which sales are made makes it profitable to sell at very low prices. More than one St. Louis magnate has ordered a pair of handsome carriage horses from a distant market in order to obtain something exceptionally fine, only to have his order executed through a St. Louis dealer or broker at an additional expense to him of the commission charged by the foreign house.

In live stock generally, St. Louis is a highly important market. The total live cattle receipts in 1892 were 801,111, and almost the entire receipts were marketed here. From 600 to 800 head of cattle are slaughtered daily at the National Stock Yards, and a great increase in facilities is the result of the introduction of capital from outside points. During 1892, St. Louis sold more Texas cattle than Chicago, and the prices realized were somewhat higher. In spite of the general decrease of interest in sheep-raising throughout the country, there was but a slight falling off in the receipts or shipments of sheep: nor was the volume of business in hogs materially reduced, although the flood kept a great deal of trade away from the city, in addition to which less hogs were raised. It is a significant fact that, although a less number were sold, a very much larger sum was realized than in 1891, and the condition of the market must be described as exceptionally healthy in every respect.

RETAIL ESTABLISHMENTS HERE AND ELSEWHERE. The story of the greatness of St. Louis as a wholesale and jobbing center might be continued without limit, but the few specialties selected must suffice to illustrate the general scope and extent of the business, which has assumed proportions far beyond what the most enthusiastic New St. Louisan realizes, and which is growing every month.

Before passing from the subject of trade and commerce, a reference must be made to the retail business of the city. St. Louis is without doubt the greatest shopping center in the West, and with but few exceptions the greatest in the country. The Bureau of Information recently issued a circular to 2,000 prominent citizens, asking them a series of questions as to the retail excellence of St. Louis. Among other queries was one as to the nature and extent of the assortments, and another asked for a comparison as to price. Nearly every reply was to the effect that the more one traveled the more was the conviction driven home that New St. Louis was one of the most favored cities so far as stocks are concerned, and the opinion was unanimously expressed that retailers ask less for their wares than do those of any other city for similar grades. One of the leaders of society, a lady who was born in the East, but who is now the wife of one of St. Louis' leading bankers, did not exaggerate one jot or tittle when she said:

"Every year I visit the eastern stores, and every year I become more strongly convinced that our St. Louis merchants equal in energy and result any in the United States."

Captain Cuttle's advice to his friends as to important records of fact and philosophy was, "when found, make a note of." The hint expressed so tersely by the St. Louis lady is as valuable as any proverb of the past or present, and should be "made note of" and be borne constantly in mind by every resident in the city or within a day's journey of it.

St. Louis merchants act on the principle that the best is the cheapest, and they accordingly carry the best goods in every grade, thereby acquiring and maintaining a reputation which adds greatly to their business, and which brings them in orders by mail from every direction. It is impossible to estimate how many thousands of dollars are received in St. Louis daily by retailers, but the express and freight business transacted may be taken as a fair index, and this shows that St. Louis occupies a unique position as a distributor of goods of every description required for household purposes. The store buildings of a few years ago having proved entirely inadequate to the wants of the present time, magnificent structures have been erected for the accommodation of merchant princes in various lines. Broadway and Olive street are special favorites with large retailers, and most of the large establishments are to be found on these magnificent thoroughfares, though in some lines adjoining streets are also quite popular.

The retail dry goods houses may be described as singularly massive and complete, some of the largest establishments on the Parisian Bon Marché plan having acquired a national reputation. In clothing and hats, the retail establishments are also conspicuously fine, while the most elaborate assortments of boots and shoes are to be found in numerous retail stores in the best locations in the city.

Speaking of the retail trade of the city generally, it may be said that the St. Louis merchants are specially favored by location. Not only have they a population of considerably over half a million within their own city from which to draw regular trade, but they also enjoy the trade of an immense number of suburban and semi-suburban cities, in addition to doing a large trade by express and through the mails with the residents of at least five States. Besides these excellent facilities for securing customers, they are remarkably well fixed for obtaining stock at reasonable prices. The manufactories of the city enable a large percentage of the supply to be drawn from home, and the railroad connections with the East are such as to render it very easy and convenient to receive the latest productions of the great eastern houses. The city is also a United States port of entry and receives goods from European centers direct to the consignee. Every advantage is taken of these facilities, and the latest fashion in St. Louis is never far behind the latest fashion in New York, London or Paris.

The St. Louisan on his travels and anxious to have justice done his favored city should acquaint himself with some of the most remarkable of its commercial* achievements.

----
*See also page 29.

St. Louis is the best market in America.

It is by far the best hardwood lumber market.

It is the largest soft hat market in the world.

It has the largest drug house in the world.

It sells more bags and bagging than any other city.

It is the largest interior cotton market in the world.

It is the best winter wheat flour market in the world.

It is the largest inland coffee market in the world.

It is the second primary grain market in the world.

It is the largest horse and mule market in the world.

Its wholesale grocery sales exceed $90,000,000 a year.

It has the largest exclusive carpet house in America.

It is the largest fruit and vegetable market in America.

It has the largest hardware establishment in the world.

It has the largest woodenware establishment in the world.

It is the third largest dry goods market in the United States.

It has the finest jewelry establishment in the United States.

It ships more than 75,000,000 pounds of barb wire annually.

It exports more goods to Mexico than any other interior city.

It is the best interior market in the United States for domestic wool.

It handles more than half the woodenware sold in the United States.

It receives by rail and river a million tons of merchandise every month.

It is the largest shoe distributing point in the world, with one exception.

It handles on an average nearly three million feet of lumber every working day in the year.

Its transactions in dry goods, clothing, hats and shoes are in excess of $100,000,000 per annum.

CHAPTER V.

RAILROAD AND RIVER FACILITIES.

THE BEST RAILROAD CENTER IN THE UNITED STATES.—THE LARGEST CITY ON THE LARGEST RIVER IN THE WORLD.—THE LARGEST RAILROAD STATION IN THE WORLD.

"A PROPHET," we are told, "is not without honor, save in his own country," and what is true of prophets is equally true of cities. Hence it was that the world generally was enlightened concerning the extraordinary advance of St. Louis as a railroad center, not by a St. Louis statistician, but by Mr. Robert P. Porter, Superintendent of the Eleventh Census, whose under-statement of the population of the city in 1890 proves conclusively that he is not unduly prejudiced in favor of St. Louis. In the speech delivered by the superintendent on November 21, 1891, from which quotations have already been made, he called attention to the fact that St. Louis, as a railroad center, is something of which the nation, as well as the city, can be proud. "We may throw Ohio, Indiana and Illinois out of consideration," he said, "and still have more miles of railroad tributary to St. Louis than the total mileage of the United Kingdom, of Germany, France or Austria-Hungary. Add half of Illinois, which is justly tributary to this city, and we have a railway mileage, tributary to this one great river city, equal to the combined railway mileage of the United Kingdom and Austria-Hungary. Again, take the mileage of railways centering in St. Louis, and we find it equal to the total mileage of the German Empire, and exceeding by about five thousand miles the total mileage of railways of England or of France. These are not boastful facts, but facts which point to a future far beyond that as yet attained by Europe's great river cities."

A year later, another tribute to the excellence of St. Louis as a railroad center, was paid by Mr. Julian Ralph, who, in his article in *Harper's New Monthly Magazine*, for November, 1892, said: "St. Louis has become remarkable as a centering place of railroads. The city is like a hub to those spokes of steel that reach out in a circle, which, unlike that of most other towns of prominence, is nowhere broken by lake, sea or mountain chain. Nine very important railways, and a dozen lesser ones, meet there. The mileage of the roads thus centering at the city is 25,678, or nearly 11,000 more than in 1880, while the mileage of the roads that are tributary to the city has grown from 35,000 to more than 57,000. These railways span the continent from New York to San Francisco. They reach from New Orleans to Chicago, and from the Northwestern States to Florida. Through Pullman cars are now run from St. Louis to San Francisco, to the City of Mexico, and to St. Augustine and Tampa in the season. New lines that have the city as their objective point are projected; old lines that have not gone there are preparing to build connecting branches, and several of the largest systems that reach there are just now greatly increasing their terminal facilities in the city with notable works at immense cost."

THE SITUATION IN 1890. These two quotations from the utterances or writings of outsiders, show how the railroad facilities of St. Louis are appreciated throughout the country at the present time. During the eighties the growth in the city's railroad facilities, and in the territory which it supplies with merchandise, were enormous.

During the decade the railroad mileage of Texas, which is one of the States which draws nearly all its supplies from this city, increased 147 per cent; those of Louisiana, Mississippi, and Arkansas, three more States in St. Louis territory, more than doubled during the same period, while the Indian Territory railroad mileage increased nearly four-fold. The increase in Kansas, another distinctly St. Louis State, was about eighty per cent, and through the entire section tributary to St. Louis there was a gain of 21,000 miles, or about sixty-one per cent. The following table shows the general increase in mileage, tonnage and passenger traffic of the St. Louis railroads between the years of 1880 and 1890. It was not prepared for the purpose of demonstrating the greatness of St. Louis, but is part of the official record of the census of 1890:

MILEAGE, FREIGHT, PASSENGERS, EARNINGS, ETC.	Year	Miles	Tons	Total
Mileage of railroads centering in St. Louis	1880	14,801		
Do.	1880	25,678		
Increase		10,877		
Freight received by railroads centering in St. Louis	1880		6,097,000	
Freight forwarded by railroads centering in St. Louis	1880		2,756,000	
Total				8,853,000
Freight received by railroads centering in St. Louis	1890		9,970,000	15,211,000
Freight forwarded by railroads centering in St. Louis	1890		5,271,000	6,488,000
Increase				
Mileage of railroads tributary to St. Louis	1880	35,475		
Do	1880	57,174		
Increase		21,701		
Freight tonnage of railroads tributary to St. Louis	1890		34,745,000	
Do	1890		48,596,000	
Increase				
Freight earnings of railroads tributary to St. Louis	1880		13,848,000	$70,453,000
Do.	1890		91,772,000	21,326,000
Increase				
Passengers carried on railroads tributary to St. Louis	1880		14,513,000	
Do	1890		39,871,000	18,358,000
Increase				
Passenger earnings on railroads tributary to St. Louis	1880			$23,202,000
Do	1890			29,738,000
Increase				6,536,000

These figures are bewildering in their vastness, especially when it is remembered that it is but a little more than forty years ago when work was commenced on the first railroad entering St. Louis. It is interesting at this period, and in view of the marvelous achievements of St. Louis railroads, to glance back for a moment at the early efforts to secure railroad connection of any kind for St. Louis. After the Legislature of Missouri had in the year 1849 incorporated a railway company to build a road from St. Louis to Jefferson City, with a view to its being extended out to the Pacific Ocean, local sentiment was inclined to be facetious as well as skeptical.

During the last year or two there have been many prophets who have doubted the possibility of connecting St. Louis and Chicago by means of an electric railroad which would shorten the distance between the two cities so as to bring it down to a three-hours' journey. Forty-four years ago there were as many, if not more, people who were certain that the road then projected across the State would never be built.

A FORECAST IN 1849.   While people were discussing the impossibility of the project, Mr. Thomas Allen called a meeting of the incorporators at the St. Louis insurance rooms and delivered an address which forms "mighty interesting reading" at this time. Mr. Allen asked his hearers to imagine that the road had been constructed and opened for traffic. "Let us enter," he said, "the depot or station-house, which is the largest house in the city. Here we see boxes of merchandise of all sizes, and various articles of household and family utensils, hogsheads of sugar, sacks of coffee and of salt, barrels of molasses and of whisky, kits of mackerel, boxes of raisins, bundles of paper, wagons in pieces and small carriages, kegs of nails, bars of iron, boxes of Indian goods, of shoes, hats, tar and turpentine, marked for the towns in the interior, and some for Deseret, all of which the men are at work placing in the freight train. There is none of that disorder and flurry which exists upon the levee, but all is neatness and order.

"But the bell is ringing. We will take our

ticket and step aboard the passenger train with fifty or sixty other passengers who are destined for various points along the line of the road. Off we go, with the speed of twenty-five miles an hour. We have not gone five miles when the pace of the train is slacked and we observe one or two gentlemen jumping off at the suburban residences. A few miles further is a platform and a turn-out. Here several are waiting to get off to go to their dwellings. Here also we observe a string of open cars laden with coal. We pass on, scarcely having time to observe the fine residences which city gentlemen have constructed all along each side of the road, but we stop every few moments to let off a passenger or two and take on as many more, so that our number is kept about the same. Here we pass a train loaded with wood, with a few cars of baled hay attached. The country on either side seems to be full of busy men and every farm occupied. Directly we reach a water station, where we observe immense piles of cord-wood, and many men engaged in hauling and cording. Here also is a small refreshment house, and here again we leave and take on a few passengers.

"We come in sight of the Missouri, and catch a glimpse, as we pass, of a steamboat, with a small freight and a few passengers, puffing away and hard on a sand-bar. Soon we meet a freight train loaded with pigs of lead and copper and iron from Franklin county. In about two hours from St. Louis, we are at the Union Station, where we discharge a few passengers and observe large piles of metal pigs. Though stopping now and then to leave or take on a passenger, or to supply the engine with water, we are soon in Gasconade county. We pass cars laden with cannel coal, and we discharge at Hermann Station a number of Germans and their baggage, and we observe some cars receiving freight, some of it apparently pianos, and quite a number of pipes one would suppose to be wine—all the manufacture of Hermann. We are come, however, to the crossing of the Gasconade, which is a grand bridge of solid masonry of great strength and durability. Here

is quite an important station, and we notice a number of new buildings going up on lots sold by the railway company; immense quantities of yellow pine piled up, and a number of cars attached to an engine ready to start to St. Louis with a heavy load of lumber.

"We cross the Lamine, stop at the Saline Station, and we are struck with the fine appearance of the country as we pass on and observe numerous excellent farms. We leave a few passengers at Lexington Station, a few miles south of that place, and reach our station not far from the Kansas river (Kaw river) about tea-time, having been about ten hours from St. Louis. Here our remaining passengers, to the number of about twenty or thirty, dispose themselves for the night at a good hotel, intending in the morning to be off for Independence, Liberty, Westport and St. Joseph, and other places up the river. The hotel is quite full of passengers, there being as many to go down as up, and in the station-house is a freight train ready to start. It was remarked that there was not less than a thousand tons of freight that day on this road. Now, although this be an imaginary trip, who can doubt, who knows anything of railroads, that the picture would be fully if not more than realized upon the opening of such a road? Can we do any better than to take the 2,000 shares required preliminary to the permanent organization? I am strong in the belief that if the road had been built but fifty miles, or if built to Jefferson City, it would pay."

When Mr. Allen concluded this address he locked the door, and, turning to those present, remarked that it was a time for acting and not speaking, adding a hope that the 2,000 shares of stock required would be subscribed for before the door was unlocked. One hundred thousand dollars in stock was required, for which Messrs. James H. Lucas, John O'Fallon and Daniel Page subscribed, and thus was laid the foundation-stone for a railroad which in itself has become a source of untold worth to St. Louis, and of a railroad system generally, which, as has been shown above, is equal or superior to that

A GLORIOUS REALIZATION.

of any other city in the world. The St. Louis Traffic Commission, of which Mr. C. N. Osgood is executive officer, with the title of Commissioner, has enabled full benefit to be derived from the great railroad mileage of the city, and it is largely from the reports of Mr. Osgood that the data concerning these railroads centering in the city are taken. These railroads are:

ATCHISON, TOPEKA & SANTA FE.
BALTIMORE & OHIO.
CHICAGO & ALTON.
CHICAGO, BURLINGTON & QUINCY.
CLEVELAND, CINCINNATI, CHICAGO & ST. LOUIS ("The Big Four").
ILLINOIS CENTRAL (via the Vandalia and Cairo Short Lines).
JACKSONVILLE SOUTHEASTERN.
LOUISVILLE & NASHVILLE.
LOUISVILLE, EVANSVILLE & ST. LOUIS ("Air Line").
MISSOURI, KANSAS & TEXAS.
MISSOURI PACIFIC.
MOBILE & OHIO.
OHIO & MISSISSIPPI.
ST. LOUIS & HANNIBAL.
ST. LOUIS & SAN FRANCISCO ("Frisco Line").
ST. LOUIS, ALTON & TERRE HAUTE ("Cairo Short Line").
ST. LOUIS, CHICAGO & ST. PAUL ("Bluff Line").
ST. LOUIS, IRON MOUNTAIN & SOUTHERN ("Iron Mountain").
ST. LOUIS, KANSAS CITY & COLORADO.
ST. LOUIS, KEOKUK & NORTHWESTERN ("Burlington Route").
ST. LOUIS SOUTHWESTERN ("Cotton Belt").
ST. LOUIS, VANDALIA & TERRE HAUTE ("Vandalia Line").
TOLEDO, ST. LOUIS & KANSAS CITY ("Clover Leaf").
WABASH.

These are exclusive of the transfer lines connecting St. Louis with the Relay depot on the other side of the Eads bridge. These are:

THE TERMINAL RAILROAD ASSOCIATION.
THE ST. LOUIS MERCHANTS' BRIDGE TERMINAL.
THE WIGGIN'S FERRY COMPANY (and associated lines).
THE MADISON COUNTY FERRY.
LOUISVILLE, EVANSVILLE & ST. LOUIS R. R. FERRY.
CARONDELET FERRY.

THE ATCHISON-'FRISCO SYSTEM. In discussing in detail the various railroad connections of St. Louis, they will be dealt with in their alphabetical order, as above; it being left to the reader to discriminate between the importance

of the various systems, and to decide which would be first discussed, were the classification by order of merit. The first on the list is the Atchison, Topeka & Sante Fe, which, by the absorption of the St. Louis & San Francisco road, some three years ago, obtained a direct entrance to the city, and made St. Louis one of the terminal points of the great system which controls over 9,000 miles of railroad, extending to California on the west, Texas and Old Mexico on the south, and the lakes on the north. The amalgamation of the two systems gave St. Louis another route to the Pacific Coast and also to Old Mexico, and, in addition to that, it greatly increased the railroad facilities between St. Louis and Oklahoma. By means of the 'Frisco branch to Sapulpa, St. Louis has railroad facilities without change of cars, to the northeast corner of Oklahoma, while the 'Frisco Southern Kansas line, with the Atchison connection at Arkansas City, affords a direct communication with Guthrie and Oklahoma, the two largest cities in the exceptionally prosperous and thriving Territory, concerning whose marvelous growth figures have been already quoted. The 'Frisco mileage alone covers 1,500 miles, mainly through the States of Missouri, Kansas, Arkansas, Texas and the Indian Territory. It affords rapid and convenient connection between St. Louis and all parts of central and Southwestern Missouri, and it also sends out from St. Louis daily through sleeping cars to the City of Mexico and to California. The quantity of freight shipped into St. Louis by the 'Frisco was 551,000 tons in 1892, as compared with 486,000 in 1891 and 437,000 in 1890. During the same three years the shipments from St. Louis increased from 317,000 tons to 409,000 tons. The immense quantity of raw material, lead and zinc, oil and similar products, accounts for the fact that in four years the shipments into St. Louis increased fully sixty per cent.

THE CHICAGO AND ALTON. The Chicago & Alton Railroad is a line very popular locally. It has only 850 miles of track, but every mile is a good one, and the connections with Chicago and Kansas

City are a source of great profit to St. Louis commerce, as the territory through which the road passes is rich in the extreme and an ever-increasing source of trade. During the last two or three years it has made vast improvements in its train service, and the admirable condition in which its ballasted track is kept is a source of general pride to all connected with the road. It hauls in immense quantities of coal and of grain, stock and fruit products, and it also affords admirable connection with Wisconsin and Michigan and several Eastern States. A great portion of its road has been double-tracked recently, and the road is in a condition of great prosperity. In 1892 it hauled into the city 126,000 tons of freight, as compared with 102,000 tons four years ago. During the same year, 1892, it distributed 103,000 tons of St. Louis merchandise, as compared with 91,000 tons in 1889.

THE "BURLINGTON ROUTE." The "Burlington," or the "Q," is becoming more and more a St. Louis road. Its management has of late years been thoroughly impressed with the importance of St. Louis as a shipping point, and the investments that have been made with a view to increasing connections with the city have run into the millions. This route by its own rails affords connection with the best parts of Illinois and Missouri, Iowa, Minnesota, Nebraska, Kansas, South Dakota, Wyoming and Colorado. In addition to this, it reaches by track of its own nearly every important business center between St. Louis and the Rocky mountains and Lake Michigan. Including the St. Louis, Keokuk & Western, the quantity of freight hauled into the city in 1892 was nearly 1,000,000 tons. In its shipments out of St. Louis the total tonnage reached 706,000, an increase from 435,000 four years ago, showing how immensely the distributing business has increased. The management of this road has chafed for years under what it considered its inadequate terminal facilities at St. Louis. Its East St. Louis freight terminal was extensive, but not sufficient to answer its purpose, and at a heavy outlay a site was secured on this side of the river for a freight house. It has erected and is now operating on this property one of the most convenient freight houses in the world. This has a frontage on Franklin avenue of 140 feet, and the brick building, which is four stories high, runs back 38 feet. The freight shed is 770 feet in length, and there is thus space, under cover, for five tracks, each capable of accommodating twenty cars. In other words, a hundred cars of merchandise can be handled under cover; a most important condition in bad weather, especially with perishable freight. Adjoining, there is accommodation for about 150 cars on team tracks. This road is also connecting itself with St. Louis by means of a road on this side of the river running north, crossing the Missouri river at Alton over bridges, to which reference will be made later. When this new track is opened an immense volume of business will be diverted to and through St. Louis, and the present freight returns will soon be made to look insignificant.

THE "BIG FOUR." The Cleveland, Cincinnati & Chicago Railway, known both as the "Three C.'s" and the "Big Four," crosses the States of Illinois, Indiana and Ohio. The "Big Four" system has recently acquired control of the Cincinnati, Sandusky & Cleveland R. R., Cincinnati, Wabash & Michigan Ry. and Whitewater R. R. The consolidation of the numerous independent lines of which this system is now composed has been a matter of much benefit to St. Louis, resulting as it has in large improvements in transporting facilities. The effect has been shown in the traffic returns. The road is now hauling into the city more than half a million tons of merchandise every year, and distributing St. Louis products weighing upwards of 300,000 tons per annum. It hauls into the city every year about 5,000,000 bushels of coal, and in many other ways contributes towards the city's prosperity and growth.

The Jacksonville Southeastern Railroad (the "J. S. E.") is a smaller line, which, however, is quite important to the city. Its career has not been an entirely fortunate one, and during the current year a receiver was appointed to protect certain interests. This was not in consequence of any lack of patronage, as its freight shipments increased over 100,000 tons in 1892. The road is entitled to the thanks of the city for the early enterprise it displayed in establishing terminals on this side of the river, and in the early future the road will acquire a prosperity to which it is at present a stranger.

THE LOUISVILLE AND NASHVILLE. The Louisville & Nashville Railroad is of far greater importance than its name would indicate. It connects St. Louis with the Southern and Southeastern sections, and it operates considerably more than three thousand miles of track in the very best regions of the New South. In addition to very valuable connections in Illinois and Indiana, the L. & N. connects with all the leading centers of Kentucky, Tennessee and Alabama, and also runs into the States of Florida, Mississippi, Louisiana and Virginia. In addition to its St. Louis terminus it has termini at Memphis, Mobile, Pensacola, New Orleans and other points; and among the commercial centers of the South through which it runs are Nashville and Birmingham. From St. Louis the L. & N. runs through the exceptionally fertile region of Southern Illinois and Indiana, crossing the Ohio river at Henderson, Kentucky, the Cumberland river at Clarksville, and reaching the Mississippi again at Memphis. At Nashville the main line from St. Louis connects with the Louisville and Cincinnati line and runs on to Birmingham, Montgomery, Mobile, New Orleans and Pensacola. The new work of the L. & N., in the way of railroad building, has been mainly in Southwest Kentucky, Tennessee and Virginia during the last few years. The road is a most valuable one for the exportation of St. Louis products to the Spanish-American countries, and it is a great favorite with exporters. Last year it shipped from St. Louis nearly 269,000 tons of freight as compared with 207,000 tons the preceding year, and it also brought

into the city 556,000 tons, an increase of nearly 200,000 tons in two years. It is also interesting to note that it hauled into the city about 7,000,000 bushels of coal in 1892 as compared with about 4,000,000 in 1890. The L. & N. is another of the roads which has appreciated the necessity of terminal facilities on the west side of the Mississippi river. Having acquired a block of property bounded by Broadway, Cass avenue, Dickson and Collins streets, it proceeded, toward the end of the year 1891, to construct a two-story freight house measuring 568x50 feet. The first floor has forty-two doors available for the receipt and delivery of team freight, and the adjoining team tracks afford every facility for business. The second story runs the entire length of the structure and is designed for the warehousing of freight.

THE "AIR LINE" AND THE M. K. & T. The "Air Line," as the Louisville, Evansville & St. Louis Consolidated Railway Company is generally called, connects St. Louis with Louisville, running through a very important and prosperous section of Southern Illinois and Indiana. It has hauled into St. Louis an immense quantity of merchandise and raw material, the tonnage having grown from 260,000 in 1889 to 466,000 in 1892. It has done less work in way of distribution of manufactured product. In 1889 it distributed less than 10,000 tons of St. Louis-manufactured goods. Since then the export business has increased ten-fold, but it has not yet acquired very large proportions. During 1892 it hauled into the city nearly 10,000,000 bushels of coal.

The Missouri, Kansas & Texas Railway is of greater interest to St. Louis on account of future prospects than actual developments. Within a comparatively short space of time the track connecting this system to St. Louis will be completed, bringing the enormous mileage of this system more directly within reach of the city's manufactures and staples. The principal offices of the company are already situated in St. Louis, a recognition of the fact that the States of Missouri, Kansas and Texas, from which the road takes its name, and from which it runs, are distinctly St. Louis territory. The greatest mileage of this road is in Texas, where it exceeds 800 miles. It has also 375 miles in Kansas, 300 miles in Missouri, and 240 miles in the Indian Territory. The completion of the track to St. Louis with independent terminals will make this the terminal city of a road which cannot fail in the early future to play an immense part in the destinies of St. Louis commerce.

THE BALTIMORE AND OHIO. The Baltimore & Ohio Railroad, which includes the Ohio & Mississippi, has become more distinctly a St. Louis road during the present year by the removal here of the offices of the company which were formerly situated at Cincinnati. In November, 1893, the offices were finally removed to the Rialto building, where the general passenger and general freight agents and managers took up their headquarters. The change was another admission on the part of experts of the standing of St. Louis as a railroad center, and the influence will be great on the policy of the road. The Baltimore & Ohio Southwestern Railroad by its absorption of the Ohio & Mississippi has a mileage of 930 miles, extending from St. Louis to Parkersburgh, West Virginia. The old Ohio & Mississippi proper extends from St. Louis to Cincinnati, a distance of 340 miles, with several branches which connect the city with various Illinois, Indiana and Kentucky points. The consolidation gives St. Louis another direct route to the Atlantic sea-board, and will result at an early date in greatly increased railroad facilities between this city and New York. It is too early to estimate what the influence will be on the shipping returns. The Ohio & Mississippi hauled in nearly 700,000 tons of freight in 1892, including 12,680,000 bushels of coal. It took from the city nearly 170,000 tons of merchandise as compared with 130,000 tons in 1890.

THE MISSOURI PACIFIC SYSTEM. It cannot be said too frequently that the history of the Missouri Pacific Railway is the history of the development of modern St. Louis. This chapter, dealing as it does with the present rather than with the past, is not the place to trace that history in all its details. We have seen how Mayor Darby lent impetus and weight to the railroad agitation nearly sixty years ago, and how Mr. Thomas Allen in 1849 drew an imaginary picture of the road then contemplated, which he believed would pay as a line connecting St. Louis and Jefferson City. In June, 1853, the first section of the railroad, extending to Franklin, was opened, and in 1855 Jefferson City was reached.

How insignificant do these little details seem compared with the events of to-day, when the Missouri Pacific and its connections intersect the best sections of the St. Louis territory! The Iron Mountain road was chartered somewhat later, and in 1858 the road was opened as far as Pilot Knob. In 1872 the road reached the Arkansas boundary, and since then its extensions have been numerous. A glance at the map now shows that the Missouri Pacific owned, leased and operated lines connect a greater portion of the State of Missouri with St. Louis, bring a still larger portion of Kansas in touch with the city, and also provide excellent facilities for Nebraska, Colorado, Arkansas, Louisiana and other States. St. Louis is the great terminus of this mighty system, and the work it does is best shown by the following figures, which have been extracted from the annual reports of recent years:

In 1885 the roads in this system hauled into St. Louis about 1,300,000 tons out of a total of 7,497,093 tons by all roads. In 1889 it brought in rather more than 1,800,000 tons; in 1892 the total tonnage by the Missouri Pacific system exceeded 2,250,000 tons, or more than twenty per cent of the entire receipts from all sources. Last year again it distributed no less than 1,266,000 tons of St. Louis merchandise throughout the St. Louis territory, this being again about twenty per cent of the total. With these figures before him the reader will not think Traffic Commissioner Osgood's eulogy of this road overdrawn. "This great system," he said, in his annual report for the year 1891, "yearly becomes more and more a factor in the commercial progress of this city. It has ever been among the first to extend its lines into new territory, thus constantly opening up to the commerce of St. Louis, the pivotal point of the entire system, and, therefore, the point with which its vast interests are chiefly identified, new fields of agriculture, mining, timber and stock-raising, bringing the rich products of the entire West and Southwest directly under contribution to her trade. The significance of the situation can be in a measure appreciated when it is stated that its lines traverse 5,300 miles of productive territory. It will be better understood when it is seen that by its rails St. Louis is given direct connection with the commercial centers and rich farms of Missouri; the broad corn and wheat fields and prosperous communities of Kansas; the fertile river valleys and trade centers of the richest districts of Nebraska; the mineral regions and chief cities of Colorado; the agricultural, fruit, mineral and timber lands of Arkansas; the rapidly increasing populations of the productive Indian Territory (which at no far distant day is to become equal in prosperity with any of the States on its borders); the sugar plantations of Louisiana, and the cotton and grain fields and vast cattle ranges of Texas. Through its connections it reaches to every other principal part of the West and Southwest, including the Pacific slope and Mexico. Its through passenger service to all these districts is adjusted with special reference to the requirements of the St. Louis traveler; and as this is the gateway to the entire system, St. Louis becomes the point upon which the travel from the East destined to these districts naturally converges. During the year 1891 over 200 miles of new road were constructed and added to the system, perhaps the most important portion being the Houston, Central Arkansas and Northern line, which will be in operation to Alexandria, Louisiana, its junction with the Texas and Pacific Railway, as soon as the magnificent bridge by means of which it will cross the Red river at that point is completed. This will give St. Louis immediate direct connection with New Orleans and the Gulf. St. Louis is the headquarters for the official staff of the company, and is the point from which all its operations are directed."

THREE VALUABLE SOUTHERN ROADS. The Mobile & Ohio Railway is an important trunk line connecting St. Louis with the South. It runs through the States of Illinois, Kentucky, Tennessee, Mississippi and Alabama, having its southern terminus at the port of Mobile, 644 miles from St. Louis. Its trains haul into St. Louis immense quantities of cotton, lumber, vegetables and fruit, in addition to about 4,000,000 bushels of coal every year. It has freight headquarters in St. Louis, in a building erected and owned by it for the purpose. The very best sections of what is now called the New South are traversed by the Mobile & Ohio and its branches, and its influence on the commerce of the city is marked. It brings in nearly 700,000 tons of merchandise every year, and takes away immense quantities of manufactured goods. A very large percentage of the Spanish-American trade is transacted over this road. From its southern terminus there are regular steamship lines to Tampa, Key West, Havana, Tampico, and other points, in addition to a steamship service to both New York and European ports.

The "Cairo Short Line," or, more properly, the St. Louis, Alton & Terre Haute Railway, operates nearly 250 miles of road through a territory which is tributary to St. Louis in every respect. It crosses the Southern Illinois coal fields, and hauls in 12,000,000 or 13,000,000 bushels of coal every year. It connects with the Illinois Central, and gives a direct route between St. Louis and Memphis and the most important points in the Southern Mississippi Valley. During the last two or three years it has inaugurated a number of improvements, which have shortened the distance between St. Louis and a large number of important points. The company also operates a line between St. Louis and Paducah, Kentucky, connecting with diverging lines, also with boats on the Ohio, Tennessee and Cumberland rivers. The recent completion of the Paducah, Tennessee & Alabama R. R., built by St. Louis capitalists, from Paducah to

Hollow Rock, Tennessee, has opened up a new territory to this market, and through a connection with the N., C. & St. L. Ry. at Hollow Rock, Tennessee, has formed a new short route to the Southeast. The policy of the management of this line is liberal, and it has at all times been found to be alive to the interests of the trade and commerce of St. Louis. The headquarters of the company are located here, and the local facilities have been largely improved by the erection of a new freight warehouse, and otherwise.

The St. Louis Southwestern Railway, formerly known as the St. Louis, Arkansas & Texas, but almost invariably described as the "Cotton Belt," is a St. Louis line, with its headquarters in this city, where its principal officers reside. The 1,200 miles of its track are of immense value to St. Louis, for they bring within easy access of the city a large number of important towns and a vast area of territory tributary in every respect to St. Louis. The mileage of the main system is 580 in Missouri and Arkansas, 40 in Louisiana, and 610 in Texas. But by the number of its important connections its importance to St. Louis is largely enhanced. Its own rails reach a group of the most popular and progressive cities of the Southwest, viz.: Little Rock, Pine Bluff and Camden, Arkansas; Texarkana; Shreveport, Louisiana; Fort Worth, Waco, Tyler, Corsicana, Greenville and Sherman, Texas. Lumber, cotton and live stock are the items of freight it contributes most largely to the St. Louis market, in addition to all the other products of agricultural sections it traverses.

TO THE ATLANTIC AND THE LAKES. The Vandalia, or the Terre Haute & Indianapolis Railroad, is another of the very extensive systems connecting St. Louis with the eastern roads. Running between St. Louis and Indianapolis, it there connects with the great Pennsylvania system. It has also connections between St. Joseph, Michigan, and Terre Haute, Indiana, and thus becomes valuable to St. Louis commerce in a variety of ways. This road also handles St. Louis freight destined for the Erie system, and its business has become so great of late years that during 1891 and 1892 it found it necessary to build and open a large freight depot on this side of the river between O'Fallon street and Cass avenue. The Vandalia hauls into St. Louis every year 11,000,000 or 12,000,000 bushels of coal, and its general freight business is also very large.

The Toledo, St. Louis & Kansas City Railway, known as the "Clover Leaf," forms an important factor in the St. Louis railroad system. It runs a distance of 450 miles to Toledo, Ohio, also operating over 250 miles of water lines between Toledo and Buffalo. This road connects St. Louis directly with Buffalo, Toledo, Belfast, Decatur, Marian, Kokomo, Frankfort, and many other important towns, besides passing through a very large area in which commerce and manufacture are both well represented. Since the gauge of this road has been changed from narrow to standard, its importance has largely increased, and it has improved its St. Louis connection by constructing a very useful freight depot on the west side of the river between Broadway and Second street, at the intersection of Brooklyn. A great increase in business has resulted from this enterprise, and the popularity of the road in St. Louis is very great.

THE WABASH SYSTEM. The last of the St. Louis roads which will be mentioned specifically is the Wabash, which connects St. Louis with twenty-one cities, each of a population more than 10,000, and a total population of 2,500,000. The Wabash Eastern and the Wabash Western, which are now combined under one management, have 731 miles in Illinois, 500 in Missouri, nearly 400 in Indiana, 125 in Iowa, 105 in Ohio, and 80 in Michigan, figures which show very plainly the immense value of the system to St. Louis. Every day it starts through sleeping cars from the Mississippi to the principal cities on the Atlantic sea-board and Canada; to the principal cities on the shores of the northern lakes; to Chicago, St. Paul, Minne-

apolis, Des Moines, and Denver, to say nothing
of the hundreds of intervening points. The
through freight service is unique in its completeness; so much so that its cars bring into
the city every year nearly 1,000,000 tons of
freight, distributing more than 500,000 tons
of merchandise. It brings from the Illinois coal fields over 7,000,000 bushels of coal
yearly, and the returns from all sources are con-
tinually increasing. This is strictly a St. Louis
road, with headquarters in the city. It has
within the last two or three years greatly increased its freight terminal facilities on this side
of the river. The old switching yard on North
Market street has been changed into a large
loading and unloading yard, and an outside yard,
with a capacity of a thousand cars, has been
established just east of Bellefontaine cemetery.
This road has excellent terminal facilities and
entrances to the city, and thus is able to haul
unlimited quantities of merchandise without
difficulty.

THE EADS BRIDGE AND TERMINALS. One of the most significant tributes paid to New
St. Louis since it emerged
from comparative dullness, has been in the increased terminal facilities provided by the railroads centering in the city and by the large
increase in the number of roads having freight
depots on this side of the river. As far as possible
controversial subjects are avoided in this work,
but it is impossible to overlook the fact that the
bridge and terminal monopoly which prevailed
for ten or fifteen years was prejudicial to the
city's commercial growth. It seems ungener-
ous to state this in plain words and without an
explanation, for it is obvious that, although this
monopoly retarded progress and enterprise, the
facilities provided by the Eads bridge have been
worth, and are still worth, countless millions to
the city. This bridge is one of the great things
familiarity with which has bred, if not contempt,
at least neglect of appreciation. Its construction was a work of enterprise of the most
noble character, and the bridge itself is one of
the finest in the world. The bridge was built
on solid rock, and it is an invulnerable fortress,

capable of bearing almost any weight and with-
standing the force of any flood. It consists of
three graceful arches of steel, each 520 feet in
length. Huge piles of masonry rest on solid
rock, and the piers are between 91 and 127 feet
below high-water mark. The masonry in this
bridge measured 69,000 cubic yards; the iron
used weighed 6,300,000 pounds, and the steel
arches came within two-thirds of that weight.
The bridge is two-stories high, the first story
being used by railroads, and the upper story
forming a splendid highway for vehicles between
St. Louis and East St. Louis, and the States of
Missouri and Illinois. Something not contemplated by the designers has lately been added,
and an electric road now affords additional facilities of communication between St. Louis and
its thriving suburb on the east side of the river.
The bridge is 2,225 feet long between its abutments, and its clearance above the St. Louis
directrix is 55 feet. It took seven years to construct and was finally finished in 1874. In the
same year the tunnel was constructed connecting the eastern approach at the foot of Washington avenue with the Mill Creek Valley, and
a union passenger depot was established.

We have said that much as the management
of this bridge has been criticised from time to
time, the value of the bridge to the city's commerce has been enormous. The unfortunate feature was the terminating of the roads from the
East on the east side of the river. Freight from
the East was billed for years to East St. Louis and
brought over the river by the company owning
the bridge and terminal facilities. In addition
to the sentimental objection to a city of the
first class being ignored in bills of lading and
receiving from the East second-hand through a
comparatively small city, the commerce of the
city was handicapped by the additional charges,
and as New St. Louis gained strength and form
the clamor for additional bridge facilities to destroy the monopoly became very strong. In
1886 the Merchants' Exchange, which had been
giving the matter attention for years, brought
the agitation to a focus, and a committee was
formed, consisting of Messrs. S. W. Cobb, C. C.

Rainwater, John R. Holmes, John Whittaker, D. R. Francis, John D. Perry and John M. Gilkeson. This committee succeeded in obtaining a charter from Congress, which was approved by President Cleveland in February, 1887. In June of the same year the necessary franchise for terminals was obtained from the city of St. Louis, and general rejoicing at the certainty of early emancipation from the difficulties complained of were the result. On April 24, 1886, Messrs. S. W. Cobb, John R. Holmes, John M. Gilkeson and C. C. Rainwater filed the necessary application with the Secretary of State for the incorporation of St. Louis Merchants' Bridge Company, and on April 26th the company's subscription books were opened.

THE SECOND BRIDGE ACROSS THE MISSISSIPPI. The act of Congress already referred to authorized the construction of the bridge provided that no bridge should be constructed across the Mississippi river within two miles above or below the Eads bridge, and as the result of this restriction, which in many ways has proved advantageous to the city, the new bridge was planned in the northern manufacturing section. A bridge without terminals would be of little value, and hence the application to the municipal authorities for franchise for terminal tracks; the rights were freely given, and have since been extended, with a result that the company has been able to complete the system of very admirable terminals. The St. Louis Merchants' Bridge Terminal Railway Company was formally established in August, 1887. The length of the railroad was specified in the charter as fourteen miles, and the life of the corporation was fixed at fifty years. Work was commenced on the bridge early in 1889, and was completed the same year, the bridge being opened for traffic in 1890. It is a handsome light structure of immense strength. The piers rest on hard limestone rock which was leveled for the purpose and thoroughly cleaned of all new shale, clay and sand. The caissons were solidly packed with concrete, and limestone from Bedford, Indiana, was used to within three feet of the low-water line; above

this level to the high-water line Missouri granite is used, and above this, Bedford limestone. The dimension stone was laid in Portland cement mortar, and the backing in Louisville cement. In order to make a less abrupt break in the grade between the level grade of the bridge and that of the approaches, the two river piers were raised so that the clear height in the center of the central span is fifty-two feet above high water, instead of fifty feet as required by the act of Congress, and the height at the end of the shore spans is about four inches less. This gives a much better bridge from a navigation standpoint than the law contemplated.

On the west end of the bridge the approach crosses Ferry street twice. The crossing nearest the bridge is made by a viaduct resting on cylinder piers; the crossing furthest from the bridge is a deck span 125 feet long resting on masonry piers. There is one other street overhead crossing which is made by masonry abutments and steel girders. The intermediate space between the structures are either solid earthwork or a substantial timber trestle. On the east end of the bridge, between the 425-foot length of permanent structure and the overhead crossing at the Chicago & Alton, Bee Line and Wabash railroads, and east of this last named structure to the earth embankment, the intermediate spaces are filled with a wooden trestle. The bridge at the crossing of these three railroads is made by two masonry abutments on which rest a 175-foot span and a 40-foot steel girder. The entire bridge and approaches is built for double track. The style of the three spans of the main bridge is a double intersection pin-connected truss with horizontal bottom-chord and a curved top-chord. The entire structure is of steel, except pedestals and ornamental parts, which are of cast-iron, and nuts, swivels and clevises, which are of wrought iron. The steel was required to stand an ultimate tensile strain in the sample bar from 63,000 to 70,000 pounds per square inch, with an elastic limit of not less than 38,000 pounds. Finished bars, selected by the engineer, were subjected to a breaking test, the requirement

being an elongation of ten per cent before breaking. The structures are so proportioned that
under all possible conditions the material cannot
be subjected to injurious strain.

THE MERCHANTS'
BRIDGE TERMINALS.
At the end of the east
approach there are three
connecting lines, one to
the north, connecting with the three railroads
above mentioned; and one to the east, on the
line of the east approach extended, connecting
with the Toledo, St. Louis & Kansas City Railroad; one to the south, connecting with the
Venice & Carondelet Belt Railway and the
East St. Louis & Carondelet Railway, through
which belt railroads connection is made with
the Vandalia, the Ohio & Mississippi, Louisville & Nashville, and all other roads which
reach St. Louis.

The west approach connects with the Wabash
Railroad, and also with the lines of the St. Louis
Transfer Company. The system also has a connection with the Chicago & Burlington Railroad on both sides of the river, and is connected
with the St. Louis & San Francisco and other
railroads. By franchises more recently obtained, it has acquired the right to construct a
belt line circling the city, and crossing every
road entering it from the west. A great deal of
work has already been done on this road, and
the improvement in shipping facilities is
marked. The Merchants' bridge is connected
with the Mill Creek Valley tracks and the
Union depot by means of an elevated structure
along the river front and across the intervening
city blocks. By means of this connection, it is
probable that in the early future an overhead
route will be established between the river and
the Union depot for all passenger trains. This
probability has been increased during the last
year by the establishment of a *modus vivendi*
between the two bridge and terminal companies.
While the Merchants' Bridge and Terminal
Company was increasing the city's terminal
facilities, the older corporation also showed
great enterprise, immensely increasing the mileage of its tracks and the extent of its accommodations. During the year 1893 it was found

that unnecessary expense was being incurred
in duplicate systems of terminals, and an agree-
ment was arrived at whereby the competition
between the two systems was terminated. It
must be left to future historians to decide whether
this step was an unmixed blessing to the city
or not. It is an event of too recent occurrence
to be dispassionately considered at this time of
writing. Opponents of the amalgamation con-
demn it as the re-establishment of a monopoly
which it took seven or eight years of work to
overcome, and to this feeling may be attributed
a revival in the fall and winter of 1893 of the
project to construct a third bridge across the
Mississippi at St. Louis. A charter was obtained for a bridge in Carondelet several years
ago, and soundings which have been made
within the last few weeks indicate that the project has not been entirely abandoned.

The amalgamation or absorption, whichever
may be the correct legal term, is defended by the
parties most interested and also by a large section of the business community, on the ground
that the combined system of terminals with two
bridges, will afford facilities for the rapid handling of merchandise unequaled in the past. The
influence of the Merchants' bridge, and of the
agitation against the billing of freight to East
St. Louis from the East, has been seen in the
immense number of freight depots on this side
of the river, which have been constructed during
the last three years. These depots will continue
to play an important part in the railroad business of the city, in spite of the removal of competition between the two bridges. It takes
more than a few months to change customs in
force for years, and the freight depots on the
west side are only just beginning to be appreciated at their full worth. Another argument,
strongly in favor of the amalgamation which
has just been effected, has relation to passenger
traffic. The immense number of passenger
trains between St. Louis and eastern points has
caused the capacity of the tunnel to be overtaxed, and for other reasons an overhead route
to the new Union depot would be hailed with
general satisfaction. According to the theories

of well-informed railroad men, a large proportion of the passenger traffic would be diverted to the Merchants' bridge and would proceed from its western approach, either by means of the elevated railroad already referred to, or by the belt road, which would take the trains in a westerly direction, and bring them into the Union depot from the west. This latter route would necessarily increase the distance somewhat, but it would take passengers through the residence portions of the city, and make little difference in the time occupied by the journey.

TWO NEW BRIDGES IN 1894. The railroad and bridge facilities of the city will be largely strengthened by the new bridges in course of construction across the Mississippi and Missouri rivers a few miles north of St. Louis. One of these is known as the Bellefontaine bridge, and crosses the Missouri river three and a half miles from the Mississippi. The bridge, which is rapidly approaching completion, is a splendid structure, about 1,780 feet in length. It is supported by five piers, and will be a bridge of exceptional strength. The other bridge is at Alton, over the Mississippi river. It is also being rapidly pushed forward to completion, and will be used as a means of securing a northern inlet to the city for the "Burlington" and other roads. The influence of these bridges on the railroad system of the city and its eastern and northern connections will be enormous, and already it is being felt in a variety of ways. At Alton, they have enlivened the real estate market and encouraged the laying out of additions. That there will be many more is a certain fact. The "Burlington" is famous for fostering its suburban traffic and, out of Chicago especially, gives particular attention to it. The plan of building up such business is to be adhered to here, and it is easy to prophesy that within two or three years we shall see the entire line of the road between St. Louis and Alton built up with lovely suburban homes. Many have already taken advantage of the prospect in view and bought large tracts of land with the ultimate purpose of making suburban tracts of them,

while some others have built upon the wayside, hoping to reap their reward after many years. It has been announced that the "Big Four," the Chicago & Alton and the "Burlington" systems will use the Alton and Bellefontaine bridges. There are others also who have come into the fold since, and have contracted, or will contract, to use them. Besides the M. K. & E. and the M. K. & T. systems, together with the St. Louis, Keokuk & Northwestern on the south, there is also the St. Louis & San Francisco to use it for east and west-bound freights, and it is surmised that another one will before long make a contract with the owners of the two bridges. From the north and east, in addition to those already named, there are the Jacksonville Southeastern, which will probably come into Alton direct by the "Bluff Line;" the "Santa Fe," which will come by the same route; possibly the Illinois Central also, via the "Bluff Line;" while the Wabash will build to the Belt Line, via Edwardsville crossing, and connect with the bridges; and it is quite likely that the Pennsylvania will build from Highland or Greenville, which lie directly east of Alton, and use the bridges as the rest will. In any event, it is certain that they will have plenty of traffic and be a most important factor in the commerce of St. Louis, as well as of Alton.

The two bridges, it is understood, are to be free, except a yearly rental charged roads not interested in the building of them, and rates may be made independent of the Eads, Merchants' or any other method of crossing the Mississippi. At Lamothe Place there is to be an important transfer station with plenty of side-tracks, where the transfers of east and west-bound freight cars will be made and new trains be made up, as also at East Alton. All in all, the new bridges, when completed, will be the most important accessions to the business of St. Louis since the building of the Eads and the Merchants' bridges. They will involve a saving of fifty miles and a week of transfer, opening up a new suburban territory and offering many other advantages too numerous to mention here, but which will develop as time moves on and the bridges and their connections are built and put into operation.

The work of building these bridges, as a total, far surpasses the entire labor of building the Eads bridge, and, with their connections and terminals, it forms one of the most majestic conceptions of modern times. Two bridges not more than four miles apart, the distance from Alton to St. Louis reduced to sixteen miles, many miles of railroad through what was considered an impassable country, subject as it is to annual overflows, all concentrating at one point for the general good and direct benefit of themselves and St. Louis, is a result which five years ago was laughed at, and even sneered at, by many of the most well-informed people.

THE LARGEST PASSENGER DEPOT IN THE WORLD. It will thus be seen that the railroad facilities of St. Louis are at the present time magnificent, and that in the immediate future they will become even more distinctly superior to those of any other city. It is therefore strictly in order that New St. Louis should have a Union depot better and more gigantic than can be found elsewhere, and this it is to have. Simultaneously with the publishing of this work there will be opened the finest depot in the world, and its builders have decided to adopt the European and eastern appellation and call it the "St. Louis Union Station." Nothing but never-ceasing care has enabled the enormous passenger traffic for the last few years to be carried on at all, let alone safely and promptly, at the old Union depot on Twelfth street, and ten years ago a new depot was determined upon. In 1886 the movement took definite shape in the formation of the Union Depot Company by the Missouri Pacific, the Cleveland, Cincinnati & St. Louis, the Iron Mountain & Southern, the Louisville & Nashville, the Ohio & Mississippi and the Wabash. It was not designed that the promoting companies should use the new structure and tracks exclusively, but upon them fell the responsibility of the great task. Jay Gould took a personal interest in the proposition, and many discussions as to the form to be adopted

took place. The platforms of the old depot run east and west, and the through system is used; the platforms of the new station run north and south, and it is designed on the terminal and "pocket" plan. The step was not taken without mature deliberation, and that the wiser counsels prevailed is generally admitted. Mr. William Taussig, the president of the company, and Mr. Theo. C. Link, the architect, will ever be spoken of with pride by St. Louisans for designing and giving to St. Louis *the largest Union Railroad Station in the world.*

There is no exaggeration in this expression. The St. Pancras Station in London is generally spoken of as an exceptionally large depot, but is less than half the size of the new station at St. Louis, which also covers more ground than the two magnificent depots of the Pennsylvania road at Jersey City and Philadelphia put together. Ranked in order of area the seven great representative depots of the world are:

	Total Area in Square Feet.	Approximate No. of Acres.
New Union Station, St. Louis	606 by 700 feet	424,200	10*
Union Depot, Frankfurt, Germany	552 by 600 feet	331,200	8
Reading Railroad Station, Philadelphia	360 by 800 feet	288,000	7
Pennsylvania Railroad Station, Philadelphia	306 by 647 feet	197,982	4½
St. Pancras Station, London	240 by 700 feet	168,000	4
Pennsylvania Railroad Station, Jersey City	256 by 653 feet	167,168	4
Grand Central Station, New York City	200 by 750 feet	150,000	3½

The depot and sheds together cover six city blocks, bounded on the north by Market street, on the south by the Mill Creek Valley tracks, on the east by Eighteenth street, and on the west by Twentieth street. The total area covered is equal to ten acres, and 200,000 men could stand under its roof at one time. No less than 12,000,000 pounds of steel, 2,500,000 feet of lumber, 5,000,000 bricks, 3,000,000 nails, 100,000 cubic feet of stone, 200,000 roofing tile and 50,000 square yards of plastering have been

*Including sheds, buildings, &c., the area covered is really about twelve acres.

used in the work, and the total cost of the structure, including the purchase of the site, exceeds $4,000,000. A detailed description of a building of this magnitude is well-nigh impossible, but some of the most striking features must be recorded. At Eighteenth street there is an entrance-way and stair-case fifty feet wide, but the main entrances are on Market street, where carriages can drive in through a semicircular drive-way to the approach to the grand stair-case. The basement of the depot is on a level with the tracks under the train-shed, and the first floor is a little above the Market street level.

Passengers to the city cannot fail to be impressed with the grand waiting-rooms through which they will pass. The general waiting-room has a floor area of 10,000 square feet, and is of exceptional altitude. The decorations, both of the walls and the ceiling, are appropriate and costly, and in the center there is to be a Bureau of Information, at which questions of all character will be answered. The grand waiting-room, on the first floor above, has an area of 12,000 square feet, and is sixty feet high. The decorations of this room are magnificent, and no less than 3,000 incandescent lights will be used for its illumination. The ladies' parlors, which are now practically completed, are also models of excellence; and the general offices, railroad, telegraphic and otherwise, are of the most perfect character. When the Municipal Assembly granted the necessary authority for closing the streets running through the ten-acre tract now covered by the depot, it was stipulated that the main building should cost not less than $800,000. The actual cost of this portion of the work has not been made public, but it is so far in excess of the minimum named in the franchise, that those who took the precaution to put in the figures feel now that their ideas of the work proposed were extremely conservative.

PLAN OF THE UNION STATION SHED. The train-shed is more remarkable than the building itself. It is 606 feet wide, nearly 700 feet long, and 100 feet high. The roof of the shed forms an arch of 600 feet radius, the height varying from 30 feet at the sides to the 100 feet already mentioned in the center. The roof is supported by forty-four outer columns, forty-four intermediate columns and twenty-four middle columns of great strength. The roof is almost entirely of glass, of which there are used altogether 120,000 square feet in the work, all of St. Louis manufacture. An extension to the train-shed calls for 42,000 square feet of space, and will give the depot facilities for handling an unlimited amount of traffic expeditiously and safely. The number of tracks provided for in this shed is thirty-two, twice as many as are to be found in the Pennsylvania depot at Philadelphia, and nearly twice as many as in the large depot at Frankfurt, Germany. Between the tracks will be hardwood platforms, twelve feet in the clear. As already mentioned, the tracks run into the depot from south to north, and the platforms parallel the tracks, bounded at the southern end by fences and gates. Along the Eighteenth street side there is also a fifty-foot platform for the exclusive use of promenaders, who will not be allowed to go on the platforms.

Seventy feet from the rear depot wall a baggage-room extends 300 feet southward. This will be the most complete quick-service room in the country, and will be so great an improvement over the accommodations hitherto enjoyed by the travelers through St. Louis that comparison is out of question. One more feature of the depot must be mentioned, because of the ingenuity of which it gives evidence, and also of the immense advantages that will accrue. This has relation to the system of tracks and their entrance to the sheds, which have been so arranged that no engine will come under the massive roof. In the good days to come, locomotives will be equipped with smoke-consuming devices, but even then they will be objectionable under cover. Now, they give forth volumes of smoke and make a variety of unpleasant noises, and their room is far preferable to their company; and it is a splendid feature of the new depot that the air in the sheds will always be perfectly clear and pure. The thirty-

two tracks will vary in length from 400 to
1,200 feet, and they will converge into a bottle-
shaped junction or throat at the south end.
A train coming in from either direction will run
past the shed; the engine will be reversed and
the train backed in over the curved "Y" to
its respective track. No switching will be
required, as the trains will be made up and
ready to resume their respective journeys in
either direction when required. The switches
will all be controlled by the lever-locking system, from a switch-tower of considerable height.
There will be no possibility of collisions, and
the service will be improved and expedited in
the most pronounced manner.

If the arrangement already described, whereby
all passenger trains will enter the city via the
Mill Creek Valley from the west, is carried out,
the system will be still greater in its simplicity.
At the first opening of the depot, however, the
Wabash, Missouri Pacific, Iron Mountain, Keokuk, Colorado, and San Francisco trains, with
others using their tracks, will come in from the
west under the Twenty-first street bridge, passing the shed entrance and then backing in as
described. The Wabash Eastern, Chicago &
Alton, "Burlington," "Cairo Short Line," "Big
Four," Illinois Central, Louisville & Nashville,
Louisville, Evansville & St. Louis and Baltimore & Ohio trains will at first run up the Mill
Creek Valley from the eastern approach, pass
under the Eighteenth street bridge, and back
into the shed and depot from the west.

The official announcement has been made that
the depot will be open for traffic next March
(1894), and there seems every reason to believe
that the promise will be carried out and that the
magnificent depot will be in use before the summer travel commences.

**THE IMPORTANCE
OF OUR
RIVER CONNECTIONS.** The extraordinary railroad facilities of St. Louis
have, to a great extent,
overshadowed its river
facilities, and have caused sight to be lost of the
fact that St. Louis is the chief port in 18,000
miles of inland waterways. In years gone by
the river was the making of St. Louis, and al-

though the city's greatness is due more to the railroads than to the river, no treatise on the greatness of St. Louis will ever be complete without
a reference to the river and the enormous traffic
that it has witnessed. "There is no warrant,"
to quote from the memorial presented by the
Merchants' Exchange in 1892 to the Fifty-
second Congress, in favor of the deepening of
the river channel between St. Louis and the
Gulf, "for the assertion that in this age of railroads rivers have lost their fascination and
influence over the people, and that it is as easy
to build up a great and populous city at a distance from navigable water as upon its shore.
The history of settlements in this country, as
well in the last forty years of railroad making,
as in the one hundred and fifty that preceded it,
attests the continued ascendency of navigable
streams and lakes over the popular mind, and
their great value in commercial, industrial and
distributive economics. The same forces that
located New York at the mouth of the Hudson,
Philadelphia on the Delaware, Baltimore on the
Patapsco, New Orleans and St. Louis on the
Mississippi, Pittsburgh, Cincinnati and Louisville
on the Ohio, and Chicago and Milwaukee on
Lake Michigan, before railroads were thought
of, have assisted to build up Minneapolis, St.
Paul, LaCrosse, Winona, Dubuque, Davenport,
Rock Island, Muscatine, Keokuk, Hannibal,
Quincy, Cairo, Memphis and Vicksburg on the
Mississippi, Evansville, Owensboro and Paducah on the Ohio, and Kansas City, Leaven-
worth, St. Joseph, Omaha, Council Bluffs, Sioux
City, Pierre and Bismarck on the Missouri; and
it may be observed that in the settlement of the
newer portions of the Mississippi Valley in the
last half century, it has ever been the rule to
found the leading cities and towns on rivers and
lakes, if there were rivers or lakes within reach,
unless special agencies dictated a different location. And it is a fact not without significance
that the cities, founded on the waterside, which
were leading cities as far back as 1830, have
maintained their pre-eminence in the face of
railway influences, and are leading cities in
1892. Pittsburgh, at the head of the Ohio, con-

tinues to be the largest city in Western Pennsylvania; Cincinnati, on the Ohio, and Cleveland, on Lake Erie, are the largest cities in Ohio; Chicago is the chief city of Illinois, St. Louis and Kansas City of Missouri, Louisville of Kentucky, St. Paul and Minneapolis of Minnesota, Omaha of Nebraska, Memphis and Nashville of Tennessee, Little Rock of Arkansas, Vicksburg of Mississippi and New Orleans, Shreveport and Baton Rouge of Louisiana—and there are good reasons for believing that these cities, all located on the waterside, will continue to maintain their ascendency in their respective States for generations to come."

The actual population of the Mississippi river States alone is 18,500,000, while the population of the Mississippi Valley States is over 28,000,000. The region drained by the Mississippi and its tributaries embraces one-half the States in the Union and nearly one-half the population, and the immense value of the city's river location can easily be understood when this fact is taken into consideration. According to the census of 1890 upwards of 31,000,000 tons of freight were carried during the year 1889 on the Mississippi and its tributaries, the principal commodities and the tonnage of each being as follows:

COMMODITIES.	TONS.
Coal	10,632,109
Forest Products	10,531,189
Merchandise	5,886,259
Wheat	1,068,504
Cotton	686,635
Iron Ore	536,647
Cotton Seed and Oil	392,988
Corn	266,071
Sugar and Molasses	189,829
Animal Products	169,470
Stone and Gravel	158,453
Clay and Sand	141,464
Manufactured Iron	122,060
Mill Products	88,129
Hay	78,635
Other Grain	51,308
Fruits and Vegetables	23,091
Tobacco	17,707
Pig Iron	5,506
Oils	3,128
Ice	4,000
Cement, Brick and Lime	1,231
Total	31,054,423

The river equipment of the streams with which St. Louis has direct traffic and large proprietary interest embrace upwards of 1,300 boats, with an aggregate tonnage of 480,000, the actual of weight of freight moved on them amounting to about one-half the total given above.

PROSPECTS OF INCREASED RIVER TRAFFIC. It could scarcely be expected that the river traffic to and from St. Louis would show a large increase when the immense railroad freight returns are taken into consideration, but considerably upwards of 1,000,000 tons of freight are received at the city and shipped from it every year. The returns would be infinitely larger but for suspensions of traffic caused by low water, and for several years the efforts of the Merchants' Exchange have been directed towards the securing from the Federal Government a measure of justice in the matter of river improvement. The movement, warmly supported by Mr. E. A. Noonan, during his administration as mayor, came to a definite head in the years 1891 and 1892, when the executive committee of the commercial and manufacturing associations of St. Louis for the improvement of the Mississippi river secured the introduction of a bill appropriating $8,000,000 annually for the improvement of the river. This bill passed the Senate, but owing to the strong opposition in the House, it was deemed inadvisable to run the risk of pushing it, and in its place there was obtained an appropriation of $4,000,000 per annum for four years, for continuous work on the Mississippi river from St. Paul to New Orleans. This work is now in progress, and a concerted effort will be made to have the appropriations continued indefinitely until St. Louis becomes a seaport, and until the river is navigable at all periods of the year, except when closed by ice.

The high water of the year 1892 reduced the river tonnage considerably. During the months of April, May, June and July the average stage of the river at St. Louis was about twenty feet, as compared with zero of gauge in the year 1863, and again in December, 1893. This latter indicated about twelve feet of water in the channel in the harbor of St. Louis, with four and sometimes only three feet of water in places between here and Cairo. The arrivals and departures at and from the port of St. Louis during the last twenty years are as follows:

YEARS.	ARRIVALS.		Tons of Freight Received.	Tons of Lumber and Logs by Raft Received.	YEARS.	DEPARTURES.	Tons of Freight shipped.
	Boats	Barges				Boats.	
1892	2053	1090	556,980	130,220	1892	2013	502,215
1891	1881	1019	450,050	142,090	1891	1845	512,930
1890	1927	1274	530,790	132,910	1890	1910	617,985
1889	2195	1474	543,990	127,695	1889	2211	712,700
1888	2079	1244	537,955	130,855	1888	2076	510,115
1887	2361	1272	652,880	213,165	1887	2328	637,060
1886	2087	1269	570,205	200,785	1886	2102	561,895
1885	1878	1030	479,065	217,860	1885	1828	534,175
1884	2018	999	520,350	240,330	1884	2018	514,910
1883	2240	1185	629,225	231,285	1883	2140	677,340
1882	2537	1110	802,080	271,490	1882	2487	769,905
1881	2426	1525	852,410	356,020	1881	2340	884,025
1880	2871	1821	893,860	198,315	1880	2866	1,038,350
1879	2360	1471	688,970		1879	2392	676,445
1878	2322	1291	714,700		1878	2348	614,675
1877	2150	660	644,485		1877	2156	597,676
1876	2122	683	688,755		1876	2118	600,225
1875	2201	743	663,525		1875	2223	639,095
1874	2332	951	732,765		1874	2364	707,325
1873	2316	1020	810,055		1873	2303	783,256

CHAPTER VI.

RAPID TRANSIT AND ITS INFLUENCES.

THE EARLY STRUGGLES OF OMNIBUS AND STREET CAR COMPANIES.—THE INTRODUCTION OF CABLE AND ELECTRIC POWER.—EFFECT ON IMPROVEMENTS AND VALUES.

THE STREET CAR service of St. Louis is now equal to that to be found in any city in the world, and in many respects it is far superior. It has more special features than the street car service of any other city, and it runs some of the most handsome cars in the world. During the year 1893 the use of horses and mules for street car traction was put a stop to in the down-town sections of the city, and the three roads which were the last to fall in line with the procession commenced the regular running of electric cars during the summer. Now every main line is operated by electricity or cable, and there are

nearly 300 miles in operation, while the total number of passengers carried each year is about 100,000,000. To realize what this means it should be borne in mind that to maintain an average of 100,000,000 passengers per annum it is necessary for the cars to haul a number equal to one-half the city's entire population every day, Sundays included. Before describing the splendid equipments of to-day, a brief reference must be made to the early days of omnibuses and street cars in St. Louis. The first omnibus was run without any concerted system or plan about fifty-five years ago. A local paper in 1838 speaks of the handsome style of an omnibus run by Mr. Belcher, but it was not until 1844 that an omnibus service of any extent was established. Mr. Erastus Wells and Mr. Calvin Case in that year established an omnibus line, which is referred to in a local paper on June 11, 1845, in the following terms:

"It is but a few months since our opinion was asked as to the probable profits of an omnibus to be run in certain parts of the city. At that time no omnibuses were run in the city. The experiment was attempted. The first was started by Messrs. Case & Wells, to run from the National Hotel on Market street, to the ferry at the upper end of the city. We believe it has been successful as could have been expected from a new undertaking. At first people were a little shy of it; some did not think it exactly a genteel way of traveling the streets. These scruples have entirely disappeared, and everybody now rides in them, and is glad of the opportunity. Messrs. Case & Wells manifest a determination to keep up with the encouragement given them, and have lately put on their line a new and beautiful omnibus, manufactured in Troy, New York. It is a fine specimen of workmanship, and is a very comfortable carriage. In addition to the line above mentioned, we now have regular lines running from the National Hotel to the Arsenal, along Second street; a line from the Planters' House to the Arsenal, along Fourth street; a line from the corner of Fourth and Market streets to the Camp Springs, and a line to the Prairie House. All seem to be doing a flourishing and profitable business, and they prove to be a great convenience to persons residing in distant parts, and to those having business to attend to in remote parts of the city. They have contributed not a little to give an increase of value to real estate lying at a distance from the center or business portion of the city."

In 1850 Erastus Wells, with Calvin Case, Robert O'Blennus and Lawrence Mathews formed a combination which purchased and operated all the omnibus lines in St. Louis. In the following year there were six lines in existence, as follows: First, from the Arsenal to Carondelet; second, from the corner of Market and Second streets to the Arsenal; third, from the corner of Main and Market to Camp Springs; fourth, from the corner of Broadway and Franklin avenue to Rising Sun Tavern; fifth, from the corner of Market and Third to Bremen; sixth, from Bremen to Bissell's Ferry. The omnibuses from these points started every four to ten minutes, and the lines comprised in all ninety omnibuses, 450 head of horses, four stables and about 100 hands.

THE FIRST STREET RAILROAD TRIP. In January, 1859, a meeting was held to discuss the question of the building of street railroads, and the sense of the meeting was so strongly in favor of the innovation that local enterprise was at once directed towards the incorporation of companies for building and equipping street railroads. In the following May the Missouri Railroad Company was organized, and Mr. Erastus Wells became its president, a position he occupied for more than twenty years. By July the road was constructed as far as Twelfth street, and on the 4th of July the first car was run over the track. In these days of street railroads running trains five, and even fifteen, miles, the excitement which the first trip created on the six-block route seems remarkable and almost humorous. The literature of the day tells us that the first car was a beautiful vehicle, light, elegant and commodious, having cost $900, including freight from Philadelphia, where it was constructed. "Mr. Wells, president of the road, then took the reins," we are told, "and, after a jerk or two, the first car moved slowly but steadily up the track amidst loud shouts and cheers from the crowd. Troops of urchins followed in its wake, endeavoring to hang on, and we fear unless this is prevented in the future, serious accidents may occur." The journey appears to have been accompanied by great difficulties, the car leaving the track several times, but Tenth street was finally reached, "the track having been cleared of stone only that distance." It took many years to bring the Missouri Railroad system up to its present standard, but Grand avenue was reached during the seventies by both Olive and Market streets.

The St. Louis Railroad, or the Broadway line, was also started in 1859, as was the Citizens' Railway, which originally ran as far west as Garrison avenue. In 1864 the road was extended to the Fair Grounds, and in 1881 along the St. Charles rock road to Rinkelville. The extension of this road between King's Highway and Rinkelville is still operated by horses on a single track with turn-outs. It is shortly to be reconstructed and equipped as an electric road, but in the meantime it gives an interesting insight into the original system of street railroads in St. Louis as compared with the magnificent equipment of to-day. The People's road was also constructed along Fourth street in 1859, and five years later it was extended to Lafayette Park. In 1882 it was further extended to Grand avenue. The first step towards the formation of the Union Depot system of street railroads was made in 1862, when the track was laid from Fourth and Pine streets to Gravois road. So many extensions have taken place since, that the road has become a general South St. Louis means of transportation, and it has just completed a line to Carondelet on the high ground. The year 1864 was an important one in street railroad history. It saw the building of the Benton-Bellefontaine Railroad as far as the water tower, and also the commencement of work on the Lindell system, now one of the largest in the United States. Cars were run on both the Washington avenue and Fourteenth street branches early in 1867, the first named road having for some years its terminus at Ware avenue.

The Union Railway was organized the following year and track was laid as far as Hyde Park. Ten years later the road was extended to the Fair Grounds. In 1871 the Cass Avenue and Fair Grounds Railway was organized, and in June 1875 it was first operated. On October 25, 1874, some excitement was caused by the running of the first two-story car in the city. This was on the Northwestern St. Louis Railway, which became absorbed by the Mound City

Railway Company, whose cars were first operated in 1866. The South St. Louis Railway Company was incorporated in 1876 at about the time of the adoption of the scheme and charter. By the purchase of the Carondelet Street Railway Company, it connected Carondelet with St. Louis, running due south.

Another company, not strictly a street railroad company, but of equal importance to the city, is the St. Louis Transfer Company, originally known as the Ohio & Mississippi Transfer Company. This was chartered in 1859, and has provided admirable transfer and omnibus facilities for passengers, baggage and freight ever since, keeping pace with the growth of public sentiment and the improvement of transfer facilities generally.

THE SERVICE OF OLD ST. LOUIS AT ITS BEST. This in brief traces the origin of the magnificent street railroad facilities of St. Louis to-day. In 1882, when, as we have already seen, Old St. Louis began to merge into New St. Louis, there were in operation fourteen street railroads, which carried about 30,000,000 passengers during the year, or less than one-third the total carried now. The following table, based on the 1882 returns, will give some slight idea of the small beginning upon which the street railroad system of New St. Louis was based:

	Miles Operated	No. of Horses and Mules	Cars Operated	Reported Valuation
Baden	3	17	8	$ 6,820
Benton & Bellefontaine	6	132	42	48,720
Cass Avenue	8	193	30	83,810
Citizens'	13	296	56	94,520
The Lindell	10	401	70	159,430
Missouri	8	295	56	122,960
Mound City	6	83	22	22,880
People's	8	250	30	59,110
St. Louis	14	442	66	125,860
South St. Louis	12	75	23	32,510
Tower Grove & Lafayette	3	93	20	25,050
Union	8	210	21	63,660
Union Depot	10	366	68	75,870

The influence of New St. Louis at once began to be felt in the street cars. As seen above, Grand avenue was generally the terminus of railroads running west, and the extension of the Lindell Railway as far as Vandeventer avenue by means of a loop running west on Delmar avenue, north on Vandeventer, east on Finney and south on Grand, was regarded as quite a work of enterprise. Bobtail cars—the popular name for the unpopular diminutive cars, whose drivers are compelled to act in dual capacity as drivers and conductors—were run, and, although the road proved a great convenience, it was not pushed to its full limit. The Market street road was also extended as far as Forest Park, and on Sundays through cars were run, though during the week the much-despised bobtail cars did duty on the extension.

St. Louisans, visiting other cities and observing the successful operation in them of street railroads operated by rapid transit in the shape of cables, became impressed with the fact that horse and mule traction was too slow for a great city like St. Louis, and the question of rapid transit began to be discussed here very freely. As we have seen in a preceding chapter, the railroad magnates strongly objected to the proposed innovation, and a vigorous outcry was also raised by the conservative and timid element. It seems strange that emancipation from the old rut should have been inaugurated by Indianapolis capitalists, but such was the case, and in 1884 the first franchise was granted for a cable road. The promoters had acquired the title and interest in the narrow-gauge road which ran from the intersection of Grand avenue and Olive street to the interesting city of Florissant, seventeen miles out in the country. That this road was intended for much greater things than it had achieved, was evidenced by its title, which was the St. Louis, Creve Cœur & St. Charles Railway Company, to which corporation the privileges were granted by the Municipal Assembly after a bitter fight.

THE FIRST CABLE ROAD FRANCHISE. Ordinance No. 12,852, approved by Mayor Ewing in 1884, should ever be regarded by St. Louis property holders and citizens with something akin to veneration, because it sanctioned the first step towards the emancipation of the city from the rule of horses and mules on its street car tracks, and because the work done under it gave a marked impetus to the new growth of the city. The franchise granted the company permission to lay a cable track between the junction of Sixth and Locust streets and the intersection of the narrow-gauge road with Morgan street, at a point a little west of Vandeventer avenue. The precautions taken against damage to the city and private property in the construction of the road were somewhat remarkable, and showed that the warnings of those who had prophesied dire disaster as the result of the innovation had not been thrown away on the city legislators. The limits of speed specified in the ordinance were also indicative of the spirit of the times. East of Twelfth street no car was to run faster than six miles an hour; between Twelfth street and Garrison avenue a speed of seven miles was permitted, and west of Garrison avenue eight miles was allowed. These speed regulations would have required the use of three different cables, with drums at Twelfth street and also Garrison avenue; but before the road was opened wise counsels prevailed, and a more reasonable uniform speed-limit was made.

Those who resided in the city at the time will remember with great interest the construction of this road. It was built in the most substantial manner then possible, but by a slow, tedious and expensive process, without the use of the devices of more recent years which had made cable-track laying far more speedy and practicable. As an event typical of the times, the laying of the first cable in the conduit is worth mentioning. The local papers devoted to the work a large amount of space, and considering the immense crowds which witnessed the work, the event was certainly one of more than ordinary interest. The cable was placed in position late in the winter of 1885–86, and the first cable train was run at the commencement of spring following. The excitement which the experiment created will ever be remembered. On the first Sunday of the road's operation it beat the record in the matter of passenger hauling, although its equipment was by no means complete. The popularity of the road was so great that even after the novelty wore off, people willingly walked four or five blocks out of their way to ride in the cars, and a career of extraordinary prosperity appeared to be certain. The "impossible" route added to the difficulties of running the road, but although a great many passengers were thrown into each other's laps, and some few were thrown on to the sidewalk at the sharpest curves, these little drawbacks did not materially injure the road's traffic receipts. The most objectionable and dangerous point was at Grand avenue and Morgan street, where a double curve seemed to defy the efforts of the engineers to devise means to keep the cars on the track. This trouble was finally obviated by the purchase of the property at the southeast corner, and the moving several feet south of the house situated upon it, so as to enable the track to be relaid without a perceptible curve at all.

The road's progress was also interfered with by a calamitous fire, which destroyed its entire equipment before it had been in operation more than a year. Horse cars were run for a short time, and finally a fresh supply of cars was obtained and traffic was resumed. The road was finally sold, at a handsome profit to the original promoters, and it passed into the control of Boston capitalists. Sufficient money was not spent to keep up the track, and the competition of adjoining roads which in the meantime had been equipped with cable power, reduced the earning capacity of the pioneer rapid transit road of St. Louis to such an extent that it passed into the hands of a receiver. About four years ago Messrs. Charles H. Turner, S. M. Kennard, Clark H. Sampson and other capitalists were convinced of the possibility of reconstructing the road with electricity and making it pay handsomely. They secured a controlling interest in the corporation, reorganized it as the St. Louis & Suburban Railroad, and at once decided upon the gigantic enterprise of equipping the road its entire length with electricity. The narrow-gauge suburban service was exceedingly unsatisfactory and entirely inadequate, and the reorganizers determined to run a double-track electric road as far as the city limits and a single-track electric road from that point to Florissant, the tracks to be doubled on the county section as soon as the traffic justified the outlay.

THE FIRST COUNTY ELECTRIC ROAD. The necessary legislation was obtained, and the long and tedious task commenced. Electric cars were run as an extension to the cable service in 1891, and in 1892 the great work was completed and a through service of electric cars established between Sixth and Locust streets and the city limits at Wells Station, with an excellent county extension to Normandy and Florissant. This road is now the longest electric road in the world operated from one power-house, and the enormous increase in its receipts since the change of motive power has more than justified the enterprise and anticipations of the reorganizers.

The history of this road has been traced at some length because of its exceptional influence on the city's rapid transit facilities and also on its general growth. Before leaving the subject, it is of interest to add that in addition to being the longest electric road operated from one power-house, it was the road selected by the government for the experiment of street railroad postal cars. The experiment has proved a perfect success, and now three trips are made daily, with sub-postoffices established along the line of route. The delivery of mail is expedited very largely by the change, and national interest has been attracted by the experiment, which, however, can hardly be regarded as an experiment now. The company already transacts a freight and express business west of Vandeventer avenue, and at an early date this service will be extended down-town.

But we are somewhat anticipating history. The railroad companies which had opposed the cable franchise found their worst fears fulfilled, and the traffic returns of parallel lines in 1886 showed the necessity of prompt action. During the year nearly every road of importance obtained the right to change its motive power, and the year 1887 saw much work done. Among the first roads to lay cable, and the first to re-construct, was the Olive street branch of the Missouri, which cabled its tracks right out to Forest Park, instead of having its western terminus at Grand avenue, as hitherto. The reconstruction was a lengthy piece of work, but it was duly accomplished, and subsequently both the other sections of this system have been equipped as electric roads. This Missouri system alone now carries half a million passengers a month, and its business is constantly increasing.

It has just erected a magnificent depot and pavilion close to the Blair statue in Forest Park for the convenience of the thousands of passengers its cars haul daily, and the popularity of the route will be still greater when this building is ready for use. There are few street railroad lines in the country which run so nearly in a straight line, and which traverse such a thickly settled and highly improved territory. Starting from Fourth and Olive, close to the Merchants' Exchange, and some of the finest office-buildings in the city, it runs directly west up Olive street, passing the Federal building and the Exposition, and continuing on its western course, within a block a great portion of the way of the finest boulevard and drive-way in St. Louis. Although this was one of the first cable railroads constructed in St. Louis, it is also the most modern in character, and the most successful in operation. No money was spared in building the road, which is kept in the highest state of repair, with a power-house of unlimited capacity, and a determination on the part of the management to provide accommodation as nearly perfect as possible. The cars, those used both for summer and winter, are excellently upholstered, and are kept scrupulously clean, while the trains run at such frequent intervals that people who are in a hurry use them even if it compels a walk of a few extra blocks. The service is so excellent in every respect that, although electricity has entirely supplanted the cable in the estimation of the people, there is an exception in this instance, and the Olive street road is as much liked as the best electric road in the city.

RAPID TRANSIT TO THE PRINCIPAL PARKS. The Missouri Company has also an electric road running in a straight line to Forest Park. This road, formerly known as the Forest Park & Laclede Railroad, starts from the southern front of the court-house, and runs up Market and Chestnut streets, reaching the park by the former thoroughfare, some few blocks south of the cable terminus. It is also the only street railroad corporation in St. Louis running to both Forest Park and Tower Grove Park, the two most popular recreation and breathing spots in the city. Tower Grove Park is reached by the Missouri Company's electric road, which starts from Fourth and Market and runs by a very direct route to Shaw's Garden, being in fact the only railroad which carries passengers right to the gates of the great botanical garden which has made St. Louis popular and famous among students of natural beauty everywhere. The western terminus of this road is at the northern entrance to Tower Grove Park, and its passengers thus have the advantage of reaching both the garden and the parks without change of cars or delay of any kind.

Simultaneously with the cabling of the Olive street road, the Citizens' Railroad was changed to cable. Nor was this all. Easton avenue between Prairie avenue and King's Highway was neither improved nor graded, and the company proposed as a matter of course to lay its conduits only as far as city improvements made it possible. The property owners, however, clubbed together and had the street graded to King's Highway. The company was a party to the transaction, made King's Highway its western cable terminus, and thereby doubled and trebled the value of property along the avenue. The company's branch to the Fair Grounds was also cabled, but in 1893 the conduit was removed and electric power substituted; another tribute to the conquering tendency of the latest of modern inventions. Under the same management as the Citizens' are the Cass Avenue, Northern Central and Union lines, to all of which reference has already been made, and all of which were equipped with electricity during 1892. The combined system serves the north-west portion of the city very thoroughly, and hauls immense numbers of passengers to the Fair Grounds and races.

One of the most indispensable, and, as we have seen, one of the very oldest roads in the city is the Broadway. Unlike the other roads referred to, which run more or less east and west, this road runs from north to south, connecting the manufacturing section of North St. Louis with the manufacturing and brewing section of South St. Louis, and passing through not only the business section of the city, but also through some of its most thickly settled residence wards. Although before this road was reconstructed for rapid transit, electric roads had established their popularity, the immense number of trains to be run over the track made the management prefer a cable, which was laid during the years 1889 and 1890. The cabling of the road was a very costly undertaking, but the work was done in the most efficient manner possible, and the road is a model in every respect. Visitors to St. Louis who desire to visit the new Merchants' bridge, the old and the new water-works, the cemeteries, all in the northern section of the city, find the Broadway cable convenient for the purpose; while it is also a popular route to the great breweries of the south end.

The Lindell, or Washington avenue, Railroad was among the first to feel the influence of rapid transit competition, as the new cable road paralleled its line within a few blocks almost its entire length. Experiments were tried in 1887 with a storage battery electric car, which, however, was not a success. Shortly afterwards Mr. George D. Capen and other local capitalists secured control of the road, and having unlimited faith in the future of St. Louis proceeded at once to map out what looked like a daring scheme, not only of reconstruction, but also of extension. Electric power was selected as the motor, and the main line track was extended on Finney avenue as far west as Taylor. From this point two branches were constructed, one running on Delmar boulevard to DeBaliviere avenue and

then south into Forest Park, where a magnificent pavilion has been constructed providing a handsome ornament to the park, and being of immense convenience to passengers visiting the city's great breathing ground and pleasure resort. The other branch was constructed out west on Page boulevard, piercing a district hitherto a stranger to street railroad facilities of any kind. The enterprise of the road did not stop at this point. Recognizing that St. Louis was in need of north and south railroads, or cross-town lines, the management obtained municipal legislation and proceeded to construct, some three years ago, the Vandeventer avenue line, which connects the Fair Grounds with the Mill Creek Valley tracks.

INTRODUCTION OF THE TRANSFER SYSTEM. The opening of this road was a matter of special interest to St. Louis, because for the first time it introduced into the city on a comprehensive scale a system of transfers, whereby a passenger can make a continuous journey by more than one car without paying an additional fare. During 1893 the company has also completed and opened a street railroad on Taylor avenue from its junction with Finney into the northwestern wards, with the intention of extending it at an early date to the cemeteries on the north and the railroad tracks on the south. Also, during 1893, it has opened a new road passing the new Union Station, crossing the Eighteenth street bridge and providing facilities for residents in the Compton Hill district. It also has a second road to Forest Park via Chouteau avenue, and has altogether one of the most comprehensive and extensive street railroad systems in the United States. Its power-house is one of the largest in the world, and it has also excited the interest of street railroad men everywhere by its patented vestibule street car, which affords easy ingress and egress through a vestibule in the center of what is really a combination of two full-sized electric cars. No returns are available for the entire Lindell system. During the third quarter of 1893 it carried nearly 4,000,000 passengers, and its completed system is probably carrying at least 1,500,000 passengers monthly.

Another road which has obtained running powers past the new Union Station is the Union Depot Company, which now embraces not only the numerous roads running into the southern wards, but also the Mound City Railroad and the Benton & Bellefontaine Railroad. This gigantic system of railroads, with upwards of sixty miles of electric track, thus runs from the extreme south of the city to the cemeteries in the extreme northwest, with branches in almost every direction, and a system of transfers which enables passengers to travel right through and across the city for one fare. Its latest extension is now nearly completed. It intersects the highest ground in Carondelet, and affords unlimited facilities for transportation. No road has a more interesting history than this great system and the parts which help to make up the whole. In its early days all the hardships of bobtail bars and insufficient service were felt, but during the last few years these complaints have all been rendered unnecessary, and the equipment is now excellent. The power-house from which these different branches are operated is of exceptional size, and its capacity is taxed to the uttermost. By its absorption of the Mound City and Benton & Bellefontaine roads, the company also acquired two other large power-houses. The business transacted by the roads in this system is nearly, if not quite, 20,000,000 passengers per annum.

A COMPARISON BETWEEN THE ROADS OF OLD AND NEW ST. LOUIS.

The People's Railroad, originally constructed to Lafayette Park, was cabled some three years ago and extended along Grand avenue to Tower Grove Park. Now an electric road is being constructed along Grand avenue, connecting the various roads which run on or across that thoroughfare, and providing a third parallel cross-town road of great usefulness. At the present time there are in the city 240 miles of street railway in actual operation, and 43 more in course of construction. In other words, early in 1894 there will be about 300 miles of

street railroads in operation, as compared with less than 120 miles in 1882. This wonderful increase in itself is a striking tribute to the growth and importance and wealth of New St. Louis, and it would be so if the question of mileage alone were considered. But the increase in value has been far greater than the increase in mileage, because, while in 1882 the tracks were laid as cheaply as possible, and the motive power was horses and mules, the roads in 1893 are equipped in the most costly manner known, and the motive power is more than two-thirds electricity, with about forty-three miles of cable road.

The enterprise of the railroad magnates has been more than rewarded, for the traffic has increased in a most remarkable manner. In 1885, the last year of the horse-car reign, the number of passengers carried by the St. Louis street railroads was a trifle in excess of 41,000,000. Estimating population at this stage at 410,000, each inhabitant of the city, on an average, rode in a street car a hundred times during the year. In 1891 the number of passengers carried had increased about 100 per cent, and in 1892 the number of passengers carried amounted to 91,500,000. In other words, the average number of rides taken by every inhabitant of St. Louis was about 200 during the year. The returns for 1893 are not yet complete, but they will certainly approximate 100,000,000 for the year. The total for the first six months was more than 48,000,000, and the following table gives the traffic for the quarter ending October 1:

	Miles operated October 1.	Number of Trips Made.	Number of Fares Collected.
Union Depot	55	158,367	4,612,404
Lindell	41	323,242	3,845,936
Missouri	24	297,600	3,712,257
St. Louis	20	211,410	3,067,721
Citizens'	15	185,246	2,215,793
Cass Avenue	27	150,896	2,121,410
St. Louis & Suburban	19	33,863	2,057,175
Southern	15	88,560	1,520,307
People's	10	58,404	1,260,078
Jefferson Avenue.	3	23,116	565,413
Baden	3	5,720	127,940

This shows a total of more than 25,000,000 passengers carried during the quarter.

RAPID TRANSIT AND THE CITY MAP. It only needs a glance at the city map to-day and the maps as published ten years ago, to see how remarkable has been the influence of rapid transit on the building up of the city. Those visiting St. Louis during the years 1892 and 1893, after an absence from the city of eight or ten years, have been astounded at the changes effected. Specific reference has already been made to the effect of the cable construction on Easton avenue. This thoroughfare was little more than a country road ten years ago. The single-track street car line was laid on one side of the road, and the service was anything but satisfactory. There were a few stores on the street, but they were general country stores, without specialties in any line. To-day Easton avenue is one of the most important thoroughfares in the city. It forms part of the direct road from the Mississippi river at St. Louis to the Missouri river at St. Charles, and, thanks to the influence of the cable, that portion of the St. Charles rock road which is now known as Easton avenue, is a busy thoroughfare, with hundreds of stores and private dwellings. Several attempts have been made to state in figures what benefit the cable road has been to Easton avenue, but sufficient data are not at hand to make any calculation approximately accurate. It is certain, however, that property which could not be sold at $10 a foot before the reconstruction, now has buyers in abundance at $50, $60 and $70, with higher prices for corners. Farther out on Easton avenue where property ten years ago could be bought by the acre, $20, $25 and $30 a foot is now paid.

The general equipment of the roads running due west with rapid transit facilities, and their extension beyond Grand avenue, has remodeled that section of the city which lies west of Vandeventer avenue and north of Forest Park. In the old days this exceptionally desirable property was inaccessible except to those who owned carriages. Even in 1885 there was no street car accommodation in the district named west of Vandeventer avenue. The enterprise of the

St. Louis & Suburban and Lindell Companies, as well as the cabling and extension of the Olive street line, has made this property as easy of access as it was formerly difficult. The result has been a complete transformation. The streets and boulevards between Vandeventer and Taylor avenues are all built up with costly improvements, including elegant mansions, while west of Taylor avenue the number of delightful homes is constantly increasing. West of King's Highway, in old horse-car days, the territory was unexplored and unknown. There were several large country mansions with extensive grounds, but as a residence section for the masses it had yet to be born. Encouraged by the railroad companies, acre after acre has been covered with attractive homes, the Cabanne and Chamberlain Park districts vying with any in the country for beauty and elegance.

The conversion of the horse car lines running south and southwest has also transformed those sections of the city. It was formerly so difficult to get to Carondelet that most people living in St. Louis knew little or nothing concerning the beauties of this section of the city. The high, healthy ground is now being built up with residences of all descriptions, and, thanks to the admirable street railroad facilities, the population is being increased at a surprising rate. In the northwest and the north, the street railroads have opened up several square miles of hitherto inaccessible property. The improvements are continuing, and, indeed, the good work of the rapid transit roads in this direction is yet in its infancy. In no respect does New St. Louis differ in appearance from Old St. Louis more than in its residences and residence sections, and the change has been brought about almost entirely by rapid transit.

POSSIBILITY OF AN EXTENSION OF THE CITY LIMITS. One more influence of improved street railroad facilities must be recorded. The St. Louis & Suburban electric road, as already mentioned, runs as far into the county as Florissant, and all along the line of its route it has built up suburban districts.

Nominally, Normandy and Ramona are both in the county, but practically they are part of St. Louis. Powers have also been obtained to construct electric roads into various other sections of the county. A road has already been finished to Clayton, the county seat, and two other corporations have been formed to construct railroads, to be operated by electricity, through the strictly urban section of the county west and southwest of the city. As a result of this, it is proposed to, as early as possible, extend the city limits so as to take in Jefferson Barracks on the south, Kirkwood on the southwest, Clayton on the west and Ferguson on the northwest.

The new limits as thus proposed would add an area to the city of about 51,200 acres, or eighty square miles. It would bring in all the suburban towns fostered by present and projected electric roads, including Ferguson, Woodland, Normandy, Jennings Heights, Ramona, College View, O'Fallon, Clayton, Rosedale, Kirkwood, Glendale, Webster, Luxemburg and Jefferson Barracks, and within the area named there is a population of nearly, if not more than, 50,000. The present financial condition of that portion of St. Louis county included in the limits named greatly simplifies the question of annexation. If the boundaries named above should be adopted the city would have an area of 89,962 acres, or about 140 square miles. It would add, at a low estimate, $25,000,000 immediately to the taxable values, yielding a revenue of about $500,000. The proposed line has been drawn so as to continue along the high ground, and within five years much of the new territory would be the most desirable property in the city. The rapid transit to suburban localities is the best in the United States, and whether the territory is annexed or not it will practically be a part of the city within a short time.

CHAPTER VII.

SOME AIDS TO PROGRESS.

THE VEILED PROPHET, AUTUMNAL FESTIVITIES ASSOCIATION, ILLUMINATIONS, EXPOSITION AND FAIR.—CONVENTIONS.—COMMERCIAL ORGANIZATIONS.

THE HISTORY OF CITIES, ancient and modern, fails to record a duplicate to the enterprise of New St. Louis in the matter of entertaining strangers and providing lavishly for their amusement. It was in 1878 that the Veiled Prophet commenced his series of annual visits to St. Louis, and from the first these visits have been made the basis of hospitality of the most lavish character. The mystery of the Veiled Prophet has been kept entire from the first, and although it is generally known that the enormous expense of the pageant and ball is borne by a secret organization composed of the principal capitalists, manufacturers and merchants of St. Louis, their exact identity is a matter of surmise, and the correctness of the guesses need not be discussed. Certain it is that the men who thought out and then raised the money to carry out the idea, have contributed nobly towards the city's re-birth and second growth, and that they have earned the good-will of all. The pass-word of the Veiled Prophet is, or should be, "unselfishness." The idea is a beautiful one, for it is borrowed from ancient or legendary history, and is designed to perpetuate the poetic story, which ought to be true if it isn't, that there used to exist a Veiled Prophet who was surrounded only by whole-souled men who gave up their lives to good works. Before the circle of followers was enlarged, the new-comer was compelled to look into a magic mirror which laid bare to the prophet's gaze his very thoughts and feelings. Hence the court was made up of generous, open-hearted men, devoted to the service of their fellows.

WHAT THE VEILED PROPHET HAS DONE.

It is very much the same with the Veiled Prophet's Association. The members subscribe freely to the expense account, but do not take their reward by means of printed and advertised subscription lists; indeed, no man can be found who will admit having donated a single dollar to the annual pageants. Millions of visitors have come in to see the sixteen annual parades, and thousands have tripped the light fantastic toe at the grand balls. It seems a trifle debasing to try to reduce to a cash basis the benefit the city has derived from the visits and the festivities. In the first place, they have lifted St. Louis out of a rut and broken down that Chinese wall which was always thought to encircle what was even then the metropolis of the Mississippi Valley. Then, they have made hundreds of thousands of people acquainted with the city, and have fostered the habit of annual visits to it. Both these influences have been of almost incalculable value; but when the prophet's power was used to raise New St. Louis out of the old city, the true force and value of that power came to be appreciated. The part played by the prophet in this work has already been discussed, and need not be enlarged upon here. The good work has continued year after year until in the fall of 1893 there seemed to be a feeling that the prophet had outlived his usefulness, and that St. Louis was too important a city for the annual pageant. At first it was thought that this feeling was, if not general, at least extensive, and it was semi-officially announced that the Veiled Prophet would appear no more. The outcry that followed showed that the sentiment was held only by the element, to be found in every city, which is much more ready to criticize than to invent or work, and it is now generally understood that the Veiled Prophet will appear next October, as usual.

A detailed description of the annual pageant would be impossible, nor is it practicable to describe the annual balls at which the wealth and beauty, not only of St. Louis and the West, but also of the East, are represented. It is no exaggeration to say that thousands of society men and women look forward to the event with excitement for months before it takes place, nor is it too much to say that the annual ball is absolutely unique. Beyond this and a passing reference to the beauty of the invitations and programmes, nothing can be said here.

More space must be devoted to the illuminations which have made St. Louis famous all over two continents. Some little work in street illumination was done when the prophet first appeared, but it was not until 1882, the year so marked by changes from old to new, that St. Louis first illuminated its streets in a comprehensive manner. The sum of $20,000 was subscribed for the purpose, and the illumination committee of that year had a task of no small magnitude to overcome, for it had to originate as well as to perfect. So far as the United States was concerned, St. Louis was the pioneer in the matter of street illuminations, no other city having made an effort in the direction, and it became necessary to look to Europe for hints and ideas. Careful inquiry in Paris showed that in even the gay French capital nothing had been attempted on anything approaching the scale determined upon in St. Louis, and even the much-talked-of illuminations of Brussels and Venice were experimental and insignificant compared with the new western idea. In London, Japanese lanterns and an occasional colored globe, constituted the idea of street beautification by night; and the St. Louisans who had crossed the Atlantic in search of information and designs returned with very little of the former and still less of the latter, the fact having been demonstrated that the apparently primitive efforts of the preceding year in St. Louis had excelled the best on record in the carnival cities of the Old World, besides having been entirely without precedent in those of the New.

STREET ILLUMINATIONS. It is fortunate for St. Louis, and also for the United States, that there was nothing found worth copying in the carnival cities of Europe, for the Carnival City of America proceeded at once to originate, and to spring at one bound into the lead as an entertaining city, achieving, even twelve years ago, a triumph it could have scarcely hoped for had it followed in the wake of other cities instead of leading the way itself. Twenty thousand dollars having been subscribed in 1882, one hundred and forty skilled plumbers were engaged, and gas-pipes and arches were placed along and over the sidewalks and across the streets. Twenty-one thousand globes of different colors were purchased, and for the distance of about forty-four blocks in the business section everything was got in readiness for a magnificent display and for a dazzling show of many-shaded lights.

The most sanguine expectations of the promoters of the enterprise were more than realized, for tens of thousands of spectators gazed with admiration on the display evening after evening, and hundreds of European tourists, who were attracted by the novelty and magnitude of the undertaking, pronounced it the most gorgeous street spectacle they had ever witnessed, and so infinitely superior to the best Old World productions as to make anything in the nature of comparison out of the question. A well-known official of the Crystal Palace at Sydenham, near London, England, was among the visitors who enjoyed the first grand street illumination the world had ever seen, and his verdict was that not even in the Crystal Palace grounds, nor in the gardens at South Kensington, had any approach towards such magnificence been made. Other visitors of equal experience endorsed this expression of approval, and no one has yet been found to express a contrary opinion. In 1883 the illuminations were repeated, and the area covered being increased several blocks; and in the two following years the work of improvement went steadily on. In 1886, the year of the Knights Templars Conclave at St. Louis, upwards of $22,000 was collected and ex-

pended in illuminations, which were made more dazzling than ever by the free use of electric lights. In 1887 the gathering of the Grand Army, followed by the visit of President and Mrs. Cleveland, stimulated St. Louisans to still greater efforts; the subscription exceeded $26,000, and the streets were rendered more dazzling than ever.

This feature was continued, and the plan of illumination gradually improved until the end of the eighties, when the impression spread that the illumination had served its purpose, and for two years this feature was omitted. The result was something like what happens to a business man who, having achieved a reputation by advertising, suddenly comes to the conclusion that he is spending too much money and shuts down on advertising expense. Such a man generally resumes advertising quickly on a more liberal scale than ever. So did St. Louis.

THE AUTUMNAL FESTIVITIES ASSOCIATION. In 1891 a mass-meeting was held, which is probably without a parallel in the world's history. It was called by the proclamation of the Veiled Prophet. The object of the meeting was to raise $1,000,000 to be expended during the World's Fair period for the general good of the city. Mr. Samuel M. Kennard presided at the meeting, and the attendance was large and representative. Indeed, the element which had succeeded in establishing New St. Louis was present in full force, although there were plenty of old men for counsel, as well as young men for war. The objects in view were largely three-fold. One, which may be described as the immediate outward and visible sign of the proposed work, took the shape of festivities for the current and two following years of a character never before attempted in St. Louis, the idea being to celebrate the Columbian quadro-centenary on the streets of St. Louis. The second object of the proposed association was to secure the erection of a new fire-proof hotel to cost not less than $1,000,000, and the proposed association was authorized to offer a bonus for this purpose. It was also designed to spend about one-third of

6

the money raised in advertising St. Louis in a
dignified manner, and thus enlightening the world
as to the progress made by the city since it decided to throw off all allegiance to tradition and
to map out for itself a new career as the future
metropolis of the mid-continent.

The success of the meeting was remarkable.
Just as, more than forty years ago, a few public-
spirited St. Louisans met together and made the
construction of a railroad into the city a possibility, so did a larger number of large and small
capitalists in May, 1891, insure the success of
an enterprise at least as important and daring.
It was not expected that the million dollars
would be raised in the room, but a very splendid
beginning was made. Two subscriptions, each
for $10,000, were announced, followed by others
of $7,500, $5,000 and smaller sums. A spirit of
enthusiasm was spread over the meeting, which
soon extended over the city and guaranteed the
success of the movement. Before the meeting
adjourned the St. Louis Autumnal Festivities
Association was formed, with the following officers: President, S. M. Kennard; first vice-president, E. O. Stanard; second vice-president,
F. A. Wann; third vice-president, John S.
Moffitt; fourth vice-president, Rolla Wells; fifth
vice-president, Clark A. Sampson; secretary,
Frank Gaiennie; treasurer, Walker Hill; execu-
tive committee, A. D. Brown, R. P. Tansey,
D. D. Walker, J. C. Wilkinson, S. C. Bunn,
Jacob Furth, W. T. Haydock, M. C. Wetmore,
W. F. Nolker, George E. Leighton, T. B. Boyd,
Charles M. Hays, Goodman King, C. D. Mc-
Clure, M. Bernheimer, T. K. Niedringhaus,
H. J. Meyer, Jonathan Rice, August Gehner,
J. J. Kreher, C. H. Turner, L. D. Kingsland,
H. C. Townsend, R. M. Scruggs, Festus J.
Wade, Jerome Hill, A. T. Kelley, George D.
Barnard, D. S. Holmes, W. H. Woodward,
Patrick McGrath, J. Specht, W. H. Thompson
and George M. Wright.

Six committees were formed to deal respect-
ively with finance, advertising, transportation,
programme, illumination and hotel. Mr. John
S. Moffitt, who had been at the head of most of
the collecting funds for illuminations in prior

years, was appointed chairman of the finance
committee, which at once proceeded to attempt
the so-called impossible task of raising enough
money to carry out the plans of the promoters
of the organization. Every professional and
mercantile interest in the city was classified and
nearly a hundred sub-committees were appointed
to assist in obtaining subscriptions. Extraordinary success followed the efforts. A spirit of
rivalry of the most friendly character was established between the different trades and professions, and not to subscribe to the fund was to
form an exception to a remarkably general rule.
That the Old St. Louis spirit was well-nigh
dead was proved by the fact that the collectors
only met with four rebuffs during their entire
work. A hundred thousand dollars was secured
the first week, and the work went on throughout the summer in the most satisfactory manner.
Not only did the capitalists and employers of
labor subscribe freely, but the laborers themselves came forward and contributed. Nearly
every member of the police force and of the fire
department, in addition to hundreds of traveling
men and clerks, joined the procession, and the
city acquired a proprietary interest in the association which it could not have done had the
money been raised from the few instead of the
many. A generation hence the list of subscribers
to the Autumnal Festivities Association will be
looked upon as a roll of honor, for while it may
be true that

> The evil that men do lives after them,
> The good is oft interred with their bones,

this cannot be said to be the case with organizations of what are sometimes incorrectly
described as a "boom" order. Hence, while
the good influences of the festivities association
are manifest to-day, they will be ten times more
so twenty and fifty years hence, when much of
the good seed sown during the last two and a
half years will have borne fruit a hundred and a
thousand-fold. The work of collection was continued during 1892, but the financial uneasiness
in 1893 made it impossible to solicit new subscriptions. Fortunately, the remarkable manner
in which St. Louis weathered the storm enabled

the association to collect almost every dollar promised it, and a total of more than $600,000 was received, including as cash the large sums generously donated by the local newspapers for advertising purposes.

Mr. J. C. Wilkinson became chairman of the illumination committee, which provided for St. Louis during the years 1892 and 1893 the most magnificent street illuminations ever attempted in this or any other city. Space prevents a detailed description of these illuminations. More than 70,000 lights, half electric and half gas, were used for the purpose, and the down-town streets were made a veritable blaze of light. The electrical panorama which were seen on the widest streets, and at the most conspicuous points, excited the admiration of the hundreds of thousands of visitors who were attracted to the city by them. Mr. Wilkinson earned the praise of every one by the ingenuity of the designs and by the determined manner in which he insisted upon novelties being produced in the face of technical objections and forecasts of certain failure.

THE BUREAU OF INFORMATION. Mr. Goodman King was appointed chairman of the advertising committee, the name of which was changed to the Bureau of Information in consequence of the vast scope of its operations. As the writer of "Old and New St. Louis" is the secretary of this bureau, Mr. Julian Ralph, whose able and comprehensive article in *Harper's New Monthly* has already been referred to more than once, will be quoted as to its work and operations: "The bureau," says Mr. Ralph, "has offices in St. Louis, and has also arranged to open others in London and other cities in pursuit of a systematic effort to advertise the commercial, social and sanitary advantages which St. Louis possesses. It may cause a smile to read that Chairman King and Secretary Cox report, in a circular now before me, what work the Bureau of Information has done 'to correct any false impressions which have been created by the too great modesty of St. Louisans in the past.' But they are right, for, as compared with its rival, St. Louis possessed

that defect, and the frank admission of such a hated fault shows how far removed and reformed from retarding bashfulness that city has since become. The bureau reports that it is causing the publication of half-page advertisements of St. Louis, precisely as if it were a business or a patent medicine, in sixty-two papers,' circulating more than a million copies; that it has obtained reading notices in all these dailies; that 'articles on St. Louis as a manufacturing and commercial metropolis and as a carnival city' are sent out every day; that arrangements are being made for a weekly mail letter to 500 southern and western journals, and that once or twice a week news items are sent to the principal dailies of the whole country. It was found that St. Louis was not fairly treated in the weekly trade reports published generally throughout the country, and this source of complaint has been removed. Invading the camp of the arch-enemy—Chicago—the bureau has caused a handsome 'Guide to Chicago' to add to its title the words, 'And St. Louis, the Carnival City of America.' It is also getting up a rich and notable book to be called 'St. Louis Through a Camera' for circulation among all English-speaking peoples. The local service for the press telegraphic agencies has been greatly improved, 'and the efforts of the bureau to increase the number and extent of the notices of St. Louis in the daily papers throughout the United States have continued to prove successful,' so that 'instead of St. Louis being ignored or referred to in a very casual manner, it is now recognized as fully as any other large city in America.'

"I have described the operations of this association and its most active bureau at some length because they exhibit the farthest extreme yet reached in the development of the most extraordinary phase of western enterprise. There we see a city managed by its people as a wide-awake modern merchant looks after his

*This was comparatively early in the bureau's issue. It subsequently made use of the columns of more than 4,000 American newspapers, periodicals and magazines, and issued 60,000 copies of the book spoken of in this article as being "got up."

business. It is advertised and 'written up' and pushed upon the attention of the world, with all its good features clearly and proudly set forth. There is boasting in the process, but it is always based upon actual merit, for St. Louis is an old and proud city, and there is no begging at all. The methods are distinctly legitimate, and the work accomplished is hard work paid for by hard cash. It is considered a shrewd investment of energy and capital, and not a speculation. If we in the eastern cities, who are said to be 'fossilized,' are not inclined to imitate such a remarkable example of enterprise, we cannot help admiring the concord and the hearty local pride from which it springs."

THE NEW PLANTERS' HOUSE. Another committee which has achieved remarkable success is the hotel committee, of which Mr. M. C. Wetmore is chairman. Authorized to offer a bonus of $100,000 for the erection of a fire-proof hotel on approved plans and on an acceptable site, at a cost of not less than $1,000,000, it proceeded at once to make its mission known and to invite offers from corporations and capitalists. Various propositions were made, but no actual advance was made until a number of local capitalists, including several members of the association, joined together, purchased the old Planters' House, removed the old structure and commenced the erection of a fire-proof hotel, which is now nearly completed and which can be described as one of the finest hotels in America, with an unlimited number of new ideas and improvements in it. One of the great events of 1894 will be the opening of this magnificent hostelry, which will cost by the time it is ready for opening nearly $2,000,000. It bears as little resemblance to the old Planters' House as New St. Louis does to Old St. Louis, and, indeed, the two buildings may well be taken as types of the correct thing forty years ago and now. The hotel fronts on Fourth street, and is bounded by Pine and Chestnut streets. It is ten full stories high, and its front is designed in the form of an inverted E, with two recessed courts so arranged that of the 400

apartments nearly every one is a front room. The style of internal decorations is not finally settled, but it will be as fine as money can procure; and the hotel will be a source of admiration not only in St. Louis, but through the entire West. Various names were suggested for the hotel when it was designed and while it was in course of erection. It has, however, been called, by general consent, the New Planters' House, a name which it will probably retain, although it was at one time proposed to call it the Columbian Hotel, a name which would have been very appropriate and which would have served as a perpetual reminder of the date of the building's erection. This detail, however, is not of such great importance as the hotel itself, and, having got this latter, St. Louis is not worrying itself greatly over the minor question.

The Autumnal Festivities Association was formed for three seasons, those of '91, '92 and '93, and while these pages are in press it is practically winding up its operation and terminating its work. In some shape or other it will, however, be perpetuated; for an association of a permanent character will certainly be formed during 1894 to carry on the work inaugurated by the festivities association and to so large an extent successfully accomplished.

One exceptionally useful influence of the association will be found in the increased facilities it has provided for the accommodation of delegates to conventions. St. Louis has earned the title of the Carnival City of America in consequence of the lavish nature of its festivities and entertainments, and it has also long been known as the City of Conventions, because its phenomenal hospitality and its exceptional railroad facilities have made it the most popular city in the country for the holding of conventions, political, social and commercial. As long ago as 1867 a River Convention, with delegates from over twenty States and Territories, convened in the old Mercantile Library Hall, which was one of the largest public meeting places in the West. The convention laid the foundation for many improvements which the Federal government has since carried out on the Mississippi river. Railroad conventions of great importance, but less national in character, had been held before, but this gathering excited almost universal attention. In the winter of 1872 a National Commercial Convention was held. In 1875 a National Railroads Convention was held, and many measures of importance decided upon. The unvarying success of the local entertainment committees in making delegates comfortable resulted in a strong effort being made to secure the holding of the Democratic Nominating Convention in St. Louis in 1876, and there was a general feeling of satisfaction when the telegraphic news announced that the Democrats proposed to nominate the next President of the United States here. The convention was held, and was a marked success, as was also the great River Convention of 1881.

THE GREAT CONVENTION YEARS. During the eighties conventions followed each other in rapid succession. In 1885 a Cattle Convention of great importance was held, and 1886 and 1887 were the banner years of St. Louis in the matter of conventions. In the former year the physicians, photographers and butchers of the United States met successively in annual convention in the Exposition Hall, and enjoyed not only satisfactory and well-attended business meetings, but a glorious time of recreation as well, the citizens never tiring of subscribing to entertainment funds. The convention boom of 1886 culminated in the Knights Templar Triennial Conclave, during which carnival reigned supreme. An immediate outcome of the success of the 1886 convention season was the selection of St. Louis for the Grand Army Reunion in 1887. This was followed by a visit from President and Mrs. Cleveland, whose welcome was one they will never forget. The festivities were on a high order, and attracted enormous crowds. In 1888 the Democratic party held its Nominating Convention in the Exposition Building, where the National Saengerbund also met.

Passing over several important gatherings, mention may be made of the grand Odd Fellows'

Convention in 1891, which was a success beyond expectation. In 1892 the People's party held its organizing conference in the city, and during the same year an important Nicaragua Canal Convention was held. In 1893 the National Electric Light Association held its convention in the city, and the Exposition was besieged with applications for standing room to hear Nicola Tesla describe his triumphs over the mysteries of electricity. The furniture manufacturers, the saddlers, the florists, and the builders, as well as many other commercial organizations, met in convention in the city during the year, as did also an important monetary and trade convention of the Western States. During the fall the Autumnal Festivities Association also entertained the foreign commissioners to the World's Fair, and other delegations of importance were seen here.

A history of St. Louis and its conventions alone could be written and provide material for a large volume. All that has been attempted is to show how thoroughly St. Louis is entitled to the name "Convention City," and how admirably it has learnt its lesson as to how to entertain.

THE TEN-TIMES SUCCESSFUL EXPOSITION. St. Louis holds the record of ten consecutive annual expositions, each of which has more than paid its own expenses. It had long been accepted as a proved fact that no city could maintain an exposition year after year successfully. Even London, by far the largest city in the world, and the first city in which an international exposition was ever held, has failed in more than one attempt to maintain a successful annual display of manufactured and artistic goods; and in nearly every large city in this country an exposition building, diverted from its original use to manufacturing or store-room purposes, stands out in bold relief in silent testimony to another failure. But in all the bright vocabulary of St. Louis, is no such word as "fail," and the Exposition has proved a success every year since it was first opened, namely, in 1884. In 1883 a number of gentlemen met at the Mercantile Club, and after talking over the possibility of erecting an exposition building and holding an annual exposition, decided to ignore the difficulties and make the attempt. The entire funds for the work were raised locally, and although the bulk of the money was subscribed in the form of stock, it is only just to the original investors to state that they had little or no hope of return, and were actuated more by a spirit of local pride and enthusiasm than a desire to obtain a good investment. The nominal cost of the Exposition Building, which was built during the years 1883-84 on a six-acre site on Olive and St. Charles streets, between Thirteenth and Fourteenth streets, was $750,000, but so much money has been spent in perfecting the structure that $1,000,000 should be named as the approximate actual cost. The building is too well known to all St. Louis people to need a detailed description. The large music hall has 3,507 numbered seats, and on special occasions will accommodate twice as many people. The space intended for general displays is very large and admirably arranged, and from the first the Exposition was a success.

It was opened in September, 1884, and during the season, which lasted six weeks, over 500,000 people passed through the turnstiles. Every year it has repeated its triumph, and nearly 6,000,000 people have paid admission fee since the first opening. For several years Patrick Sarsfield Gilmore and his famous band furnished the music every season. In 1892 Col. Gilmore commenced the season with his band of 100 pieces, and just as he was enjoying the triumph of his life, that life ended with painful suddenness and the Exposition suffered severely in consequence. In 1893 John Phillip Sousa commenced a three-years' engagement with his unrivaled band, and during the season Madame Scalchi and other artists of international repute assisted in the concerts. The attendance in 1893 far exceeded expectations. It had been feared that the competition of the World's Fair, added to the general financial depression, would have resulted in a serious falling off in attendance, and the loss on the season was debated

very freely by those to whom ignorance is never bliss, but rather the reverse: Long before the close of the season it became evident that there would be a handsome surplus, and when the season closed there remained a profit considerably in excess of $25,000—a wonderful achievement when the exceptional difficulties of the year are taken into account. Twenty years hence the work of the Exposition management will be appreciated much more highly than it is to-day, but even now it is generally realized that the men who have made the Exposition a success and who have enabled the entire bonded indebtedness to be paid off, deserve the thanks of the entire city. The first president of the Exposition was Mr. Sam. M. Kennard, who bore the burden and heat of the day for nine years and then insisted on being allowed to retire. He was succeeded by Gov. E. O. Stanard, who gave to the duties of the office the careful attention which has marked his honored career. He in turn was succeeded late in 1893 by Mr. T. B. Boyd. Too much credit cannot be given to General Manager Frank Gaiennie, whose success in 1893 must be regarded as phenomenal and by whose efforts some of the choicest exhibits at the World's Fair have been secured for the local display of 1894 and 1895. This promises quite a change in the appearance of the Exposition next year; and in view of the enterprise of the management, there seems no reason to doubt that the St. Louis Exposition will continue year after year with unabated triumph.

Although not what may be termed a New St. Louis institution, the St. Louis Agricultural and Mechanical Association deserves credit for the yeoman service it has rendered year after year. At one time the St. Louis Fair was one of the greatest events in the West, and although neither the city or country fair is the attraction it once was, the St. Louis Fair continues the greatest thing of its kind in the world. The building of the new Jockey Club House, and the erection and opening of the new grand stand are more strictly of the newer order of things, and some very excellent racing has been seen in

St. Louis. The Veiled Prophet has assisted the institution in a variety of ways, and has timed his visits so as to make them come in Fair week, or the first complete week of October.

The opening of the finest base-ball park in America in 1893 serves as a reminder of the fame St. Louis base-ball players have obtained. Although not now world's champions the "Browns" are still great ball players, and a third world's championship flag will in the near future float over Sportsman's Park.

TRAFFIC COMMISSION AND SPANISH CLUB. More strictly commercial than these agencies are the Traffic Commission and the Spanish Club, already referred to. The Traffic Commission, as at present organized, is a most useful body, and it has done work for St. Louis commerce which it would have taken many years to accomplish by individual effort. It has insisted upon justice to the city in the matter of freight rates, and has succeeded in adjusting an immense number of irregularities and discriminations against this city. By its aid hundreds of miles of territory have been added to the district easily accessible to St. Louis trade, and it is still continuing its good work in a variety of ways. The commission has permanent offices in the Equitable Building, and is under the active management of Traffic Commissioner Osgood, a railroad man of unlimited experience and marked ability.

The work of the Spanish Club has already been enlarged upon. It is an institution which has somewhat hid its light under a bushel in the past, and although it has increased railroad and river connection between St. Louis and Mexico, secured reduction in rates amounting to quite a substantial percentage, and more than doubled the trade between Mississippi and Spanish-American points, but a comparatively few people appreciate the extent of its work and its triumphs. The club has now handsome quarters in the Columbia Building. Its president is Mr. L. D. Kingsland, and its secretary Mr. S. L. Biggers, both of whom have traveled extensively through Spanish-speaking countries.

The assistant and acting secretary is Mr. Bernard Mackey, for many years in the consular service.

The Citizens' Smoke Abatement Association is another organization designed to aid the trade as well as the salubrity of St. Louis. Nearly all the coal used for manufacturing purposes in St. Louis is bituminous, and the quantity of smoke sent out by the countless chimneys is very destructive to stocks of merchandise, in addition to being objectionable from both the standpoints of health and comfort. As the result of prolonged agitation, the Citizens' Smoke Abatement Association was formed some two years ago. It has succeeded in obtaining legislation against the emission of smoke. An immense number of boiler-plant owners have co-operated with the association and abated the smoke without waiting for legal proceedings. Those who failed to fall in with the procession are now being proceeded against in the courts, and although in a manufacturing city like St. Louis there will always be a certain amount of smoke, the smoke nuisance will be so far reduced as to be practically abated.

THE MERCHANTS' EXCHANGE. During the last few months the Merchants' Exchange has purchased the building, a portion of which it has occupied for several years. The Exchange is the successor of one of the oldest commercial institutions of the West. In 1836 a meeting of merchants and traders was held and the St. Louis Chamber of Commerce established. It did not resemble in any way our present Merchants' Exchange, being rather a large market and commission house, with arrangements for arbitration in disputes. In 1847 ground was purchased at the corner of Third and Chestnut streets for the purpose of erecting an exchange building, and in 1849 the Merchants' Exchange was established and carried on more or less in connection with the Chamber of Commerce. The Millers' Convention was formed shortly afterwards; and the Millers' Exchange, established at Nos. 9 and 11 Locust street, was the first exchange in the United States established for the purpose of bringing together buyers and sellers of grain. In 1855 a movement was started which resulted in the erection of the Exchange Hall, on Main street, which for many years was the great center of trade in the city. During the war political differences led to the organization of the Union Merchants' Exchange, a name which was retained until 1875, when it was changed to the Merchants' Exchange of St. Louis, and all the organizations were practically amalgamated. In 1874 the corner-stone was laid for the present Chamber of Commerce, which still continues to be one of the finest exchanges of its character in America. The grand hall is 221 feet in length, 92 feet wide and 80 feet high. The ceiling is perhaps the most appropriate and handsome in the country. It is finished in elaborate fresco work, with paintings in the panels. In their general details these are strikingly magnificent. The north panel is conspicuous for its characteristic types of England, Germany, Italy, France, Scotland and other nations of the Old World in the central group, with others surrounding. The southern panel has types of Asiatic and African countries, and on the cornice are the States of the Union, designated by name.

The Exchange membership includes some three thousand of the leading men of the city. The first president of the Chamber of Commerce was Mr. Edward Tracy. He was succeeded by Messrs. Wayman Crow, George K. McGunnegle, W. N. Morrison, Alfred Vincent, R. M. Henning, Henry Ames, E. M. Ryland, R. M. Funkhouser, D. A. January and William Mathews. The following gentlemen have served as presidents of the Merchants' Exchange:

1862 HENRY J. MOORE.	1878 GEORGE BAIN.
1863 GEORGE PARTRIDGE.	1879 JOHN WAHL.
1864 THOMAS RICHESON.	1880 ALEX. H. SMITH.
1865 BARTON ABLE.	1881 MICHAEL McENNIS.
1866 E. O. STANARD.	1882 CHAS. E. SLAYBACK.
1867 C. L. TUCKER.	1883 J. C. EWALD.
1868 JOHN J. ROE.	1884 D. R. FRANCIS.
1869 GEORGE P. PLANT.	1885 HENRY C. HAARSTICK.
1870 WM. J. LEWIS.	1886 S. W. COBB.
1871 GERARD B. ALLEN.	1887 FRANK GAIENNIE.
1872 R. P. TANSEY.	1888 CHAS. F. ORTHWEIN.
1873 WM. H. SCUDDER.	1889 CHAS. A. COX.
1874 WEB. M. SAMUEL.	1890 JOHN W. KAUFFMAN.
1875 D. P. ROWLAND.	1891 MARCUS BERNHEIMER.
1876 NATHAN COLE.	1892 ISAAC M. MASON.
1877 JOHN A. SCUDDER.	1893 W. T. ANDERSON.

Mr. George H. Morgan has been secretary and treasurer since the year 1865.

The Builders' Exchange is the successor of the Mechanics' Exchange, another institution which has done good service in concentrating and developing the trade and commerce of St. Louis. It was originally organized in 1839; it was reorganized on a wider basis, under the name of the Mechanics' and Manufacturers' Exchange and Library Association of St. Louis, in 1852. In 1856 there was another reorganization, and the exchange was established very much on the basis on which it exists to-day. In 1879 its headquarters were at 106 North Fourth street, and later its headquarters were on Seventh street, between Chestnut and Market. Upwards of a year ago, it moved into elegant offices in the Telephone Building, where it continues to exercise a most beneficent influence on the building and kindred trades and interests of the city. It is universally regarded as one of the permanent institutions of the city of St. Louis, and is devoted to the building and material interests of the city, affording an opportunity to its members and all engaged in the building business to enjoy the great advantage of having a meeting place in the central part of the city for the consideration of questions of importance relating to trade matters, lettings, and so forth. The hall is so large that it is used for conventions and similar gatherings. Mr. Richard Walsh is the secretary, and the 1893 president is Mr. Wm. J. Baker.

The limits of space forbid a detailed history of the Real Estate Exchange, Coal Exchange, Brewers' Association, the Associated Wholesale Grocers of St. Louis, the Retail Grocers' Association, the Furniture Board of Trade, of which mention has already been made; the Cotton Exchange, the Wool and Fur Association, the Live Stock Exchange, the newly-formed Wholesale Clothing Association, and of the other organizations designed to aid the city's commerce in various directions. St. Louis is fortunate in both the number and extent of these associations, and the influence of their work has been felt in a large variety of ways.

CHAPTER VIII.

FINANCE AND BANKING.

NEW ST. LOUIS AN IMPORTANT FINANCIAL CENTER.—BANK CLEARINGS.—TRUST COMPANIES
AND BUILDING ASSOCIATIONS.

E HAVE ALREADY seen that St. Louis is the great manufacturing and commercial center of a district even larger than that which is generally described as the Mississippi Valley. It is equally true that St. Louis is the great financial center of a district almost as large. The banks of St. Louis are known throughout the entire country for their solidity and for the conservative policy which has characterized their management. The year 1893 was a peculiarly trying one for banks, and from every large city in the Union there came reports of distrust and uneasiness, followed, in very many cases, by records of actual suspension. None of the cities of the first class went through the ordeal entirely scathless, with the single exception of St. Louis, where there was not a single bank failure, nor even a suspicion of insolvency. Had it not been for the reports telegraphed from other cities, and the doleful forecasts of impending national calamity, St. Louis would have gone through the year without any knowledge of the panic, and its financial institutions would have done their ordinary business just as if it had been a great boom year. As it was, the reports of disasters elsewhere naturally led to timid depositors withdrawing money from the banks, but thanks to the solid rock foundation of these institutions, the withdrawals did not cause them any alarm, and, although the reduction in the amount of loanable capital necessarily hampered commercial progress, all demands were promptly met; and it was proved that, with all its energy and enterprise,

New St. Louis is just as solid and substantial as the unduly conservative Old St. Louis used to be.

The history of banking institutions in St. Louis need not be traced at any great length in this work. In 1816 the Missouri *Gazette* wrote on "the opulent town of St. Louis, with a capital of nearly $1,000,000," but went on to complain that there was no bank in the city to foster business, although the territorial legislature had granted a charter for one three years before. The banks of St. Louis and of Missouri, to which reference has already been made, were established soon after this, and the use of peltry and hides in place of money began to die out. The Bank of the State of Missouri appears to have done the bulk of the banking business for some time after this, and in November, 1829, this institution, in consequence of the suspension of a number of eastern banks, passed a resolution that in the future it would receive and pay only its own notes and specie on the notes of specie-paying banks. Something of a local panic followed, and on November 13th a meeting was held to take into consideration the action of the bank. A number of the prominent capitalists of the city, including George Collier, E. Tracy, Pierre Chouteau, John Walsh, William Glasgow, John Perry, Henry Von Phul, John Kerr, G. K. McGunnegle, Joseph C. Leveille and John O'Fallon, with great public spirit pledged themselves to indemnify the bank against any loss it might sustain by the depreciation in notes. The offer was somewhat discourteously declined, and as a result the Bank of the State of Missouri was practically boycotted, and the St. Louis Gas

Light and the various insurance companies transacted most of the banking business.

Private banking houses sprang into existence about this time, and the financial troubles of 1853 and 1854 were reflected on this city. In January, 1855, there was a run on several private banks and some of a more public character; but once more the public-spirited men of St. Louis came forward and checked the run by guaranteeing deposits in the banking houses of Lucas & Simonds, Bogy, Miltenberg & Company, Tesson & Dangen, L. A. Benoist & Company, J. J. Anderson & Company, Darby & Barksdale and the Boatmen's Savings Institution. The panic was at an end and business was resumed as before. In 1857 there was a renewal of trouble, but once more it was met in the same generous-hearted manner. After the war the banking institutions of St. Louis gathered strength, and until the panic of 1873 the local financial needs were well met. In that year $300,000 of "brown-backs" were issued. They took their name from the fact that owing to the dearth of currency, Mayor Brown recommended the Council to issue warrants to the extent of $300,000. The proposition was accepted and the warrants or notes issued. The financial transaction was a unique one, and served its purpose remarkably well. Confidence was restored, and although there was further difficulty in 1887, that year may be named as the last in which there was any serious trouble with St. Louis banks.

ST. LOUIS A CENTRAL RESERVE CITY. Early in the year 1887 St. Louis was made a central reserve city and a depositary for national banks of other cities. This recognition by the Federal government of the importance of St. Louis as a financial center has had the effect of making St. Louis exchange used much more generally throughout the entire West and Southwest, and a very much larger number of banks in other cities have included St. Louis financial institutions in their lists of correspondents. Several of the largest firms have still further emphasized the importance of St. Louis by remitting their personal checks on city banks for the payment of accounts due in other cities. This practice has not yet become as general as it ought to be, and efforts have been made during the last two or three years to make the practice universal. Some firms still adhere to the old practice of purchasing exchange on New York and remitting the same in payment of accounts, a practice which involves a loss in illegitimate bank clearings of several millions per month.

A large majority of the city banks favor the remitting of personal checks in preference to the purchase of exchange, and their influence is being gradually made perceptible in the right direction. In the days of Old St. Louis it was quite a usual practice for large firms to keep a banking account in New York, and to pay all eastern accounts by checks drawn on their New York banks. This plan is obviously unjust to a city of the magnitude of St. Louis, and, although it will take several years to make the remission of St. Louis checks to all outside points general, it is gratifying to know that very few firms now adhere to the plan of checking on New York instead of on banks of their own city. Considering the high financial standing of St. Louis banks and the central location of the city, St. Louis checks ought to be accepted at par in all parts of the country, and they are done so when any attempt is made to insist.

Only once has New St. Louis seen a bank failure. That was eight years ago, and was the result of a personal breach of trust, and not of commercial or financial depression. The last statement as to banks and banking capital in Old St. Louis shows that the capital and surplus was $13,492,964; the savings and time deposits, $8,901,522; the current deposits, $32,827,489, and the circulation, $632,850. This was in 1882, and at the present time the banking business of the city has gained such proportions that the capital of the national banks alone exceeds $26,000,000; the surplus and profits, $3,000,000, and the loans and discounts, $23,000,000. The following official statement of the twenty-six leading St. Louis banks, is one of which the city is naturally proud, and it shows very clearly the financial solidity of New St. Louis:

OFFICIAL STATEMENT OF THE TWENTY-SIX LEADING ST. LOUIS BANKS.

RESOURCES.

BANK.	Currency and Coin.	Checks and Exchange.	Loans and Discounts.	Bonds and Stocks.	Real Estate, Furniture and Fixtures.	Expense.	Overdrafts.	Totals.
Bank of Commerce	$1,499,834.30	822,593.48	$5,844,068.25	724,071.37	$ 530,000.00	$	1,922.06	$9,422,489.46
Boatmen's	1,124,463.89	492,778.79	5,481,271.46	259,050.24	508,321.85		75,313.85	7,941,200.08
Fourth National	971,840.56	284,638.56	3,290,032.37	664,610.00	20,237.65	43,002.25	3,074.15	5,277,435.54
Continental Nat'l	938,732.01	789,427.04	2,909,671.38	508,703.79	50,000.00		418.22	5,196,952.44
State Bank	767,174.68	187,645.34	3,200,664.04	286,327.73	44,269.91		6,225.28	4,552,206.98
St. Louis National	591,333.88	748,350.84	2,675,309.12	56,000.00	211,000.00	6,871.77	21,160.64	4,310,076.25
German Savings	365,262.70	398,865.11	2,745,923.50	490,000.00	63,131.37		5 691.89	4,068,264.57
Mechanics'	695,871.13	501,640.90	2,659,568.56	3,523.00			1,120.10	3,861,732.69
Commercial	1,050,234.63	329,782.42	2,171,975.88	4,977.10			3,929.08	3,560,899.00
Laclede National	545,478.65	410,756.88	2,370,824.61	69,500.00	50,663.97	24,863.15	1,108.49	3,473,195.75
Third National	430,001.64	332,629.92	2,081,922.00	94,612 50	180,000.00		5,883.80	3,135,048.86
German-American	607,324.95	230,664.55	1,651,002.83	480,200.00	30,000.00		536.72	2,988,729.05
Franklin	294,702.05	181,108.27	1,625,649.52	654,630.00	134,000.00		2,830.91	2,892,920.75
Merchants' Nat'l	522,275.47	197,538.00	1,934,707.56	58,000.00		23,752 30	1,486.42	2,737,760.65
Lafayette	310,846.93	209,344.09	1,715,367.17	224,300.00	500.00		5,329.80	2,465,687.99
Am. Exchange	183,691.91	161,661.00	1,643,539.27	3,200.00	126.04		10,471.22	2,002,693.04
Northwestern	86,344.60	121,270.59	1,120,462.51	352,127.68			1,315.10	1,689,520.47
Nat. B.of Republic	233,519.29	213,515.33	1,044,564.68	60,850.00	17,500.00		394.46	1,600,343.66
Bremen	69,563.45	145,169.29	691,123.06	265,500.00	19,000.00		567.54	1,190,923.34
Mullanphy	80,518.10	33,386.70	825,103.15	154,513.24	37,831.46		2,316.80	1,133,589.45
Chemical National	130,599.73	98,535.95	796,249.37	57,000.00	10,000.00	231.41	3,328.66	1,095,945.12
International	138,265.30	36,220.15	589,943.72	64,289.04	59,789.62		278.54	888,786.37
Citizens'	219,601.25	66,614.37	514,212.46	5,825.92	9,879.94		2,062.41	818,196.35
South Side	140,485.39	92,015.38	441,790.23	113,386.00	3,800 00		1,906.02	793,381.02
Southern Com'l	12,192 95	21,729.67	205,314.79	5,797.77	10,774.48		406.90	256,216.59
Jefferson	37,143.65	4,160.42	121,190.05		1,000.00		2,235.19	166,629.31

LIABILITIES.

BANK.	Capital.	Surplus and Profits.	Circulation.	Individual Deposits.	Bank Deposits.	Time Deposits.	Bills Payable.	Totals.
Bank of Commerce	$3,000,000.00	884,604.10	$ 45,000.00	$3,032,192.97	$1,578,014.63	882,667.76	$	$9,422,489.46
Boatmen's	2,000,000.00	641,535.60		3,012,400.10	365,475.66	1,921,797.72		7,941,200.08
Fourth National	1,000,000.00	848,179.38	45,000.00	1,787,154.64	1,153,921.30	393,179.32	50,000.00	5,277,435.54
Continental Nat'l	2,000,000.00	259,883.20	45,000.00	1,624,577.00	1,133,084.84	134,407.46		5,196,952.44
State Bank	650,000.00	1,197,089.44		2,081,305.70	233,281.73	391,530.11		4,552,206.98
St. Louis National	1,000,000.00	190,212.43	45,000.00	1,315,403.76	1,596,269.47	163,190.59		4,310,076.25
German Savings	250,000.00	524,511.87		1,515,772.84	30,590.72	1,528,843.32	218,545 82	4,068,264.57
Mechanics'	600,000.00	688,200.91		1,745,793.81	361,269.48	402,128.08	64,340.41	3,861,732.69
Commercial	500,000.00	530,219.79		2,202,074.07	311,934.74	15,770.49		3,560,899.09
Laclede National	1,000,000.00	194,711.75	45,000.00	1,401,134.39	745,693.38	86,356.23		3,473,195.75
Third National	1,000,000.00	330,987.82	45,000.00	1,045,050.27	714,005.77			3,135,048.86
German-American	150,000.00	661,019.38		1,394,191.49	137,085.75	646,432.43		2,988,729.05
Franklin	200,000.00	462,931.61		1,037,768.63	216,781.45	975,439.06		2,892,920.75
Merchants' Nat'l	700,000.00	246,972.51	45,000.00	1,064,005.75	475,241.28	206,541.11		2,737,760.65
Lafayette	100,000.00	251,284.69		957,325.52	3,918.01	1,153,359.77		2,465,687.99
Am. Exchange	500,000.00	357,738.61		798 090.16	184,152.81	92,752.67	69,958.79	2,002,693.04
Northwestern	100,000.00	134,699.66		414,822 85		1,040,597.76		1,689,520.47
Nat.B.of Republic	500,000.00	24,442.86	45,000.00	443,197.04	503,411.11	84,292.65		1,600,343.66
Bremen	100,000.00	137,000.00		402,521.75		551,401.59		1,190,923.34
Mullanphy	100,000.00	160,885.98		334,220.24	9,374.43	529,108.84		1,133,589.45
Chemical Nat'l	500,000.00	36,288.98	45,000.00	344,345.80	90,669.33	79,642.01		1,095,945.12
International	200,000.00	84,872.94		400,853.64	56 73	203,003.02		888,786.37
Citizens'	200,000.00	71,665.38		415,230.67	10,783.35	120,516.95		818,196.35
South Side	300,000.00	35,323.13		306,311.61	17,228.41	134,517.87		793,381.02
Southern Com'l	100,000.00	14,069.33		91,034.38		51,112.88		256,216.59
Jefferson	100,000.00	3,239.65		59,556.56		3,833.10	6.59	166,629.31

It is universally conceded by experts that the St. Louis banks keep themselves in an exceptionally solid position. The statement on the preceding page was prepared during the financial depression, and shows the institutions at their worst, instead of their best. Yet, the available funds for the surplus reserve averaged forty to forty-four per cent, as compared with less than twenty-five per cent in New York, and similar percentages elsewhere. The number of banks in St. Louis does not increase rapidly, but it is observed that those already in operation increase their facilities for doing business steadily, and one after the other they secure more handsome, commodious premises for the transaction of their business. Some of the most desirable corners in the city are now occupied by banks, and during the last few months several important changes of location have taken place.

In addition to banks proper, St. Louis has three very large trust companies, which are transacting a banking business of great importance, as well as acting as trustees and executors and filling in many other ways a want long felt in financial circles. These institutions do not at present make use of the Clearing House directly in their transactions, and hence the business of that institution is not increased to the extent that the business done would appear to indicate. This last-named institution was organized in 1868, and has continued without interruption since. The first president was Mr. W. E. Burr, president of the St. Louis National Bank, who was succeeded in 1873 by Mr. Charles Parsons. In the same year Mr. Edward Chase became manager, and for the last twenty years he has conducted the vast transactions of the Clearing House Association with marked ability. In 1875 an amendment was made to the constitution making the minimum capital of members $150,000, a conservative policy which is still maintained.

As already mentioned, the returns of the St. Louis Clearing House do not adequately represent the financial transactions of the city. This is largely because of the comparative diminutive amount of speculation and dealing in options in St. Louis as compared with other more reckless centers. There is also an absence of any attempt here to make the figures better than they really are. Thus, in some centers checks are issued with the endorsement that they are payable only through the clearing house, and hence all purely local transactions become added to the total. Also, in St. Louis it is the almost invariable practice to pay wages in cash and not by means of checks, as is a common practice in many industrial centers. In addition to this, it is the practice of the St. Louis banks to pay their daily balances to each other in currency. In many cities the certificate given by the Clearing House to banks, showing the amount coming to them on the balances from other banks, are treated as checks and cleared the following day, so that the amount of the balances of one day is added to the total clearings of the next. It is really a question of arithmetic and book-keeping only, but the subject is worthy of mention, because it is important St. Louis people should realize that every dollar returned as being cleared represents that amount of actual business.

In spite of this strictly conservative policy, the bank clearings of New St. Louis have steadily increased. They averaged considerably less than $60,000,000 a month when the change from the old to the new took place. In 1886 they averaged a little less than $70,000,000 a month, from which year they gradually increased until the year 1892, when they averaged a trifle over $100,000,000 per month. The year 1893 opened up most auspiciously in the matter of banking business. December, 1892, had broken the record in the bank clearings, with a gain of $7,000,000 over the preceding year; the returns for the first month of the new year were $16,000,000 larger than the preceding January, and the returns for the first quarter were very largely in excess of the corresponding period of any preceding year, being more than forty-five per cent greater than 1886.

The table on page 93 shows the bank clearings for the current year, and for the seven preceding years.

BANK CLEARANCES.

MONTH.	1886.	1887.	1888.	1889.	1890.	1891.	1892.	1893.
January	$ 65,215,966	$ 71,441,522	$ 73,489,445	$ 84,139,804	$ 94,715,140	$ 97,620,745	$ 98,855,246	114,721,817
February	56,865,185	64,016,573	73,682,245	72,500,989	85,143,841	82,018,043	97,370,011	93,519,692
March	62,407,170	75,820,934	75,136,605	79,774,733	87,236,790	89,648,649	99,186,662	108,371,973
April	63,523,300	73,773,478	72,004,856	71,892,175	93,455,536	89,499,582	103,381,629	107,761,070
May	70,800,052	79,768,875	73,797,050	83,738,646	100,925,642	90,605,844	94,008,641	109,154,296
June	62,760,710	75,821,594	69,957,876	83,333,370	92,250,636	87,120,315	90,575,498	95,321,231
July	74,369,918	74,227,069	67,134,909	82,207,885	92,940,902	95,688,688	100,027,298	82,506,431
August	70,449,412	77,007,133	75,230,076	81,869,687	88,342,008	97,504,202	105,289,130	68,744,079
September	71,543,696	74,537,207	78,265,484	80,511,105	93,532,926	97,411,603	101,702,686	75,437,705
October	69,822,165	74,855,029	83,430,317	95,632,681	99,714,641	104,135,739	106,999,568	86,439,652
November	68,375,951	72,757,656	72,291,801	81,020,747	94,534,031	97,808,462	108,090,990	96,174,462
December	74,660,537	80,500,961	86,054,204	87,840,838	97,781,118	110,239,721	117,662,598	
	$810,759,062	$894,527,731	$900,474,878	$987,522,629	$1,118,573,210	$1,139,599,573	$1,231,571,963	

A most gratifying event of the last four or five years is the increased standing of St. Louis as a money center. The stability of rates in St. Louis has attracted general attention. Manufacturing establishments in search of locations have been largely induced to locate here because of the certainty of obtaining accommodations when required. More than that, the city's loaning business has extended over a much larger territory. Boston has for years advanced money for enterprises throughout the entire country, and St. Louis recognizes with gratitude the assistance the great New England town has rendered many of its valuable enterprises. Now St. Louis is in the habit of accommodating not only western and southwestern cities, but also many of the large eastern cities to which we used to look in years gone by. During the year 1892 this business gained very rapidly. During the preparations for the World's Fair a very large amount of money was taken out of St. Louis for the purpose, and more recently loans of large amounts have gone to Denver, Kansas City, Dallas, Galveston and other western and southern centers.

As a very powerful lever in raising New St. Louis to its present position socially, commercially and financially, the building and loan associations deserve special notice. Philadelphia used to claim a monopoly of the distinction of being a city of homes. New St. Louis competes with it for a right to the name, and it is probable that the percentage of inhabitants owning their own homes is now fully as large

in the metropolis of the West and Southwest as in the City of Brotherly Love. It was the building associations that helped thousands of Philadelphians to become home-owners, and it is the same agency that has reduced the ranks of the renters and increased the number of owners in this favored city. It is unnecessary to devote space to the origin of building associations in St. Louis. Some that were established during the last years of Old St. Louis have recently accomplished their purpose, furnished a home to each member who persevered in his effort to obtain one, and more than kept faith with their original members. It was not, however, until New St. Louis had been thoroughly established, and the new order of things had become generally accepted, that the number of building associations became large enough to exert any very important influence upon the growth and development of the city. During the years 1886, 1887 and 1888, associations were started in large numbers, and a great majority of them have done magnificent work, both for their members and for the city. Some of the more recent ones formed have fallen into the error of promising rather more than they can possibly fulfill, but they have, by the reduction of their charges, made home-buying exceedingly easy, and to their influence may be attributed the transformation of several districts within the city limits and out in the country to settlements of comfortable homes and substantial, if not costly, houses.

CHAPTER IX.

BUILDING IMPROVEMENTS.

ONE HUNDRED MILES OF STREET FRONTAGE BUILT UPON IN THREE YEARS.—HISTORY OF
THE FIRE-PROOF OFFICE-BUILDING ERA.—INVESTMENTS IN IMPROVEMENTS
AND THEIR INFLUENCE UPON VALUES.

ENTION HAS already been made of the influence of rapid transit and of building associations in increasing the area of the residence sections of St. Louis, and although it is probable that the street railroads are entitled to the bulk of the credit, it is certain that the expansion of the city's financial institutions and the general work of the building associations have given to the building industry an impetus during the last five or six years which has been much too general and far-reaching in its character and operation to be described as a "boom." The year 1892 was the banner year of St. Louis' building, for during it the enormous sum of $20,000,000 was expended on buildings actually completed, to say nothing of those in course of construction on January 1, 1893. The total number of building permits issued during the year was 5,497, and as evidence of the character of the improvements it may be mentioned that only twenty per cent of the permits were for frame buildings. The nominal value of the improvements, as shown by the building commissioner's book, was about $17,000,000, but this is no criterion of actual value because of the invariable undervaluation. In St. Louis the cost of a permit to build is calculated upon a percentage of the alleged value of the proposed building, and the habit of underestimating is a natural result of this rather inconsistent rule. It is probable that the sale-price of the buildings authorized to be erected during 1892 was

$25,000,000, so that the estimate of $20,000,000 actually expended on completed structures is quite a reasonable one. The lot frontage covered by new buildings in 1892 was 201,440 feet, equivalent to a single row of buildings thirty-nine miles long. This means that thirty-nine miles of street frontage was actually built upon, and the effect of the change on the aspect of the city can easily be appreciated even by those who have not been fortunate enough to go over the ground for themselves. The lot frontage covered in 1891 was thirty miles, and that of 1890 was nearly as great, so that during the three seasons the mileage of built-up streets in St. Louis was increased nearly 100 miles, an achievement of which the city is naturally proud and which it will be hard for any other city to duplicate.

To grasp the real import of these astounding totals, it should be remembered that the aggregate value of the buildings authorized to be erected in 1878 was $2,432,568, and even in 1882 the total was only $6,163,545. After this the influence of improved streets, rapid transit, building associations, and New St. Louis ideas generally began to be more apparent, and in 1889 the aggregate values mentioned in the building permits ran into eight figures. Since that time the increase has been very rapid, the total being nearly $14,000,000 in 1891, nearly $17,000,000 in 1892, and close upon $9,000,000 for the first six months of 1893. The values given as rough—and it may be added parenthetically, carefully undercalculated—estimates by the projectors of new buildings on applying for permits during the actual life of New St. Louis exceed in the aggregate $120,000,000, and it is believed by competent valuers that the buildings erected under these permits have cost at least $200,000,000. Little wonder, under these circumstances, that the appearance of New St. Louis of 1893 is entirely different from that of Old St. Louis in 1883.

RAPID INCREASE IN VALUE OF TAXABLE PROPERTY. Many old buildings of considerable value have been removed to make room for new ones, and hence the increase in the assessed valuation is not quite so large. But since 1878 the total has about doubled. The 1894 valuation will certainly exceed $300,000,000, as compared with $245,000,000 in 1890, and $165,000,000 in 1880. The city comptroller estimated the value of the city's real estate in 1890 at $141,000,000 more than the assessed valuation, and the estimate was a conservative one. Upon this basis the value of the real estate in the city is now nearly, if not quite, $400,000,000, while it is doubtful if that sum would purchase nearly all the realty in St. Louis. These figures are too large to be easily grasped, but they show as no argument could demonstrate, how stupendous has been the city's building growth since its second birth.

Reverting to the character of buildings, it may be mentioned that the number of new structures erected in 1890, 1891 and 1892 was about 14,500, of which only 4,000 were frame. The percentage of frame houses to brick has been gradually decreasing. In the eighties about one-third of the new buildings were constructed of lumber, as compared with little more than a fifth at the present time.

The immense number of buildings constructed since the census was taken is of special interest as bearing upon the question of population, and justifies the claim made by directory publishers and canvassers, that the number of inhabitants has increased much more rapidly during the last three years than during any corresponding period of time in the history of St. Louis. Besides the activity in the erection of new build-

ings, great enterprise has been shown in the improvement and enlarging of existing structures. The real estate sales for the year 1892 reached, as shown in the records, a total of $62,000,000, or a great deal more than $1,000,000 a week. Upwards of 40,000 deeds were filed at the office of the recorder of deeds during the year, and nearly 8,000 deeds of trust were released. During the same year 120,000 feet of land was subdivided, but the subdivision did not keep pace with the building, and as a result there were seven miles less of unbuilt-up streets at the end of the year than at the commencement. Acre property within the city limits is getting very scarce, and the demand for residence property has grown so rapidly that values do not compare at all with those of a few years ago. The extreme western district is now very largely built up, and the price at which lots are held is restricting improvements to those of a very costly character. In the extreme northwest, the extension of the Benton-Bellefontaine road and its equipment of electricity, together with the construction of the Belt Railroad has caused an awakening, and the sales in this section have been very large in consequence. A number of New St. Louis men have made their homes in the extreme south of the city, where building has been carried on with great activity and where the vacant lots are becoming more and more scarce.

Another characteristic of the new buildings, in addition to the more general use of brick and stone, is the improved architectural excellence and the increased value generally. In the residence portions of the city, which were more especially referred to in the opening remarks of this chapter, the change is remarkable. About eighteen months ago a large delegation from the National Press Association was entertained in St. Louis, and the visitors were driven over the city in carriages placed at their disposal. They were not asked their opinions as to the city, but voluntarily expressed them; and the sentiment was unanimous that in no part of the world were so large a number of architectural styles represented as in St. Louis. Coming from men and women who have traveled from Maine to California, and many of them from New York to London, Paris, Berlin, Vienna and Florence, an expression of opinion of this kind naturally has weight; and when one of the most inveterate Bohemians in the crowd said that there was more home-pride in St. Louis than in any other city he had visited, the sentiment was warmly applauded by his companions and appreciated by his hearers. The greatest ambition of a successful St. Louis manufacturer, merchant or professional man seems to be to build for himself a palatial home and to surround it with all the luxury and beauty which money can procure.

BIRTH OF THE LOFTY OFFICE-BUILDING ERA. "Ground costs money and air does not," remarked Jay Gould on one occasion when discussing the number of stories of which buildings should be composed. Old St. Louis did not appreciate the importance of this fact, and the buildings in the city were seldom more than six stories high, and very frequently only four or five. New St. Louis, on the other hand, has made high buildings a specialty, and although sky-scrapers twenty stories high have not found favor here, the most popular office-buildings are those which vary in height from ten to fourteen stories. Both types of St. Louis are still represented in its commercial and professional buildings. In the extreme eastern section of the business quarter, where at one time all the important transactions of the "Future Great" were planned and carried out, there are still to be found a number of substantial buildings four or six stories high with few, if any, modern conveniences, with slow elevator service and with a minimum of light. Many of these buildings are still in good order, and hence the old-style office-building dies hard, although the competition of the new type of building is felt very keenly.

Ten years ago this old-style office-building was regarded as the correct thing, although in other cities the theory which Jay Gould subsequently expressed so concisely had been appreciated and the air was being encroached upon with considerable rapidity. Now, however, New St. Louis is represented by more than twenty office-buildings of absolutely the first class, and these are not surpassed in any other city, although, as already mentioned, extremes of height such as are found in Chicago or New York have not been attempted here. In addition to the score of buildings specially deserving mention as types of the New St. Louis idea, there are others of recent construction almost as magnificent and embracing every improvement calculated to increase the capacity of the structures and the convenience of the tenants. An excellent municipal ordinance forbids the erection of a building in St. Louis more than 100 feet in height unless its interior construction is absolutely fire-proof. Hence the new office-buildings are in no sense of the word fire-traps, but are rather to be looked upon as safer than the small buildings they have superseded, which had but indifferent means of egress in case of fire, and whose material was more or less combustible—and generally more.

The era of the fire-proof office-building in St. Louis dates back to about the year 1885, when the Equitable Building on Sixth and Locust streets was enlarged and heightened. This fine structure was originally six stories high. It was the pioneer of modern office-buildings in St. Louis, and was regarded by every one who saw it as a distinct advance on anything yet attempted in the Mississippi Valley. Being absolutely fire-proof and exceptionally well arranged, there was quite a run on its offices, and instead of tenants being sought, the only difficulty the management had to contend with was filling the demands of applicants. It was decided to have the foundation and walls carefully examined and to increase the height from six to ten stories if the plan were endorsed by competent engineers. The examination proved that the structure was strong enough to bear the weight of six additional stories easily, but the original plan was carried out, and the Equitable Building raised its head ten stories high, a monument to the enterprise of its owners and to the determination of

New St. Louis to have the best of everything that science had perfected. To-day the Equitable Building does not rank among the very highest St. Louis buildings, but in 1885 and 1886 it was looked upon with as much admiration as the Union Trust Building is now.

The Laclede Building is generally regarded as the pioneer of the lofty fire-proof buildings of St. Louis. There were a great many projects about the year 1885 looking to the erection of buildings of this character, but the first scheme of magnitude involved the erection of a ten-story building, to be known as the Union Building, on the southwest corner of Olive and Fourth streets. In the winter of 1885 and 1886 the old improvements of this corner were torn down, and it was announced that a large body of Chicago capitalists were behind the scheme, and were about to erect a building of gigantic proportions. Fairy tales concerning the proportions and decorations of the new building abounded, but local suspicion was aroused when the excavations were left untouched week after week, and the final announcement that the wealth of the capitalists had not materialized, caused more regret than surprise. The unrealized hope was not only an eye-sore, but also a source of ridicule, and a number of St. Louis capitalists, who did not boast of fabulous wealth but who had a reputation for completing every project with which they connected themselves, took hold of the enterprise and erected the Laclede Building. The Laclede Building is not the palace covered by the plans of the Union Building, but is a first-class office structure, fire-proof throughout, and constructed of Missouri granite, iron and brick. The hall walls are of polished Berdillo marble and plate glass, and the halls and ceilings are of marble. The building was watched with great interest while in course of construction, and when it was finished its elevator capacity, arrangements for ventilation and for the transaction of business, as well as the completeness of its furnishings, not only excited the admiration of St. Louis people generally, but encouraged the perfecting of projects for a number of similar and even superior buildings.

7

At about the same time the Commercial Building was designed. In the early days of New St. Louis the southeast corner of Sixth and Olive streets was encumbered by improvements of a very inferior character, many years behind the times. A syndicate was formed and a lease negotiated for ninety-nine years, at $20,000 a year, with a clause that a building to cost not less than $200,000 should be erected on the site within the space of three years. As a result of this undertaking, the Commercial Building was designed and completed, the cost of construction being about three times the minimum stated in the lease.

The Commercial Building has since been outclassed in height, but it is still looked upon as one of the most substantial and convenient office-buildings in the West. Missouri granite and St. Louis pressed brick, two of the best building materials to be found in the world, were used in the exterior construction, with the columns, pilasters and lintels of iron. The building is absolutely fire-proof, and has 192 office-rooms. Georgia marble was used largely in the corridors and wainscoting, and a perfect system of elevators, four in number, was put in. Like the Equitable and Laclede, the Commercial Building was in its early days visited by hundreds of spectators, and even now our best office-buildings are regarded as an attraction by sojourners in other cities.

It is not suggested that the three buildings first mentioned were actually the three first to be completed and occupied, the order being rather that of the negotiations which resulted in the inauguration of a rule which has changed the aspect of down-town St. Louis and attracted the admiration of all. Olive street, in the neighborhood of the Federal Building, was largely reconstructed during the days of the fire-proof office-building awakening. Work was commenced on the Odd Fellows' Building, on the corner of Ninth and Olive streets, very early in the revival. The building is almost faultless in its construction, and the summit of its tower is 236 feet high. Missouri granite, both rock-faced and polished, was used in the construction of the first story, and the seven stories above are of St. Louis pressed brick. Iron and steel pillars and girders were freely used, and the entire work is exceptionally massive and lasting. The foundations are so strong that they would probably hold a building nearly twice as high as the one now upon them. The corridors are tiled with white marble, and the wainscoting is of the best Georgia gray and white marble. The building, which cost over $600,000, was completed in the spring of 1889. A portion of it is occupied by the Odd Fellows' halls, offices and library, but the offices available for the public are occupied by professional and business men, and are replete with every convenience.

Adjoining the Odd Fellows' Building, and erected almost simultaneously with it is the Fagin Building, unique in its features and a structure which has been both praised and criticised by experts. It is unlike any other office-building in the city, and the front is constructed almost entirely of granite and glass. It is ten stories high, and the available space in the interior is 1,052,000 square feet. The building, despite some early criticisms, is strong and attractive. Its plan involves an abundance of light, and, although its entrance is not as attractive and handsome as a building of such altitude and cost would seem to demand, it is a grand building and has undoubtedly had its influence in a most important direction on the office-building work of St. Louis.

On Eighth street, also opposite the Federal Building and almost at the corner of Olive, is the Turner Building, which, it is claimed, was the first building erected in St. Louis fire-proof in every part. It is less lofty than some of its neighbors, but is a very handsome, substantial structure, with every possible convenience for its tenants.

The American Central Building, on Broadway and Locust street, was reconstructed during the same period, and the Bank of Commerce Building and a large number of factories and what may

be termed individual business establishments were also erected. The year 1889 found the office-building question practically settled and down-town St. Louis equipped with structures and offices handsome enough to do credit to any city and apparently numerous enough to meet every demand. It was even suggested that the work had been overdone and that there would be a difficulty in renting the offices in the new buildings. Looked at from the standpoint of St. Louis in 1893 the forecast appears ludicrous, for during the last three or four years the activity of the fire-proof-lofty-structure-builder has more than redoubled, and on every side there are to be seen grand edifices not then so much as contemplated.

THE HIGHEST OF THEM ALL. The highest of these most recent office-buildings is the Union Trust Building, at the corner of Seventh and Olive streets. This building, which is now practically completed, is fourteen stories high, or, if the plan of counting basement and attic, common in some cities, is adopted, there are really sixteen stories. The building occupied about a year and a half in construction, including the time devoted to tearing down the old improvements and in digging out the foundations. Much longer time would have been required but for the adoption of what is known as the steel skeleton system of construction. Without this aid to building, the walls and doors in the lower stories would have had to be exceptionally thick and massive to hold the weight, but the plan adopted obviated this difficulty and added immensely to the floor-space of the building. Pillars of rolled steel and iron are extended from the foundation to the roof, and these are all sufficiently strong, not only to hold the enormous weight resting upon them, but also to stand the strain of high winds and tempestuous weather. The floor-beams and girders are also of rolled steel riveted to the uprights, and the whole building is thus one united mass, the strain being divided over an immense area. The precautions taken in the design to secure rigidity have proven entirely successful, and the building is now as solid and substantial as though it stood but two stories high.

The building is fire-proof in fact as well as in name. Hollow fire clay tile was used largely in the construction, and the stair-cases and even the elevator guide-posts are of incombustible material, so that in the event of fire nothing but desks, chairs, window-frames and doors would burn. The building has a frontage of 128 feet on Olive street and 84 feet on Seventh street, with the advantage of a wide alley, which practically gives it three fronts. The internal court, fronting southward on Olive street, adds to the frontage so much that, although there are 300 offices in the building, the windows of each one opens direct into the air, if not sunlight. Two hundred and forty offices face the streets, and these are being rapidly occupied by tenants. The external construction is of buff terra cotta for the two lowest stories, buff brick to the thirteenth and terra cotta at the summit. The appearance is unique and somewhat peculiar, and the material used is of a character to withstand the attacks of smoke and dust and retain its color almost indefinitely. Two thousand tons of iron have been used in the construction, and there are more than seven miles of steam, water and escape pipes in the building. Three miles of electric wire were also used in the equipments, and about 25,000 square feet of marble and mosaic were required. The halls and corridors are richly decorated with marble, and the windows are of polished plate glass. The elevator service is exceptionally good, and in every office there is a hot and cold water supply service. A million dollars has been mentioned as the probable price of this lofty and remarkable structure, but, although a detailed statement has not been published, there can be no doubt that the outlay has been very largely in excess of the sum named.

SECURITY BUILDING AND NOONDAY CLUB. The Security Building, on the southwest corner of Fourth and Locust streets, while not so lofty as the Union Trust, is probably the most magnificent fire-proof structure in the West. It is ten stories high,[*] and its roof 156 feet 9 inches above the sidewalk. In its construction only the most costly materials were used, and the building cost considerably in excess of $1,000,000. The internal decorations are on a par with the magnificent outside work, and the building has a substantial, valuable appearance which excites comment from every visitor. The entrance to the elevators, from a most attractive and unusually convenient rotunda, is artistic in the extreme; and the mosaic floors are æsthetic enough for an art museum or a picture gallery. The offices are replete with every possible convenience, and are as elegant as money could possibly make them. The tenth floor is occupied entirely by the reception and dining-rooms of the Noonday Club, one of the latest additions to the commercial clubs of St. Louis. It was established in 1893, with 300 members, consisting of presidents and leading members of some of the largest and most wealthy firms of the city.

The Security Building fronts on Locust street, with two wings extending south, one on the east, and one on the west side. The club rooms are thus divided into three divisions. The central portion contains the restaurant, which on special occasions is converted into a banqueting hall. This room is finished in light colors, verging to a very pale brown and cream white. The west wing contains a regular lunch-room, with the kitchens overhead, in what may be described as the attic addition to the building. The lunch-room is finished in harmonious colors, and has windows on three sides. The billiard hall is equally well provided with light. The floors have been varnished into a glossy cherry color, and the walls are painted a deep wine-red, the ceiling being pale green. The appointments of the club, generally, are thoroughly in keeping with the design of the organization, and with the general elegance and excellence of the building in which it is situated.

---

[*] Only complete and full-sized floors are counted. The Security Building has also a basement and an attic, and hence might be spoken of as a twelve-story building. It is always the rule in St. Louis to understate, rather than exaggerate.

TWENTY-SIX BUILDINGS COSTING MORE THAN $500,000 EACH. Mention has already been made of the three exceptionally magnificent new structures of St. Louis—the Union Depot, the City Hall and the New Planters' House. In this chapter a few representative buildings of the New St. Louis type have been selected. It has not been attempted to refer to every large building constructed during the last five or six years, because even a brief description of these would occupy the space allotted to several chapters. Only those who have given the question careful attention realize the stupendous nature of the work the local builder and contractor has done. It is important to bear in mind that early in the present year there were actually in course of construction more than twenty-six buildings, each averaging in cost more than $500,000. These included an immense number of new factories to take the place, in some instances, of buildings which had ceased to be available for the purposes desired, and also to provide accommodation for increased business and new firms. Prior to this date there had been erected, in addition to those already mentioned, such magnificent structures as the Bell Telephone Building, in which the Builders' Exchange has its headquarters; the new Globe-Democrat Building, and the Roe, Houser and Oriel buildings. The twenty-six buildings referred to as being either in course of construction or having contracts completed at the commencement of 1893 were as follows, the prices given being those named in the building permits, which, it will be seen, aggregate about $14,000,000:

New Planters' House, twelve stories, Fourth street, between Pine and Chestnut streets, $1,000,000; the Colonnade, ten stories, comprising a hotel, theatre and arcade, an office-building and a Turkish bath establishment, to occupy a half block on Ninth street, between Olive and Locust streets, $1,100,000; a hotel, not yet named, ten stories, on Ninth street, corner of Pine street, $500,000; Imperial Hotel, ten stories, corner of Market and Eighteenth streets, $1,200,000; City Hall, in old Wash-

ington Park, fronting on Market, between Twelfth and Thirteenth streets, $2,000,000; new Union Depot, Market street, south side, between Eighteenth and Twentieth streets, $1,000,000;* Hammett-Anderson-Wade's Columbia Building, southeast corner of Eighth and Locust streets, $300,000; Mills & Averill's building, on Chestnut street, twelve stories, $600,000; Patterson Building, southeast corner of Olive and Twelfth streets, ten stories, $250,000; Fair Building, southwest corner of Seventh and Franklin avenue, $150,000; Nelson Building, south side of St. Charles, east of Twelfth, eight stories, $100,000; Hoyle Building, southwest corner of Third and Locust streets, $75,000; McCormack Building, north side of Chestnut, between Eighth and Ninth streets, $75,000; Interstate Investment Co.'s Building, southeast corner of Ninth and Washington avenue, $100,000; Benoist Building, southeast corner of Eleventh and Olive streets, $75,000; F. A. Drew Building, southeast corner of Twelfth and St. Charles streets, $125,000; Culver Building, southeast corner of Twelfth and Locust streets, $90,000; new Board of Education Building, northwest corner of Locust and Ninth streets, $400,000; Rialto Building, ten stories, southeast corner of Fourth and Olive streets, $500,000; Security Building, ten stories, Fourth and Locust streets, $1,500,000; Wainwright Building, nine stories, northwest corner of Seventh and Chestnut streets, $600,000; Union Trust Company Building, fourteen stories, northwest corner of Seventh and Olive streets, $1,000,000; Puritan Building, north side of Locust, between Seventh and Eighth streets, nine stories, $150,000; Meyer Building, southeast corner of Washington avenue and Eighth street, $100,000; new Mercantile Club Building, southeast corner of Locust and Seventh streets, $500,000; Famous Building, west side of Broadway, between Franklin avenue and Morgan street, $400,000.

---

*A comparison of the permit price of this structure with the actual expenditure, as outlined on page 67, shows better than any argument in words how inadequately the building permit returns set forth the actual building expenditure.

LIBRARY AND SCHOOL BUILDING. The Mercantile Library Building was completed too soon to be included in this list. It is a fire-proof structure, on the corner of Broadway and Locust street, with the upper floors devoted to the library. Its reading-room is one of the largest and best equipped in the country, and it is a great advance on the old structure which made the library famous in former years. The Public Library Building, or, more correctly speaking, the Board of Education Building, four blocks west of this, is another lofty and valuable building, as different from the old Polytechnic, in which the Public School Library was situated, as New St. Louis differs from Old. Among the strictly 1893 buildings not already described, but which must be mentioned as remarkable evidences of the building activity of New St. Louis, is the new High School on Grand avenue. This building has a front facade 300 feet in length and 147 feet deep. Brick, ornamented with red sandstone, forms the outer walls, the front and two towers being faced with stone up to the second floor. There is an interior court 45x130 feet for light and ventilation, and the building contains, in addition to an immense number of class and study-rooms, an assembly-room about eighty feet square. Another is the new Mercantile Club Building, to which reference has already been made. This building has been erected on the site of the old club house and of Mr. Henry Shaw's mansion, at the corner of Seventh and Locust streets. It has a frontage of 127 feet on Locust street, and 90 feet on Seventh street. It is six stories high, and is constructed of Lake Superior red sandstone, resting on a granite base. The upper floors are of red brick, with sandstone trimmings. The design includes lofty balconies, and a gabled Spanish roof, giving the building a unique effect, very pleasing to the eye, as compared with the flat roof so universal in the modern lofty structures.

A block west of this club, the St. Nicholas Hotel is in course of construction and will soon be ready for occupation. This is another building in which the style of architecture differs materially from that in general use, and its appearance is sufficiently handsome and even antique to give quite a name and reputation to both Locust and Eighth streets. The estimated cost of the building is about $300,000. It is eight stories high with a balcony and a slanting red tiled roof with curved brick gables. These gables are already a source of admiration and by the time the finishing strokes have been put to the work the building will certainly be an ornament to the city. Among the peculiarities of the internal structure may be mentioned the ball-room, which is to occupy the uppermost floor. This will be one of the most gorgeous ball-rooms in the country, and is likely to be used very largely for entertainments of a public and semi-private character.

No reference to the buildings of 1893 can be complete without something more than a passing mention of the Rialto Building on the southeast corner of Fourth and Olive streets, a thoroughfare which in years gone by was the center of commerce of the city, but which in the early days of New St. Louis was rather outclassed by streets slightly more western. The new hotel, the Security and Laclede buildings and the Rialto are only four evidences of the determination of property owners to restore the street to its former commercial precedence and grandeur. The Rialto Building is ten stories high and is constructed of steel and iron encased in massive blocks of granite and red sandstone. It fronts ninety feet on Fourth street and rather less on Olive street, and its cost was considerably in excess of $500,000. The external appearance is rendered attractive by the architectural device to increase the light and capacity of the offices, and the internal arrangements are complete in the extreme, the elevator plan being remarkable for its simplicity and good service. Adjoining, and in the shadow of this building, is the Bank of the Republic structure. This bank was established on Ninth and Olive streets, where it has built up a large and lucrative connection. It has, however, decided to move on Fourth street, and has erected a building one story high and remarkably attractive in its appearance. The front is of Italian marble exquisitely carved in draped figures, and the entire roof is of heavy glass. Instead of erecting a high building and renting the upper offices, the bank preferred the more costly plan of a one-story building devoted entirely to its own use. The structure is thirty-five feet high, and each foot cost about $1,000 to construct.

IN THE WHOLESALE SECTION OF THE CITY. Among the buildings costing upwards of $500,000 and erected in 1893, was the Martin Building, on Tenth street, between Washington and Christy avenues. This is right in the center of what may be termed the wholesale district of St. Louis, and the building is designed exclusively for wholesale purposes. It occupies a space of 70x205 feet, and is eight stories high. The two first stories are in blue Bedford stone, the remainder being in light colored Roman brick with terra cotta trimmings. There is a court in the center entered through an arched gateway on Tenth street. The Collier Block is on Washington avenue, Fourth, and St. Charles streets, and when completed will occupy an entire half block, with side frontages of 150 feet on both Washington avenue and St. Charles street. The main floors are of iron columns filled in with plate glass, and the upper floors are of dark gray brick with terra cotta trimmings, surmounted above the sixth floor by a Florentine cornice.

The Columbian Club House and the new Good Shepherd Convent, although not strictly commercial structures, were in course of erection during 1893 at a total cost approximating $750,000. The Columbian Club House is situated at the corner of Lindell boulevard and Vandeventer avenue. It is a good type of the Italian renaissance style of architecture, with a facade of buff Roman brick and buff Bedford limestone. The building is four stories high and has a frontage of 114 feet. The new Good Shepherd Convent, costing nearly $500,000, is in course of construction on Gravois avenue, a little west of Grand. The tract of land was presented by Adolphus Busch, and upon it is being constructed a building in Romanesque

style, with little unnecessary ornamentation but of large capacity. The principal facade is 400 feet long, and the building is three stories high.

Space prevents a detailed description of all the elegant buildings in course of construction at the present time, or which have been built during the last three years, but enough has been written to show that capitalists have an unlimited confidence in the future of New St. Louis and are willing at all times to invest freely in buildings of the better class. And it is very important to emphasize the fact that, although the year 1893 has been in every way unfavorable for new enterprises and generally discouraging for mercantile interests, there has been no difficulty in renting the rooms and offices in the new buildings, although the apartments now number several thousand. Favorite offices in the best buildings having the very best sites and locations have been secured long before work was completed, and the rapidity with which the new buildings have filled up is a striking testimony to the expansion of St. Louis and its manufacturing, commercial and financial interests. No city on the continent has been transformed more completely by aid of the builder and contractor during the last six or eight years, yet the percentage of vacant offices in St. Louis is smaller than in any other large city. In other words, phenomenal as has been the increase in building, the demand has more than kept pace with that increase; and from every appearance it is still continuing to grow.

A COMPARISON OF REALTY PRICES. The growth of the city, and the immense expenditure on improvements, has had a marked effect on the value of real estate. There has never been any wildcat speculation in the city, and, although the transactions have frequently shown a total consideration money exceeding on an average $1,000,000 a week, and continuing for many weeks, the bulk of the investing has been for the purpose of improvement, and not for mere speculation. It is on record that the ground now bounded by Market and Wash streets, and by Broadway and Jefferson avenue, was once sold for $4,000 in cash and 2,400 levies of furs. The value of this property to-day exceeds $250,000,000, and it includes some of the most costly frontages in St. Louis. There are several frontages worth more per foot than was paid for this entire tract in the city's early days. Thus, the corner of Broadway and Olive street is estimated to be worth more than $10,000 a foot; passing up Olive street the value decreases slightly going west. Thus, Seventh and Olive ground is worth about $8,000 a foot, while at Twelfth and Olive it is worth $2,500. West of Jefferson avenue the value decreases less rapidly, and even as far west as Jefferson avenue available corners sell at $1,500 a foot front. The average value of Olive street property, between Twelfth street and Broadway, is $6,834; and between Twelfth street and Jefferson avenue it is $2,000. There are about 14,600 feet of ground on Olive street, between Broadway and Jefferson avenue. The value of the property between Twelfth street and Jefferson avenue is $19,466,000; and between Twelfth street and Broadway it is $33,249,378.

These figures, of course, do not include the value of any building improvements on the property. Olive street frontage, in the business part of the city, is regarded as the most valuable property in the city at present. Locust street and Broadway is worth $6,000 a foot. At Seventh street, Locust street property is worth $2,000 a foot; at Twelfth street, $1,500; and at Jefferson avenue, $300. The average value per foot, west of Twelfth street, is $3,166. Between Twelfth street and Jefferson avenue it is $900 a foot. The estimated value of the property on Locust street, between Broadway and Twelfth street, is $15,399,156, and between Twelfth street and Jefferson avenue it is $8,758,800. St. Charles street at Broadway is worth $4,000 a foot. At Seventh street it is worth $1,200 a foot; at Twelfth street, $1,500 a front foot. West of Twelfth street, St. Charles street is practically no street. The average value of St. Charles street property, between Twelfth street and Broadway, is $2,233 a front foot, or $10,865,778.

The corner of Washington avenue and Broadway is worth $6,000 a front foot. At Seventh street, Washington avenue property is worth $3,000 a front foot; at Twelfth street, $2,000; and at Jefferson avenue, $1,000. The average value per foot, east of Twelfth street and west of Broadway, is $3,667 a foot, and between Twelfth street and Jefferson avenue the average value is $1,500 a foot. The property east of Twelfth street, on Washington avenue, is worth about $17,596,800. The property on Washington avenue, between Twelfth street and Jefferson avenue, is worth, approximately, $14,400,000. Lucas avenue and Broadway is worth about $3,000 a foot. At Seventh street, Lucas avenue property is valued at $1,000 a foot; at Twelfth street, $800; and at Jefferson avenue, $200 a foot. The average value per foot between Twelfth street and Broadway is $1,600 a foot; and between Twelfth street and Jefferson avenue it is $500 per foot. The property on Lucas avenue, between Twelfth street and Broadway, is worth about $7,680,000; and between Twelfth street and Jefferson avenue it is worth $4,800,000. The corner of Morgan street and Broadway is worth about $2,000; Seventh and Morgan is worth $800 a foot; Twelfth and Morgan, $1,000; and Jefferson avenue and Morgan, $300 a foot. The average value of Morgan street property, between Twelfth street and Broadway, is $1,266; and the average value of Morgan street property, between Twelfth street and Jefferson avenue, is $650 a foot. The total value of Morgan street property, between Twelfth street and Broadway, is $2,560,356; and between Twelfth street and Jefferson avenue it is $6,325,800. The corner of Broadway and Franklin avenue is worth $4,000 at foot. At Seventh street, Franklin avenue property is worth $1,500 a front foot; at Twelfth street, $1,500; and at Jefferson avenue, $750. The average value per foot east of Twelfth street is $3,333; and between Twelfth street and Jefferson avenue it is $1,125. The estimated total value of the ground between Twelfth street and Broadway, on Franklin avenue, is $15,408,689; and between Twelfth street and Jefferson avenue it is $11,099,250.

**ST. LOUIS REAL ESTATE
AS AN INVESTMENT.**

These figures are selected as evidence of the growth in values. It will be noticed that they are not speculative in any way, because nearly all of the property mentioned is improved with substantial buildings, and has not been bought and sold for speculation at values based upon surmises and possible growth. In the neighborhood of the new Union Station the increase in values has been more phenomenal and more speculative. Within four years prices have increased from five to ten-fold, although purchases are made without regard to the value of existing improvements. The influence of the enterprise of the Terminal Association has been felt to so marked an extent that the neighborhood within a few blocks of the depot is being completely reconstructed, and elegant hotels, boarding-houses, stores and mercantile establishments are taking the place of the comparatively small dwelling-houses which monopolized the frontage during the last decade of Old St. Louis and the first five or six years of New. The heavy expenditure in railroad improvements in the North End has had a similar influence on values, and, indeed, at the present time, it is almost impossible to obtain property at prices approximating those that were asked five or six years ago, and even more recently. The sudden withdrawal of capital from investment during the summer and fall of 1893 did not have any material effect on values in St. Louis. The number of purchasers, of course, was greatly reduced, and sales were much harder to consummate; but holders had such unlimited faith in both the present and future greatness of St. Louis that they declined to sacrifice, and the number of "hard times" sales at cut prices was very small. St. Louis real estate was the last to feel the influence of the depression, and the first to benefit by the restoration of confidence, and the business during the winter has not been far below the average. These facts show that St. Louis is not a "boom" town, and that, as an investment for large and small sums, its real estate offers advantages not to be equaled elsewhere.

Immense fortunes have been made out of judicious investments in the city; and in still more instances substantial and satisfactory returns have been received. The reputation for solidity and conservatism in finances has helped the real estate interests of St. Louis to a marked extent. The amount of loanable capital from a distance has always been large, and one company alone, the Connecticut Mutual Life Insurance Company, has loaned upwards of $20,000,000 in St. Louis since its general awakening and revival. Mr. E. S. Rowse, who has negotiated the loans, rejoices in the fact that his books show an absolutely clean record, not a single case of foreclosure marring their pages. This company has loaned about $35,000,000 in the State, and its success and enterprise is merely quoted because of the very profitable faith in St. Louis and in Missouri which the vastness of its operations demonstrates so conclusively.

At the time of this writing millions of dollars are known to have been withdrawn from speculative investment and placed in deposit vaults, where the money is unproductive. The loss of thousands of dollars a year in interest this way naturally arouses capitalists of every grade to a sense of the error they are committing, and the indications are that a greater portion of the money will be taken from the "stockings" without further delay and invested where it is quite as safe and a thousand times more productive—St. Louis real estate. The natural consequence will be renewed and increased activity during the coming year, with countless projects of improvements and hundreds of new buildings. If this work partook of the nature of advice to investors, there would be no better ending to this chapter than a recommendation to investors to take time by the forelock and make their selections and purchases before the enhancement of values which the increased demand of the coming spring is certain to create. The speculator is not very likely to make a mistake if he selects New St. Louis as the field of his operations; while the investor has a still greater guarantee of satisfactory returns.

CHAPTER X.

MUNICIPAL DEVELOPMENT.

THE NEW WATER-WORKS.—NEW CITY HALL.--NEW ST. LOUIS, THE PIONEER IN STREET SPRINKLING AND ELECTRIC LIGHTING.

THE PROGRESS made in municipal institutions and features during the last ten years has been enormous, and the New St. Louis idea has been warmly supported and fostered by the city authorities. In the first chapter the city's incorporation and the extension of the city limits from time to time are briefly recorded, and in pursuance of the plan on which this work is based, only those features which have a strong bearing on the city's new growth will be dealt with at any length, while nothing in the shape of a municipal history of Old St. Louis will be attempted. It is impossible, however, to omit a tribute to the genuine integrity and zeal of the men who have been placed at the head of the city government from time to time. The earlier mayors were not assisted by commissioners, as now, and all the detail work passed through their hands. At this stage of the city's history the mayor is at the head of an immense body of workers, and the Board of Public Improvements has a president whose duties are as numerous as the sands on the sea-shore. The other members of the board are the street, water, sewer, harbor and park commissioners, each in control of the department from which he takes his name. The health department is managed by a commissioner who has no seat in the "B. P. I." cabinet, and among the other heads of departments are the city register, the supply commissioner and the building commissioner.

The following table, giving the names of the mayors of St. Louis since the city's incorporation, and data as to population, will be of interest, and will also show concisely how rapidly the city has grown:

Period of Administration.	Mayor	Date of Census.	Population.
1823-28	Wm. Carr Lane	1820	4,928
1829-32	Daniel D. Page	1830	5,852
1833	Samuel Merry*		
1833-34	J. W. Johnson		
1835-37	John F. Darby	1835	8,316
1838 39	Wm. Carr Lane		
1840	John F. Darby	1840	16,469
1841	John D. Daggett		
1842	George Maguire		
1843	John M. Wimer		
1844-45	Bernard Pratte		
1846	P. G. Camden		
1847	Bryan Mullanphy		
1848	John M. Krum		
1849	James G. Barry		
1850-52	L. M. Kennett	1850	74,439
1853-54	John How		
1855	Washington King		
1856	John How		
1857	John M. Wimer		
1858-60	Oliver D. Filley	1860	160,773
1861-62	Dan. G. Taylor		
1863	Chaun. I. Filley		
1864-68	Jas. S. Thomas		
1869-70	Nathan Cole	1870	310,963
1871-74	Joseph Brown		
1875	Arthur Barrett‡		
1875	James H. Britton		
1876	Henry Overstolz†		
1877-81	Henry Overstolz	1880	350,518
1881-85	Wm. L. Ewing		
1885-89	D. R. Francis§		
1889	Geo. W. Allen‖		
1889-93	E. A. Noonan	1890	a 451,770
1893	C. P. Walbridge	1893	b620,000

* Disqualified in consequence of holding office under general government. J. W. Johnson elected in his place.
† Died April 27, 1875. J. H. Britton elected to fill vacancy.
‡ Declared elected by City Council February 9, 1876, instead of James H. Britton.
§ D. R. Francis elected Governor of Missouri, and resigned January 2, 1889.
‖ Geo. W. Allen, being President City Council, became mayor.
a Federal census, generally conceded to be at least 30,000 too small.
b Directory census early in year.

**MAYOR EWING,
1881—1885.**
It was during the mayoralty of Mr. W. L. Ewing that New St. Louis commenced to exist. The pen with which Mr. Ewing signed his approval of the ordinance authorizing the construction of the first rapid-transit street railroad in St. Louis ought to have been preserved in the city archives, for, as we have seen, that ordinance enabled a complete change to be made, not only in the street railroad facilities, but also in the city itself. The next event of importance, or perhaps an event of equal importance, during Mayor Ewing's administration was the commencement of the repaving of the down-town streets with granite. This was done under the fostering guidance of Mr. J. W. Turner, who was street commissioner at the time, and whose work was of so high an order that his name has since been mentioned as a desirable candidate for almost every municipal office of importance from the mayoralty down. Mr. Turner found the streets in but an indifferent condition, not worse, perhaps, than those of other cities, but in no way suited for the heavy traffic of a busy manufacturing district. The soft roadways gave way under heavy loads, and in many instances extra teams had to be obtained to pull wagons out of holes and ruts. Reference has already been made to the opposition with which the proposal to pave the down-town streets with granite was received, but the authorities held their own, and finally the good work was commenced in earnest. In the spring of 1883 there were little more than three miles of granite paving in the city, but during the years 1884 and 1885 reconstruction on a wholesale scale was completed, and at the end of the latter year there were over twenty-two miles of granite streets in the city, with about a mile of limestone blocks, a little over two miles of wooden blocks, four miles of asphalt, five of telford and about 285 of macadam.

In his report for the year 1885, Mr. Turner went very fully into the granite pavement question. "It is needless to say," he remarked, "that the granite pavements have given great satisfaction. They have facilitated and thereby decreased the cost of transportation over our streets very largely. Houses handling large amounts of heavy goods report that it has reduced the cost of transportation two-fifths. A great deal of the objection that was raised at first against these pavements in anticipation of excessive noise has subsided; either the noise was not so great as was expected or the people have become accustomed to it. Doubtless, in narrow streets on which the traffic is very great, the noise is quite objectionable, but we have few of these; and taking the immense advantage gained by having solid and enduring pavements facilitating the operations of the commerce of the city, we can tolerate a few disadvantages arising from our new pavements. The character of our work can be considered first-class in every respect; the quality of the stone is good. We have now several varieties to select from, and the supply on the line of the Iron Mountain Railroad, within a haul of one hundred and fifty miles of the city, is inexhaustible. The price of these pavements has been gradually falling; our last lettings show a very great reduction, due to competition, resulting from new parties opening new quarries, thereby increasing the supply of stone in the market; and also due to increased capacity of and facilities for operating old quarries."

**THE STREETS
AND
THEIR PAVING.**
The wear and tear of eight years has more than borne out Mr. Turner's estimate of the high character of the work. The best laid of the down-town streets are still in perfect order, and show little or no signs of wear. The mileage of the granite streets has increased steadily every year, and Mr. Turner's successors, Messrs. Burnett and Murphy, have evinced as much enthusiasm on the subject as Mr. Turner himself. There are now some forty-six miles of granite-paved streets in the city, in addition to nearly five miles of granite-paved alleys. Limestone blocks for streets have not proved entirely satisfactory, but there are upwards of eighty-four miles of alleys paved this way, and giving good service. The mileage of telford pavement has been increased since

the revival, and there are now some thirty-three miles paved in this way, with a total mileage of improved streets and alleys exceeding 450. The streets of the city, and more especially the sidewalks, are now on the whole far better paved than those of the average American city, although the rapid increase in territory has made it impossible to keep up with the city's growth. In order to expedite improvements, the law concerning the apportionment of cost was revised in 1892, and it is now enacted that the entire cost of reconstruction shall be charged against adjoining property, regardless of its assessed valuation. As the result of this enactment, known as the "Stone law," a large quantity of improvement work has been commenced and is under contemplation, and the splendid reform in Mayor Ewing's term will soon be so developed and brought to such perfection as to cause delight to St. Louis citizens generally.

When St. Louis was first settled, the high ground on the bluffs was what attracted the pioneers, who knew nothing and cared less about the magnificent location beyond the bluffs, and how admirably the site was adapted for a great city. After the abrupt rise from the river, there is a table-land with just sufficient grade to make drainage easy, extending several miles north and south, and about three-quarters of a mile west. Beyond this right out to the city limits the ground is rolling, a succession of hills and valleys with a gradual tendency upwards, affording admirable opportunities for street laying and general draining. Had our ancestors been less conservative in the matter of extending the city limits and had they taken in fresh territory before instead of after it was platted out and built up, we should have had in St. Louis a magnificent system of rectangular streets. As it is, St. Louis is really made up of a large number of incorporated towns and villages, and as many of these had a complete system of streets before being absorbed, there are several irregularities which have given trouble to the authorities from time to time in the way of street-naming. The trees to be found in the forest around the city in its early

days suggested names for the principal streets running east and west; and to a great extent the streets running north and south have been from time to time numbered consecutively instead of being named. East of Jefferson avenue the numerical system of nomenclature is fairly regular, but west of that thoroughfare most of the north and south streets are known as avenues, and are given distinctive names, considerable confusion being caused thereby. Shortly after the adoption of the scheme and charter, there was a general overhauling of names, and at the present time a motion is before the Municipal Assembly to further simplify the system. Market street has always been the dividing line between north and south, and all numbers north and south commence from this historical thoroughfare. The numbers on the streets running east and west commence from the river, and each block has its distinctive number. The plan, on the whole, works well; and a reform now being perfected whereby street signs will be made more numerous and conspicuous, will do away with nearly every complaint.

THE BOULEVARD SYSTEM. Since Street Commissioner Turner commenced his crusade against unpaved streets in the business section, the boulevard idea has gained much strength in St. Louis. The first boulevard to be constructed was the Lindell, which is still looked upon as one of the finest driveways in the West. It connects Grand avenue with Forest Park, and is a popular driveway as well as a most desirable promenade. It is adorned with some of the most magnificent houses in the city, and is regarded by visitors as a great credit, not only to St. Louis but to the West generally. Forest Park boulevard, a few blocks south of the Lindell is, in some respects, even more elaborate than what is generally known as "The Boulevard." It has a park-like reservation in the center of the street, and when more thoroughly built up will be a strong competitor for public favor. The present street commissioner, Mr. M. J. Murphy, is responsible for a comprehensive plan of boulevards, which will add some sixty miles to those already in existence. In March, 1891, an act was passed by the State Assembly authorizing cities of more than 300,000 inhabitants—or, in other words, St. Louis, there being no other city in the State with even half that number of inhabitants—to establish boulevards with special building-line, and restricted as to the nature of the travel. The boulevards will vary in length and will provide a system of driveways unsurpassed in any city in the country. Among those already dedicated under the act may be mentioned the boulevards already described, Delmar boulevard, from Grand avenue to city limits, a distance of four miles; and Washington boulevard, a parallel street. Among those comprised in the system will be Columbia boulevard; Florissant boulevard, from Hebert street to the city limits, a distance of five miles; King's Highway, from Arsenal street to Florissant avenue, six miles; Union avenue, from Forest Park to Natural Bridge road; Skinker boulevard, skirting the city limits some six miles, and several other shorter but scarcely less important lengths of thoroughfare.

The boulevard system, when completed, will add some fifty or sixty miles to the most beautiful thoroughfares of St. Louis, which in themselves are far more attractive than the average citizen is apt to realize. A visitor from the distance seeing Vandeventer, Westmoreland or Portland place, for the first time, is enchanted with the delightful combination of urban wealth with rural beauty. The park reservations in these places, which are selected as types of others either in contemplation or in course of construction, are kept in the highest stage of cultivation. The roadways on either side of them are almost perfect, and the houses which have either been constructed or are being erected are models of architectural excellence. Taken altogether, the streets, avenues, boulevards and private places of St. Louis are unequaled, and they are an honor to New St. Louis and to the men who in the early days of the revival lent their influence and ability to a movement which has resulted so advantageously, and which promises to attain far greater excellence.

MAYOR FRANCIS, 1885-1889. The administration of Mayor David R. Francis extended over a period of great importance to New St. Louis. Mr. Francis was elected in the spring of 1885, and he continued at the head of the city government until the end of 1888, when he resigned in consequence of his election to the highest office within the gift of the State of Missouri. Politicians of every grade give him credit for encouraging every movement calculated to add to the city's greatness, and also for originating and recommending a large number of reforms and new enterprises of the utmost importance. If the ex-mayor and ex-governor were asked what was the most vital question with which he was called upon to deal while occupying the mayoralty chair, it is probable he would reply that it related to the city's water supply, which, when he took charge, was being rapidly overtaken by the city's great increase in population. The growth in population during the eighties exceeded 100,000, and it is generally conceded that the bulk of this increase took place after 1884, or during the latter half of the decade. The danger, or at least the possibility, of a water famine in the event of the slightest break-down in the machinery of the existing plant so impressed the mayor that he cordially endorsed the recommendations of Water Commissioner Whitman and lent his influence to the movement, which resulted in work being commenced to entirely reconstruct the system and furnish water settled and filtered in sufficient quantity to supply the demand of 1,000,000 people.

The history of the water supply of St. Louis is one of continual expenditure and improvement. So rapid has been the city's growth that no sooner has one system been perfected than new works have been discussed. In the early days of the city water was procured by means of wells; and about seventy years ago the problem of water-works construction began to be discussed. Work was commenced on the first water-works in 1830. They were situated in the neighborhood of Ashley, Collins and Bates streets, and the first reservoir was on

Little Mound. Engine-houses were built at the foot of Bates street, and a six-inch main laid. The enterprise was a private one, but did not prove very profitable to the investor, and the city was compelled to render financial assistance. In 1835 the works were purchased for $18,000, and before three years had expired they had proved to be altogether inadequate. Complaints are heard at the present time of the water rates being higher than necessary, but they are small compared with the early charges, despite the fact that money at that time was much less plentiful than now. Private families were charged $10 or $20, according to the number of children, and the charges for stores, offices and factories varied from $10 to $500. Early in the forties considerable improvements were made, and in 1846 a third engine was put up by Kingsland & Lightner. In 1852 the Hercules engine was put up by Gaty & McCune. In 1854 the Benton Reservoir, with a capacity of 40,000,000 gallons, was constructed, and in 1859 there were seventy miles of iron pipe, and it was announced that the water supply was abundant.

In 1865 the State Legislature passed a law creating a Board of Water Commissioners for St. Louis, and to the credit of this commission it should be stated that one of its first recommendations was the construction of a reservoir and filtering-beds at the Chain of Rocks, with a conduit to Baden. The plan was rejected in March, 1866, and was severely criticised on the ground of its being experimental and even visionary in character. Time justifies a great many projects, and after the lapse of twenty years the Chain of Rocks was finally selected as the most appropriate point for the construction of an inlet tower. Had the recommendations of the commissioners been accepted in 1865 and 1866 the city would have been richer by several million dollars and its record for healthfulness, good as it has been, would have been far better. Bissell's Point was selected as the site for the works which were necessary and work was commenced upon them. The buildings, which are still in existence and

in use, comprise two series of structures, one for the high-service and the other for the low-service system. The reservoirs have each a capacity of 23,000,000 gallons, and before the demand for water became so great that it was impossible to allow sufficient time for settling, the supply was clear as well as abundant. The Compton Hill Reservoir was also constructed, with a capacity of 56,000,000 gallons. This reservoir, being 176 feet above the city directrix, practically commands the entire city.

THE WATER-WORKS TWENTY YEARS AGO. In 1871 the system was practically completed. Accounts prepared at the time show that its capacity was, although large, far less than the demand it has been called upon to supply during recent years, and it has only been by incessant care that the wants of the people have been supplied. The new water-works, as they were called in 1871, cost the city about $4,000,000, and the valuation of the entire system and grounds was a little in excess of $7,000,000. In 1881 contracts were let for a fourth high-service engine, and during that year Water Commissioner Whitman, in his report, said: "Another question requiring consideration and the official action of the municipal authorities, is as to whether we shall continue to take the water from the river at Bissell's Point, or, in the extension of the works, they shall be planned with a view to taking the water higher up the river to the Chain of Rocks." Recommendations, such as this, followed, and Mayor Francis, as already stated, became thoroughly impressed with the importance of strengthening and increasing the service, and also of obtaining a supply from the Chain of Rocks, so as to avoid the danger of contamination by city sewers.

Not only had the population of the city increased very rapidly, but the consumption of water, per inhabitant, had also nearly doubled in ten years, increasing from fourteen and a half gallons per head per day in 1872 to about twenty-eight gallons in 1882. The collections for water license showed a still more remarkable growth, in spite of the frequent reductions in the charges, which enabled manufacturers to obtain water more cheaply than was possible elsewhere. In 1836 the annual collections were about $4,500, and it was not until the year 1840 that the total exceeded $20,000. In 1851 it was $30,000, and in 1860 it nearly reached $100,000. The collections since then have been as follows, the calculations being made to the months of April or May in each year:

Year.	Amount.	Year.	Amount.
1861	114,760 35	1878	512,053 19
1862	123,690 25	1879	550,140 60
1863	147,120 95	1880	620,280 30
1864	170,313 30	1881	660,024 75
1865	208,340 90	1882	706,145 65
1866	248,268 33	1883	719,686 37
1867	248,575 30	1884	736,694 26
1868	288,910 07	1885	759,265 53
1869	321,412 50	1886	800,325 70
1870	323,102 00	1887	808,043 25
1871	335,626 91	1888	919,975 18
1872	373,194 60	1889	952,689 25
1873	426,922 59	1890	1,017,016 20
1874	444,622 35	1891	1,132,088 40
1875	414,870 44	1892	1,173,998 30
1876	456,163 39	1893	1,235,933 30
1877	445,041 14		

THE NEW WORKS AT THE CHAIN OF ROCKS. Although the projectors of the new water-works were not aware that in the year ending April, 1893, more than $1,200,000 would be collected in water rates, they realized the impending growth of the city and predicted an enormous increase in consumption as a result both of the gain in population and in manufactures. The usual opposition was forthcoming, but with the aid of the mayor's influence a thoroughly comprehensive scheme was finally adopted, and in the year 1888 contracts began to be let for the new works. They are situated at the Chain of Rocks, about twelve miles north of the business section of St. Louis, the plan being to secure pure water by aid of an inlet tower in the river, and to draw it through a gigantic conduit to the city proper. Among the appointments made by Mayor Francis, was that of Mr. M. L. Holman to succeed Mr. Whitman as water commissioner, and upon him has devolved the great work of construction. At the present time the works are nearly completed, and the city will soon have a water supply beyond criticism. Perhaps the most magnificent feature of the new water-works and their connections, is the seven-mile conduit between the Chain of Rocks and Bissell's Point. This conduit is one of the finest in the country, and has been constructed in the most substantial manner.

The inlet tower stands well out from the shore, with which it is connected by an intact tunnel cut from the solid rock. About midway in the depth of the stream the water is let into the tunnel by means of six iron gates operated by hydraulic lifts. At low water eighty feet of the tower is visible, but at high water only about fifty feet. The tower cost about $100,000. A technical description of the works would occupy several pages, and would only be of limited interest to those uninitiated into the mysteries of engineering. It is important, however, to note that the new basins and filter-beds will suffice to settle and filter sufficient water to supply the needs of the city for the next ten years at least, and if the new works are overtaxed to the same extent as the old works, a sufficient supply will probably be forthcoming for ten years longer. Five years have already been occupied in the work, and the total cost will be in the neighborhood of $4,000,000.

We have already anticipated somewhat, as the works were only commenced during the administration of Mayor Francis. But the decision to obtain a supply several miles north of the city's sewer outlets, and to erect new works on a generous scale, marks such an epoch in the municipal growth of the city as to be deserving of more than passing mention. St. Louis is fortunate in being situated on the banks of a river which furnishes an unlimited supply of water of an exceedingly healthy character. Since it has been necessary to overtax the works, the water has not been so clear as desired, but when filtered the water of the Missouri river is at least as good as that furnished in any city in the country. Although the Missouri and Mississippi rivers reach each other in their course several miles above St. Louis, they do not thoroughly unite until they have passed the city, the denser water of the Missouri being easily distinguished from the brighter Mississippi water as the two flow side by side between Alton and St. Louis. The Missouri water is far more suitable for drinking purposes and is freer from deleterious matter, and, although it has been criticised from time to time, the best answer to such criticisms is the exceptional healthfulness of St. Louis. The following table, taken from the *Scientific American* of December 9, 1893, shows the death-rate in the cities of the world credited with a population exceeding, or approximating, 500,000, the estimated population being that of 1892:

	Population.	Deaths.	Death-rate per 1,000
London	5,849,104	55,895	19.11
Paris........	2,424,705	28,675	23.61
New York	1,801,739	23,856	26.47
Berlin	1,669,124	17,181	20.58
Chicago	1,458,000	13,590	18.95
Vienna	1,435,931	18,005	25.07
Philadelphia	1,115,562	12,249	21.95
Brooklyn	978,394	10,682	21.84
St. Louis.........	520,000	4,802	18.47
Brussels..........	488,188	4,359	17.86
Boston	487,397	5,816	23.88
Baltimore	455,427	4,806	21.10
Dublin	319,594	4,735	27.05

THE HEALTHIEST LARGE CITY IN THE WORLD. From this table it will be seen that St. Louis is the healthiest large city in the world. Countless millions have been spent in sanitary work in London, the death-rate in which city has been reduced rapidly, but it still stands higher than that of St. Louis, whose record of 18.47 to the thousand speaks volumes for the purity of its water supply and the efficiency of its sewer system. Moreover, a death-rate of 18.47 is somewhat high for St. Louis, which has begun to look at anything much above 18 as exceeding the normal.

Among the other strictly municipal reforms effected during the administration of Mayor Francis, the sprinkling of the streets by municipal contracts may be mentioned, partly because St. Louis in this, as in many other things, set an example to the entire country, and partly

because of the phenomenal success which has been achieved. It is not to be suggested that Old St. Louis allowed the dust to blow as it pleased during the summer months. There were sprinkling contractors in abundance, but they did their work in quite a primitive style. They made a contract with the owner of a house or lot to sprinkle in front of his premises, and when every property holder on a block entered into the arrangement, fairly satisfactory but very costly service was rendered. What generally happened, however, was the omission of enough street frontage to spoil the entire work. Owners of vacant property were necessarily averse to paying large sums for sprinkling, and, hence, the peculiar phenomenon of streets sprinkled in sections and patches was common. Early in the term of Mayor Francis, the question of a comprehensive system of street sprinkling became a live subject, and a charter amendment having been obtained, a sprinkling department was formed and contracts were let for sprinkling most of the streets of the city. From the first the change was popular. The saving of expense was enormous and the work far more satisfactory. In his message to the Municipal Assembly in May, 1888, Mayor Francis claimed that the problem of abating the dust nuisance had been met and solved; and the experience of the last five years shows that he was correct. A large number of delegations have visited St. Louis from other cities to inspect the street sprinkling and investigate the system, and as a result many cities have already followed in the footsteps of the metropolis of the West and Southwest. A mileage of streets covering about 450 miles is now sprinkled, and the cost is but little in excess of $150,000. It is probable that in the old system quite as much, if not more, was paid, although the service was not one-fourth as complete or satisfactory.

Space makes it impossible to mention in detail, or even in the abstract, the countless interesting and important events which transpired during the administration of Mayor Francis. The visit of President Cleveland and the general decoration and illumination of the city in his honor may be mentioned as the grandest spectacular event; and among the more strictly useful ones the completion and opening of the Grand Avenue Bridge is sufficiently important to deserve recording. Prior to the building of the bridge, Grand avenue, one of the best and most important of the north and south streets, was divided into two parts by the Mill Creek Valley tracks, the crossing of which at grade practically ruined that section of the avenue as a driveway. The new bridge, or viaduct, is a costly and handsome structure, and it has popularized Grand avenue as a driveway far more than even its projectors anticipated.

MAYOR NOONAN, 1889-1893. The unexpired period of Mayor Francis' term was filled by Mr. George W. Allen, the president of the Council. Mr. Allen was succeeded in April, 1889, by Mr. Edward A. Noonan, whose administration was made conspicuous by an immense amount of municipal enterprise. Aside from the reconstruction, with electricity as the motive power, of at least two-thirds of the street railroad mileage, the most important event of the Noonan administration was, probably, the commencement of work by the Chicago, Burlington & Quincy Railroad to secure an entrance to the city from the north, and to construct an independent system of terminals for its own use and for the convenience of roads with running powers over its tracks. This was a special hobby of Mr. Noonan, who recognized the tremendous importance of the work and who gave to it all the influence and weight the city government could lend. Scarcely less important was the final start on the new City Hall, which project had been talked of for a generation. While St. Louis had been outgrowing its water-works, it had completely outgrown the City Hall, which, although it answered the purpose for Old St. Louis, was absurdly inadequate for New St. Louis. As some indication of the growth of public sentiment, it may be mentioned that in 1849 the City Council was authorized by legislation on the part of the State to "erect a City Hall on the square of land belonging to said city, sit-

uated east of Main street, between Market and Walnut." The attempt was referred to in the Missouri *Republican* as "a foolish effort to array some feeling about the erection of a new market-house, stores, town hall and offices for the city officers on the square occupied by the old market and town hall." The "foolish effort" met with doubtful success, for four years later the same journal announced "with regret that nearly all prospects of the purchase of a lot on which to erect the new town hall had been abandoned for at least the present session of the City Council. A bill, drafted with a view to the proposed edifice, and allowing Mr. James H. Lucas $68,000 for the greater portion of the square bounded by Eleventh, Twelfth, Olive and Locust streets, has been under consideration of the Council for the past month or more, but was definitely killed at the session of Tuesday."

Temporary accommodation was obtained in the new County Court House, and it was not until the year 1868 that the subject of building a City Hall was revived. Four years later work was commenced on the building now generally condemned as inadequate, on Eleventh street, between Market and Chestnut. Mayor Brown, in a message to the Council shortly after work was commenced, expressed his regret that the city finances did not warrant the erection of a City Hall commensurate with existing needs and future growth, but he expressed satisfaction in the fact that the new building would do "indifferently well." It seems strange that only twenty years ago a building first designed to be two-stories high and to cost $48,750 should have been deemed sufficient for the city's needs, and even when the plans were changed and a third story added, the total expenditure was only $70,000, and the actual result a building which even the most loyal citizen is compelled to look upon with feelings of regret, if not contempt. In 1880 Mayor Overstolz criticised the City Hall severely. "The building now occupied by the municipal departments," he said, in his annual message, "was not intended to be permanent, was not built in a substantial manner, and does not afford the necessary accommodations. It has stood the test of use and time very indifferently, and for several years past it has cost a considerable amount annually for repairs, and its condition to-day is certainly not favorable for the safety of the valuable archives, records and other property stored therein. In character and size it is inadequate to the wants of the government, and its appearance is discreditable to a city of the reputation, wealth and influence of St. Louis."

THE NEW CITY HALL. The suggestion of the mayor was not acted upon, and possibly it is well that further delay was caused, because the idea at that time was to enlarge the Court House and make it do both for a Court House and City Hall, an arrangement which would have been a poor makeshift and a further source of regret. All through the eighties the question of a new City Hall was a live one, and shortly after Mayor Noonan's inauguration, the agitation was brought to a head and work was commenced on what promises to be one of the finest city halls in the world. The building is now nearly under roof and is being pushed forward as rapidly as possible. It is situated in Washington Square, a block and half southwest of the old hall, and two blocks north of the old Union Depot. The square had for some years been used as a park, and when the fence around it is removed, there will be enough space left on all sides of the City Hall to provide a very handsome public square. The building has a frontage of 380 feet with a depth of about 220, and will have a floor surface of 500 square feet on each of its stories. It is five stories high, and a handsome bell-tower about 200 feet high is to surmount it. The general style of architecture is of the Louis XIV. order, and the building will be similar in appearance, although much more massive and costly than the very attractive town halls to be seen in Normandy and Northern France. The basement and first story of the building are constructed of Missouri granite, the material of the upper stories being buff Roman brick, with sandstone trimmings.

The roof, upon which work is now in progress, will be of black glazed Spanish tile, lending a very handsome finish to a building which will be a distinct ornament to the city. The interior courts are being lined with white glazed brick, and the entire structure will be fire-proof throughout. In addition to the apartments in the basement, there will be 150 rooms in the hall. The Council Chamber and the House of Delegates, will each cover 4,500 square feet, and the Treasury and Collector of Water Rates departments, now so inadequate for the convenience of the public, will be even larger than these two debating chambers. The arrangements for the interior decorations are very elaborate, and as at present arranged will consist of granitoid floors for the store and filing-rooms in the basement; mosaic and marble tile flooring for corridors and the public spaces of offices; the placing of fire-proof arches between the iron joints to the building and marble flooring in working spaces of the offices. Under the head of interior finish is also included the entire plumbing of the building, including marble walls and partitions of lavatories. The general scheme of decoration consists of treating the first-story corridors of the building, the central rotunda, the Council Chamber, the House of Delegates and the Mayor's office in quite an elaborate manner, as those parts of the building are the ones seen by the casual visitor, and it was thought that they should be made more decorative than the general offices of the building. The finish in those cases will consist of scagliola art marble, and will be dignified and monumental. The working rooms of the building are treated in a strictly utilitarian manner, and, while the large amount of wainscoting necessary makes it expensive, it is strictly for the betterment of the building, there being no waste in the way of an elaborate treatment that is purely ornamental. The absence of wood finish and the substitution of marble makes the building more strictly fire-proof, and also saves the expense of keeping the woodwork presentable.

The ceilings of the first-story corridors will be a succession of flat domes. These will be

8

treated in fresco, using a dead gold finish, and
the under parts of the rotunda will be painted
an old ivory tint, with the ornamental panels and
plaster decorations picked out with gilt. The
chambers of the Council and House of Delegates
are wainscoted fifteen feet high, above which is
a wide plain belt of plaster, which is to be
painted a flat tint of old ivory. Above this belt
is an elaborate frieze of plaster, the ornaments
of which are picked out with gilt. All the
above decorations will be done in the style of
Louis XIV. All the walls above the marble
wainscoting and the ceilings of offices are
frescoed in flat tones. The cost of the building
and the internal decorations, with the furniture,
will exceed $1,500,000 and may approximate
$2,000,000.

ELECTRIC STREET LIGHTING. Another event of special
importance from a munici-
pal standpoint during Mr.
Noonan's administration was the lighting of the
city streets and alleys by electricity. St. Louis
was the first city in the United States to illuminate its alleys throughout by electric light, and
it was really the first city in the world to make
arrangements for lighting the whole of its
streets in the same way. It is scarcely necessary to speak of the earliest attempts to light
the streets of St. Louis. In 1837 the State
Legislature authorized the St. Louis Gas Light
Company to erect works for lighting St. Louis
and suburbs with gas. The charter was amended
in 1839 and again in 1845, but the clause in the
charter which was first taken advantage of was
the one which authorized the company to do a
banking business. In 1846 a contract was entered into between the city and the company,
and in November, 1847, the city was first lighted
with gas. For forty-three years gas lamps held
undisputed sway in St. Louis, but in the year
1889 a new department was added to the city
government, under the management of a super-
visor of city lighting. The contracts with the
gas companies expired on January 1, 1890, on
which day the alleys were for the first time
lighted throughout by means of the incandescent system. The electric company which had

the contract for arc lights for the streets was
not ready to commence on the same date, but
on May 1st the entire city was lighted by electricity.

During the early part of 1890 there were
erected 1,552 arc lights for the streets, 1,462
incandescent lights for the alleys, and 3,442 incandescent lights for public buildings. The
work was rapidly increased, and early in 1891
356 miles of streets and 81 miles of alleys were
thoroughly illuminated by electricity. To do
this more than 2,000 arc lights were required,
and about 5,000 incandescent lights were in use
in the alleys and in public buildings. The system has since been largely increased, and St. Louis
is certainly the best lighted city on the continent to-day.

During the last eight or ten years great progress has been made with the laying of public
sewers, and St. Louis, in addition to being
favored with good streets and excellent lighting,
has also a sewerage system which has conduced
largely to the preservation of health and the
general comfort of the inhabitants. The Mill
Creek Valley forms not only an excellent means
of entrance for the railroads from the west, but
also an unsurpassed center for a sewerage system. The Mill Creek sewer is the largest in the
world, and it receives and discharges into the
Mississippi river from the southern portion of
the city the sewerage and strong water of an
area comprising 12,300 acres. The rapid growth
of the city in every direction has made it necessary to lay off new sewer districts and to carry
on an immense quantity of new work, but the
demand has been fairly kept up with and there
are now in the city nearly 400 miles of public
and district sewers, with some twenty or thirty
additional miles constructed every year.

MUNICIPAL FINANCES. The city's finances are in a very
healthy condition. The bonded
debt on April 10th, 1892, was
$21,524,680, which was reduced during the year
by about $150,000.* Of this sum $135,000 was

---

*Since the above was written the bonded indebtedness
has been still further reduced, and now amounts to about
$21,200,000.

furnished by the sinking fund, and more than $13,000 by premiums on the four per cent renewal bonds, which were placed in London. These bonds, redeemable in twenty years and bearing interest at four per cent, were placed at $101.15, and during this year (1893) bonds of similar character to the extent of $1,250,000 were placed in London at par. This latter transaction was, taking into account the condition of the money market, even a greater achievement than that of 1892, and shows clearly how the credit of St. Louis stands abroad. The total reduction in the bonded debt within the last five years has amounted to over $600,000, and the annual interest charges have been reduced during that period from $1,131,099 to less than $1,000,000.

The credit of New St. Louis is shown by the rapid decrease in the interest it is compelled to pay on its debt. In 1888 the interest paid varied from seven to four per cent, and averaged nearly six per cent. The average in 1889 was five per cent, and now it is about four and a half per cent. The city taxation is at the rate of forty cents per $100 for the payment of debt and interest, and varies from one dollar to sixty cents for general purposes. Considering the immense amount of new public work made necessary by the city's growth and now actually in hand, the rate of taxation is exceedingly low, and may be mentioned as one of the inducements offered to manufacturers and others on the lookout for a location.

CHAPTER XI.

SOCIAL ADVANTAGES.*

A CLEAN BILL OF HEALTH AND ITS CAUSES. EDUCATIONAL FACILITIES.—ART. LIBRARIES.—
CHURCHES.—MUSIC. THEATERS. CLUBS. HOTELS. BENCH AND BAR.—
MEDICAL. JOURNALISM.

NEW ST. LOUIS is a cosmopolitan city, not only in regard to its population, but also in the matter of its achievements. If this history has accomplished its purpose, it has established the fact that New St. Louis is one of the most important manufacturing centers in the world; that it is the center of the most fertile region in America; that its railroad facilities are unsurpassed and in many respects unapproached; that it has the best rapid transit street car service in America; that its financial institutions are absolutely beyond suspicion and reproach; that it has practically reconstructed itself by wholesale building

and rebuilding, and that in municipal matters generally it has been the pioneer in almost countless reforms and improvements. The space allotted for a historical sketch of New St. Louis has already been exceeded, but the subject cannot be left without a passing reference to the social advantages, which are quite as conspicuous as those of a strictly mercantile and financial character. The city has fully appreciated the philosophy contained in the couplet:

Ill fares the land, to hastening ills a prey,
Where wealth accumulates, and men decay.

Hence it has not overlooked movements which are calculated rather to make men healthy and wise than strictly wealthy; and a large measure of success has attended the efforts thus made. There are still many reforms needed, and it

*The reader is also referred to the Chapters on Municipal Achievements and on New Buildings. Only those social advantages not included in preceding chapters are dealt with here.

would be idle to attempt to argue that New St. Louis is a model city. At the same time it compares most favorably with any other large city in the world, and although the pessimist is always abroad, many of his complaints and laments result rather from the expectation of the impossible, than any serious neglect or omission. We have already seen that St. Louis is the healthiest large city in the world. Various causes have combined to curtail its death-rate and to give it a clean bill of health. In the first place, the location of the city is favorable in the extreme. Scientists have of late derived much satisfaction from calling attention to the fact that the Mississippi river runs up hill, its source being nearer the earth's center than its mouth. If this is so, all the hill-climbing is done before St. Louis is reached, because the city directrix is 412 feet higher than the mean tide-mark of the Gulf of Mexico. The city is built on rising ground averaging many feet higher than the directrix, and hence although St. Louis cannot be described as a mountain city, it is certainly not a lowland town. Its climate is delightful in the extreme, the friendly shelter of mountains and hills protects it from cyclones and other dangerous wind storms, and its location seems to guarantee to it immunity from the intense heat of the South and bitter cold of the North. The mean temperatures for the last half century are eighty degrees for July, seventy-six degrees for August, and thirty-one degrees for January. The maximum temperature for a year rarely exceeds ninety-five, and very seldom approaches a hundred. The average daily maximum for July, the hottest month in the year, has been about eighty-eight during the last six or eight years; while the average minimum for the same month has been about eighteen degrees lower. It is important to bear these figures in mind, because during exceptionally warm spells a great deal is apt to be said about excessive heat, although it is a remarkable fact that the maximum temperature of St. Louis for a year is generally lower than that of cities some hundreds of miles further north, just as the minimum temperature is gen-

erally higher than that recorded for cities much more southern. In other words, the climate of St. Louis, as a rule, is equable and healthy, and as a health resort the city is entitled to more than a passing word of praise.

GOOD WATER AND PURE AIR. The health of the city has also been maintained by the excellence of the water supply. Efforts which can only be described as superhuman have been made from time to time to show that St. Louis water is contaminated and unfit for drinking purposes. These efforts have been crowned with uniform and signal failure, and the fact has also been established that in the rare event of an epidemic the greatest suffering is always in houses which depend for their water supply on cisterns and wells. Even now, overtaxed as are the water-works, the supply of water is more than satisfactory; and when the new settling-tanks and filter-beds are in operation, St. Louis will have a water supply as good as that of any large city in the world and above the possibility of suspicion.

Like all manufacturing cities, St. Louis suffers from the emission into the air of large volumes of what is known to the law as "dense black" and "thick gray smoke." A writer in the New England Magazine for January, 1892, says that "within ten years the temporary and exasperating evil of smoke from bituminous coal will be in a great part removed." The writer overlooked the fact that Old St. Louis has given place to New, and although only two years have elapsed since the able article from which the extract is taken was written, the smoke nuisance has already been very largely remedied and removed. Too much credit can scarcely be accorded the Citizens' Smoke Abatement Association for its work in this direction. The leading spirits in the movement, to which reference has already been made, have been Messrs. L. D. Kingsland, Clark H. Sampson, Samuel M. Kennard, A. D. Brown, E. D. Meier, C. H. Huttig, and other manufacturers and merchants, while Prof. W. B. Potter, one of the best known mining engineers and metallurgists in the United States, has lent to the movement the knowledge gained by many years' experimenting and testing. The first step taken by the association was to satisfy itself that smoke can be abated, even when bituminous coal is used, without the slightest hindrance to manufacture or commerce. This fact being finally established, it obtained legislation and inaugurated a canvass of the smoke-reducing plants of the city. Excluding hotels and private houses, several hundred offenders were listed, and moral suasion was brought to bear to prevail upon these to put in smoke-abatement devices without waiting for legal proceedings.

Already more than 500 grossly offending chimneys have ceased to deluge the air with smoke, and of the first 200 cases in which notice of prosecution was given, 195 secured a continuance, or rather a postponement, by producing satisfactory evidence that they had either abated the smoke or signed contracts to enable them to do so. Other experiments are being made with coke and smokeless coal; and although, as previously remarked, it is scarcely to be expected that St. Louis will ever be absolutely free from smoke, it is certain that long before the ten years aforesaid have expired, the city's attractiveness and healthiness will have been increased by the reduction of what has hitherto been almost a scandal, to nothing more than a sentimental grievance.

THE CITY'S PARKS. During the New St. Louis period great progress has been made in the laying out and improving of the city parks. Thanks to the forethought of legislators in years gone by, the city has a better devised park system than that of any large city in the world. There are upwards of 2,000 acres reserved for breathing grounds, and the best possible use is made of them. Forest Park, consisting of 1,371 acres, was purchased in 1874, and during the last few years it has been made far more attractive by the addition of a zoological department, while at the present time the project of raising a private fund for the erection of a museum in it is being seriously discussed. The financial stringency of 1893 has naturally retarded the enterprise, but New St.

Louis has never been known to fail in good work of this character, and there seems no doubt that in the early future the project will materialize satisfactorily. The eastern portion of Forest Park is laid out with delightful driveways, while the western portion is less cultivated and possesses rural charms very attractive to the visitor.

Tower Grove Park, consisting of some 266 acres, is a more highly improved recreation ground. It is not only a favorite driveway, but it has some magnificent statues, presented to the city by Mr. Henry Shaw. These include the first bronze statue of Columbus ever erected in this country, and also other works of art of a costly and attractive nature. Adjoining Tower Grove Park is the Missouri Botanical Garden, known generally as Shaw's Garden, which was laid out by the deceased millionaire and bequeathed by him to the city. The garden covers a space of about fifty acres, and is regarded as one of the finest botanical gardens in the world, attracting visitors from all sections. It was laid out without regard to expense, and is so richly endowed that it will be preserved for all time to come in its present magnificence. Its principal features are the main turf walk to the conservatory, the statue of Victory, the mausoleum containing Henry Shaw's remains, the grand parterre, ornamented with flower-beds and statuary, the lotus ponds, water-lily ponds and show of water plants, the lodge for the garden pupils, a grand display of cacti, palms and exotics, the Linnean house, the summer house in the fruticetum, the willow pond in the arboretum grove and herbaceous grounds, the late residence of Henry Shaw in the garden, the grape arbor in the fruticetum, and labyrinth.

The other city parks include recreation grounds in every section of the city, easily accessible by street cars. They are not described at any length here, because most of them were acquired before New St. Louis commenced to assert its influence and displace the old régime. For the same reason but a passing tribute can be paid to the police department, which is admitted to be one of the most efficient in the country, or to the fire department, which has no rival, and which has won praise from the chiefs of departments visiting St. Louis from cities in almost every section of the world.

WASHINGTON UNIVERSITY AND ITS WORK.

In educational matters New St. Louis has been as conscientiously active as in those relating to wealth, health and comfort. It is a pleasing characteristic of the West that, no matter how rapid or spasmodic the growth of cities has been, the rights of the rising generation, in the matter of educational facilities, have never been overlooked. This has been the case in a most marked degree in St. Louis, where the growth of the school system has fully kept pace with the phenomenal advance in other directions. The grandest educational institution in the city is the Washington University, which ranks among the very best colleges in the country. The charter under which the university was operated was signed by the governor of the State in 1853, on Washington's birthday. In the charter the institution thus formed was described as the Eliot Seminary, and later the name was changed to O'Fallon Institute. The constitution declared that the institution should comprise a collegiate department, a female seminary, a practical and scientific department, an industrial school, and such other departments as the board of directors might determine. It was also very discreetly ordained that there should be no instruction sectarian in religion or partisan in politics, and that no sectarian or partisan test should be used in the selection of professors or officers of the institute. It was specially desired by the seventeen men who formed the first board of directors that the university should be known by the name of the first president, but Dr. Eliot objected strongly, and after considerable wavering the board adopted his view and the university was given the name by which it always has been known during its forty years of extreme usefulness.

Dr. Eliot outlived nearly all of his colleagues on the original board of directors, remaining president of that body until the year 1887, when his illustrious career was terminated by death. It is probable that if a vote could be taken on the question, a majority of the inhabitants of St. Louis would favor the name being changed back to the original appellation. The name "Washington" has been so largely adopted throughout the country for various purposes that it does not retain sufficient distinctive qualities to be a proper name for a large university in a central western city. There has, however, been little agitation of late on the question of name, the more important question of the possibility of having to move further west in order to obtain more accommodation, having received more attention at the hands of the directors. The university is at present located on Washington avenue at the summit of the first hill above the actual bluffs. The southern wing of the building and the chemical laboratory were erected in 1855, and about the same time the Polytechnic Building was erected on the corner of Seventh and Chestnut streets for further work in connection with the university, especially in its industrial department. The Polytechnic Building still stands, though it has passed out of the hands of educational directors and is now occupied by the Real Estate Exchange and by real estate firms. At a comparatively early date the building is likely to be torn down and replaced by a more lofty and more modern structure, better adapted for the purposes of commerce and finance.

The Polytechnic Building was nearly nine years in erection, and its final cost, including the site, was $400,000. In the meantime the outbreak of the war had hampered the university's finances, and the institution found itself in debt with a building on its hands entirely unsuited for the purpose for which it was constructed. In 1868 the building was sold to the St. Louis Board of Education for $280,000, and with the money thus obtained the university proper began to make up for the time lost by the war and the mistake made in the designs of the Polytechnic. Mr. William Chouvenat was then chancellor, and during his administration the university made great progress. The Mary Institute, organized in 1859, had already been established on a firm footing, and the Polytechnic School, with technical courses in engineering and chemistry, was formed. In 1870 Chancellor Chouvenat died, and Dr. Eliot assumed the duties of chancellor as well as president. He lived to see the dream of his youth very largely carried out. The Swift Academy became separated from the undergraduate department and was established in a building of its own.

The Manual Training School, admitted to be one of the finest of its class in the world, was established on a firm footing, and has since attained popularity which has made it more than famous. The St. Louis Medical School is one of the many branches of the university; and by the will of Henry Shaw a school of botany has been endowed with facilities for studying botany unexcelled in any institution in the world. As already stated, Dr. Eliot died in 1887. He was succeeded by Mr. G. E. Leighton as president, and by Prof. W. S. Chapman as chancellor. There are between 1,500 and 1,600 students enrolled in the university, and there is every probability of a scheme materializing at an early date whereby the institution will move out in the suburbs and build for itself a larger home, more suitable in every way for the carrying out of the great work inaugurated by some of St. Louis' greatest men forty years ago.

The Washington Observatory in connection with the university is one of the most important in the world. It gives time, to use the technical expression, to thousands of public, railroad and other clocks, regulating the official time and correcting it to actual time over a larger area than any other observatory in the world, with the single exception of that of Greenwich, near London, England, from which the degrees of longitude are calculated.

THE MUSEUM OF FINE ARTS. The School of Fine Arts in connection with the university has its home in a very appropriate and attractive building situated at Eighteenth and Locust streets. A history of the early struggles of art and artists in this city would be of great interest, but it is impossible to handle it in this place in a manner satisfactory to experts. Just before the war the Western Academy of Arts was established, with Mr. Henry T. Blow as its first president. The outbreak of hostilities put a stop to the career of the academy, and it was not until 1872 that another attempt was made. In the latter year the Art Society was established, with Mr. Thomas Richeson as president. By this society many of the unique specimens on view in the reading-room of the Public Library were collected and donated. The society ceased to have any practical influence after 1878. In 1877 the St. Louis Sketch Club was established, and in 1878 Mrs. John D. Henderson formed and opened a school of design.

In 1881 the School of Fine Arts in connection with Washington University was finally established, in pursuance of the plan originally determined upon by the founders of the institution. Prior to this date the School of Fine Arts had been announced, but the year 1881 saw it located in a permanent home. On the 10th of May, 1881, Mr. Wayman Crow, than whom a more loyal St. Louisan never lived, donated to the university the magnificent structure known as the St. Louis Museum of Fine Arts. When this home for the preservation of the beautiful was constructed, Lucas place, as it was then called, was exclusively a residence locality. Since then its name has been changed to Locust street, and factory after factory has been erected on its frontage lines. In the midst of these monuments to commercial progress the museum stands out in bold relief as an exponent of an entirely different idea, and also a different style of architecture. The auditorium will seat nearly 1,000 people, and the five galleries are graced with many works of art which would have been lost to St. Louis but for the princely generosity of Mr. Wayman Crow and the zeal of those who have watched over the museum with almost tender solicitude. Prof. Halsey C. Ives, who has been connected with art movements in St. Louis for many years, is now at work on a project of far greater magnitude than any he has yet identified himself with, and students and lovers of art will have no cause to consider themselves neglected or overlooked.

The influence of Washington University and the numerous institutions connected with it has been of immense value to St. Louis in every way. Mention has been made in the mercantile chapters of this work of the importance of cementing the relations between St. Louis and the Spanish-American republics. This work is being done, not only by the agency of St. Louis business men and their representatives traveling throughout the countries named, but also by the education of quite a large number of Mexican young men at Washington University. Although there are no arrangements for students to board in the institution, a very large number of non-resident students are always enrolled, and these find convenient board accommodation close to the great seat of learning. Among the prominent business and professional men of St. Louis a singularly large percentage graduated from the University on Washington avenue, and this is also the case of many of the leading men of Missouri and adjoining States. The exact location of the future home of the university is in doubt at the present time, but its future is assured. No institution of St. Louis has done more to make the city famous and respected.

THE PUBLIC SCHOOL SYSTEM. The public school system of St. Louis ranks among the very best in the world. At the Columbian Exposition exhibits from these schools obtained eleven highest awards, and the exhibits attracted so much attention that a large number of visitors to the Fair, including officials from several States, visited St. Louis before returning to their homes for the express purpose of familiarizing themselves with the methods which had so excited their admiration. The triumph at the World's Fair was by no means a surprise to those who have taken an interest in the St. Louis schools, because the city has been looked upon for years as the pioneer in advanced studies for the masses, and the St. Louis system, as it is frequently called, has been adopted by a large number of the best cities in the country.

Without attempting a detailed history of the rise and progress of the public schools of St. Louis it may be said that their earliest triumphs were achieved during the administration of Dr. Wm. T. Harris, who was for twenty years connected with our public schools, and who has since made an international reputation as United States educational commissioner. His work in connection with the public schools was of the noblest possible character, and the excellent plan that he formulated and popularized, has not been materially varied since he left the city.

The chief difficulty with which his successors have had to contend, has been in the rapid increase in the number of applicants for admission. In 1875 there were fifty-six school-houses in St. Louis, with about 30,000 seats. In 1886 the number of houses had increased to 103, and the accommodation to a little over 42,000. In the last days of Old St. Louis, the sitting accommodation of the public schools was about 45,000, which was increased very rapidly to 50,000, which was the return in the early part of 1889. In 1890 there were 111 school-houses with 51,645 seats. In 1891 additions to the existing schools provided accommodation for nearly 2,000 more scholars, and in 1892 the opening of new schools increased the seats to nearly 57,000. At the present time the demand for new schools is being met as rapidly as possible, and during the first quarter of the school year 1893-94, the attendance reached 61,252, an increase of 3,400 on the preceding quarter. Despite the efforts of the authorities, 365 children were unable to find sitting accommodation at the schools when the last report was issued, and although work is being continued in school building and enlargement, the number of children grows so rapidly that great difficulty is experienced in keeping up with the demand.

It will be observed that during the last twenty years the accommodation has been more than doubled, notwithstanding the fact that during that period a very large number of very excellent private schools have been established. Even during the New St. Louis era there has been an increase in school attendance of more than thirty-three per cent. It now costs more than $1,000,000 a year in teachers' salaries alone to maintain the teachers' staff; and it is notorious that St. Louis pays a higher grade of salaries for teachers than any other city, the desire being to obtain the best possible tuition for children. The salaries range as high as $3,000 a year, and the system of advancement as a reward of merit has had the effect of keeping the best teachers in the city, and encouraging talented instructors from every point to come to St. Louis.

FROM KINDERGARTEN TO THE "HIGH." Commencing with the youngest children, reference may be made to the kindergarten classes, at which the attendance exceeds 5,000. Kindergartens are established in nearly all the district schools, and it is about twenty years since the experiment was commenced. The kindergarten, as found in St. Louis, is not a nursery, but is an attempt to instruct the little people in necessary study, and to lay the foundation of the education they will require in later years. Froebel's idea was to develop in each child the germ of intelligence, and the leading fundamental principle of his method is developed. "I see in every child," said he, "the possibilities of a perfect mind;" and this is the underlying principle of the kindergarten course in the St. Louis schools. The adoption of games makes it possible to accomplish the object without difficulty; and this is done with invariable success. The child is not only taught to distinguish between the colors and the different letters, figures and words, but it is also instructed in manners and polite habits, and to practice the etiquette and amenities of polite life. Prof. Long, who is now superintendent of the schools, entered very heartily into the spirit of his eminent predecessor, and the interest Mr. Long takes in the kindergarten department is largely responsible for the high state of efficiency which has been maintained.

Children enter the kindergarten class at six, though they are often found as young as five. The age at which they enter upon other departments necessarily varies, but it is found that the influence of this early tuition remains throughout their entire educational period. The enrollment in the kindergarten schools now exceeds 8,000, and it has been suggested frequently that a change should be made in the law so as to let the children commence at four, instead of six. Forty-five schools have kindergartens connected with them, in six of which the children are allowed to attend all day, while in the remainder the children attend half a day only and thus increase the number of children able to obtain education in this preliminary but important branch.

In the intermediate and higher grades, a high-class education, fully equal to that obtained in comparatively costly academies and colleges is given. It is the desire and policy of the School Board that every pupil shall pass right through the course of study from the Kindergarten to the High, but when owing to accident or otherwise, a child has to leave school after passing through the early grades, he can fill a position often nearly as well as his more fortunate brothers. In addition to a full course in reading, writing, arithmetic and national history, each child has the benefit of a complete system of calisthenics and enlightened control of discipline, and a comprehensive arrangement of those lines of instruction indispensable to people who have to make their own way in life. As in all manufacturing cities, the children are apt to leave school at too early an age, and one of the difficulties which has beset not only Prof. Harris, but also his successors, is how to crowd a full course of training which ought to occupy eight or ten years into five or six. Difficult as the task necessarily appears, it has been accomplished with great success, and the teachers deserve great credit for their triumphs in this direction. For those who are compelled to leave school prematurely, an excellent system of night schools is in operation, and some of the very best business colleges in the United States enable young men and ladies to put the finishing strokes to what may be termed a commercial training.

The Normal and the High schools are universities in everything but name, and those who are fortunate enough to be able to graduate from either can hold their own in almost any company. A St. Louis Normal diploma gives an applicant for a teacher's position exceptional advantage over his or her competitors, and many of the most successful principals in the country graduated from this favored city. There is also a Normal school for colored children who desire to adopt teaching as a profession; and education's good influence is felt in every class and by all people.

PAROCHIAL SCHOOLS AND COLLEGES. In addition to the admirable public schools of the city, St. Louis has a parochial school system which does excellent work. The city has grown so rapidly that the financial resources of the Board of Education have been taxed to the uttermost to keep pace with the growth in the number of children of school age, and were it not for the fact that the parochial schools take care of more than 20,000 children, and give them a high-class education, it would have been impossible to make both ends meet. The Catholic population of St. Louis has not neglected its duty towards the rising generation, and the amount of money it has raised for the maintenance of parochial schools reflects the greatest credit upon its sincerity and liberality.

There are more than forty parochial schools, employing nearly 200 teachers, and the average attendance is between 22,000 and 23,000. When parents are in a position to pay, a small tuition fee is charged, but a large percentage of the children are taught entirely free of charge. The teachers in the Catholic schools are taken from the ranks of the Christian Brothers, Sisters of Charity, Sisters of Mercy, and the members of various orders, and they are hence exceptionally competent in the performance of their duties. The parochial school buildings are of an improved character, and are generally well ventilated and appointed. Children are received between the ages of six and fifteen, and when they have graduated they have an opportunity of entering one or another of the numerous Catholic colleges in the city.

Without attempting to give a list of these colleges and universities, one or two must be mentioned as deserving of special praise. The Christian Brothers' College is perhaps the most prominent. The Christian Brothers came here from France nearly half a century ago and established themselves at Eighth and Cerre streets. With the birth of New St. Louis the Brothers went west and purchased a ten-acre tract at the corner of Easton avenue and King's Highway, where they erected a building of brick and stone, designed in the shape of a cross, consisting of a central edifice and four wings. It has a frontage of 370 feet, a depth of 200 feet and an elevation of 110 feet. In the center is a fine rotunda 60 feet square. Every modern convenience is provided. The college is a community in itself, and its location, buildings and grounds are not excelled for educational purposes in the Mississippi Valley. It is easily accessible by the Easton avenue cars from the heart of the city, and is just far enough out to combine rural and city life. The curriculum comprises preparatory, commercial, collegiate, literary and scientific courses. There are generally from 300 to 400 students at the college, and a corps of thirty-three professors, all of whom with the exception of three are Christian Brothers, is engaged.

The St. Louis University has been identified with St. Louis for nearly seventy years. It was originally located in a home constructed in the thirties on what is now known as Ninth and Christy avenue, but what was then looked upon as out in the woods. In 1867 a much more suitable site was purchased on Grand avenue and Pine street, where there has been erected one of the grandest educational buildings in the United States. It has the form of a reversed L, the base line being on the left instead of the right side of the perpendicular. The front on Grand avenue measures 270 feet, and all that portion of the building is devoted to college purposes. The resident portion is further west. The immense structure is built of brick and stone, and its architecture is early decorated English Gothic. It has a magnificent museum, fine laboratory and library, and all the adjuncts of a thoroughly equipped college, including a lecture-room with seating capacity of 500. The college has an attendance of about 350, and its instructors are Jesuit Fathers.

It would be interesting, if space permitted, to mention in detail the various schools and educational institutions of St. Louis; but this being impossible, the subject must be dismissed with the statement that few cities in the world are more thoroughly equipped for educational purposes than St. Louis. Men can be trained for the highest professions; and the higher education of women has been remembered and provided for in a manner which disarms criticism at the threshold.

LIBRARIES, PUBLIC AND PRIVATE. The libraries of St. Louis, if not so numerous as some of those to be found in the older cities of the East, make up in efficiency and completeness what they lack in numbers. Many of the city's prominent men have private libraries of the grandest type, and the city has two public libraries which are an honor to the municipality and a constant source of profit and entertainment to the student and searcher after knowledge. The Mercantile Library will soon celebrate its semicentennial. It has now nearly, if not quite, a hundred thousand valuable volumes, although its first report speaks with gratification of the possession of less than two thousand. Under the able management of Mr. John M. Dyer, one of the best librarians the country has seen, the library grew and prospered, and the dream of that gentleman's life was realized some four or five years ago when the new fire-proof building at the corner of Sixth and Locust was erected as a safe home for the priceless treasures owned by the association. A statue of Mr. Dyer in the library serves as a painful reminder that he died of overwork in connection with moving and rearranging the books in their new home.

Forty years ago the library built what was then regarded as a very fine hall, which was used for convention purposes again and again. It became out of date with the birth of New St. Louis, and the present building is more in keeping with the demands of the times. It is a very handsome six-story building of Romanesque character. The library halls are twenty feet in height, and the arrangements are complete in every detail.

The Public Library, which in the year 1894 will be made a free library in the full sense of the term, is a child of the School Board. For many years it was known as the Public School Library, but more recently it has been known as the Public Library, and greater effort has been made to popularize it with the public. It had its home for twenty-five years in the Polytechnic Building, purchased, occupied and finally sold by the School Board after a series of blunders which will be remembered as long as St. Louis remains a city. The library is now located in a lofty building at the corner of Ninth and Locust streets, which has already been described in this work. The number of books on its shelves does not differ materially from that at the Mercantile Library.

The St. Louis Law Library contains the best collection of legal works to be found in the West. More than twelve thousand volumes of standard legal authors, as well as other works, are to be found, and the records of decisions in different States is complete in the extreme. The libraries at the St. Louis and Washington universities have a reputation extending over the entire country; and the Odd Fellows' Library contains a collection of books of inestimable value.

CHURCHES AND RELIGIOUS INSTITUTIONS. St. Louis, while it cannot compete with Brooklyn for the title of the "City of Churches," is still admirably equipped with religious edifices of all characters and denominations. The gradual tendency of recent years has been to go west, and church after church has found a new location and a new home on the suburban side of Grand avenue. There are now about three hundred churches in St. Louis, many of them most magnificent in character. The old Catholic Cathedral on Walnut street, between Second and Third, is in a wonderful state of preservation. Its corner-stone was laid sixty-two years ago, and the Cathedral was opened fifty-nine years since. The exterior shows evidences of the ravages of time, but it is still in excellent condition, and the interior is as beautiful as ever. When first erected it was by far the finest structure devoted to religious purposes west of the Alleghany mountains, and it is still among the most interesting, if not the most magnificent, religious edifices in the country. The interior is divided into a nave and two aisles, the double row of dividing columns being in Doric style and built of brick covered with stucco.

The Rock Church, or, more properly, St. Alphonsus', on Grand avenue and Finney, is really a second cathedral. It was erected by the Redemptorist Fathers, many of whom actually performed manual labor on the structure while in course of erection. It is one of the special features of the city to which the attention of visitors is called, and it is one of the most handsome cathedral churches in the West.

The Episcopal Cathedral is also a credit to the city. The first parish of the Episcopal Church west of the Mississippi river was organized in 1819, when the population of St. Louis was only about 4,000. From that time the Episcopal Church in St. Louis has grown both in the number of its edifices, in its influence and in its church membership. In 1867 the present cathedral, on Fourteenth and Locust streets, was erected, and about five years ago it became the spiritual home of the diocese of Missouri. Aided by a magnificent endowment from an unknown source the church has been placed in a sound financial condition, and subsequently a donation of $15,000 has been made for the purpose of erecting a cathedral home or mission. The conditions of this latter donation have just been fulfilled.

Among the numerous Episcopalian churches in the city may be mentioned the Holy Communion, St. George's and St. Mark's Memorial and St. Peter's, although this is but a very partial record and does not attempt to particularize.

The Presbyterian churches are also numerous. The First Presbyterian Church of St. Louis was the first church of that denomination established west of the Mississippi river. This church was erected in 1825, and has only recently been demolished. Its successor has its home on Washington avenue and Sarah street, in a much more pretentious building erected five years ago. The Second Presbyterian Church, on Seventeenth and Locust streets, is a comparatively old building, having been erected prior to the war at an expenditure of $30,000. It is in an excellent state of preservation, and is looked upon as a very representative church. The same denomination has a splendid structure on Grand avenue, near Olive street, and a number of other churches.

SACRED EDIFICES WITH INTERESTING HISTORIES.
The Methodist-Episcopal denomination made a splendid showing in a religious census recently taken. The Trinity Church, erected in 1857, and originally known as the Simpson Chapel, holds the record of having been the only Northern Methodist church which held services regularly throughout the war. This was not the first church in St. Louis of the denomination, whose record goes back as far as the eighteenth century. The Rev. John Clark preached in St. Louis in 1798, and about twenty years later the Rev. Jesse Walker established a Methodist-Episcopal church in the city. This church eventually connected itself with the Southern branch of the denomination. The other Methodist churches in St. Louis include some edifices, not only of great influence, but also of interest in historical records. Among them may be mentioned the Centenary, at Sixteenth and Pine streets; St. John's, at Locust street and Ewing avenue, and others, some belonging to the Methodist-Episcopal Church, North, and others to the Methodist-Episcopal Church, South, both denominations being supported by prominent and influential citizens.

The Second Baptist Church, on Locust and Beaumont streets, may be regarded as the home of the earliest Baptist congregation of St. Louis. The present magnificent structure, with its excellent appointments, dates only from 1879, but the congregation which worships in it claims much greater antiquity. The Baptists enjoy the honor of having been the first to build a Protestant church in this country west of the Mississippi river, they having completed a sacred edifice near Jackson, in Cape Girardeau county, nearly ninety years ago. The same denomination has in St. Louis a church on Grand avenue at the corner of Washington, and another on the same avenue, but much farther north. It is also well represented elsewhere in the city.

The oldest religious Hebrew association in the city is the United Hebrew Congregation, which erected a synagogue just before the war on Sixth street, between Locust and St. Charles. The building was subsequently sold and converted into a commercial establishment, the congregation moving to Olive and Twenty-first streets. More recently it, or rather members originally connected with it, have erected Temple Israel and Shaare Emeth, both known as representative and handsome churches.

The Church of the Messiah, presided over by one of the ablest orators and writers in the West, represents the Unitarian idea in St. Louis. This church was erected in 1879 and 1880, the building being finally dedicated in December, 1881. In style it is early English Gothic, the blue limestone being relieved by horizontal strands of sandstone, which material is also used for the window and door trimmings.

Such is a brief record of the churches connected with the leading denominations in St. Louis. All that has been attempted has been to show that the social advantages include ample provision for spiritual training.

NEW ST. LOUIS AND MUSIC. The value of good music has been thoroughly appreciated in New St. Louis, and the best of conscientious music as compared with the purely commercial article is rapidly obtaining the appreciation it deserves. The old Philharmonic Society spent several thousand dollars in its efforts to revolutionize music and to send out missionaries into the homes, churches and institutions of the city and give a higher tone to instrumental and vocal music generally.

The Choral Society is more strictly a New St. Louis organization, and it has done splendid work for St. Louis, although it is to be regretted that much of the expense has been borne by private individuals, whose modesty has prevented the public becoming acquainted with the debt it owes them. During the last fourteen years the society has spent sufficient money to bring to St. Louis the very best soloists in the country, and its work has been so successful that the production of the "Messiah" in Christmas week of 1893, with Miss Emma Juch and other singers of national reputation as soloists, is expected to be one of the finest productions of this great oratorio ever heard in this country. This will be the twelfth production of the "Messiah" in St. Louis; and it is safe to say that for many years to come this magnificent inspiration will be heard in the western and southwestern metropolis during Christmas week. The society is educating public tastes so rapidly that it is becoming self-supporting. In 1891 the sum of $5,400 had to be raised to meet the deficiency caused by the engagement of high-class talent. In the season of 1892–93 the deficit was only $3,600, which was promptly made up, and the indications are that the season of 1893–94 will be about self-supporting.

The influence of the society has been felt in public institutions of every character. The singing in the churches in St. Louis is now exceptionally fine, and the same may be said of several of the local institutions. In another way the Philharmonic and Choral societies have shown their influence. Old St. Louis had a reputation among advance agents as being an excellent town for concert companies to miss. New St. Louis, thanks largely to the Choral Society, has a very different reputation, for any good company can secure a crowded house. During the thirty days between April 12 and May 12, 1893, there were eleven high-class concerts in St. Louis, and these received the sum of $15,000 as a reward for their excellence.

THEATERS AND CONCERT HALLS. As an amusement center generally St. Louis has a high reputation. Mention has already been made of the special attractions provided during the autumnal festival period, and a record has been made of the early struggles of the first theater constructed in the city. There are now six thoroughly equipped first-class theaters in the city, with a seating capacity of more than 12,000, independent of the 6,000 seats in the two halls within the Exposition Building. For six seasons in succession five of these theaters have been well supported, and the best theatrical talent of the country has been seen at them. St. Louis' patronage has been also liberal enough to attract the best actors of foreign countries touring in America, and the appreciation of high-class histrionic work is proverbial. At the Olympic Theater, on Broadway, opposite the Southern Hotel, Joseph Jefferson, Edwin Booth, Lawrence Barrett and Fanny Davenport may be mentioned among leaders in the profession who have played very successful engagements. The Grand Opera House, is equally popular, and here also some of the greatest performers of the day have been seen. In addition to the best American actors and actresses, such conspicuous figures in the theatrical world of other nations as Sarah Bernhardt and Wilson Barrett have been seen repeatedly. The orchestra of the Grand is exceptionally good, and, like the Olympic, the theater is first-class in every respect.

Among the newer bids for the support of the theater-going fraternity may be mentioned the Hagan Opera House, erected about two years ago. The Hagan is a novelty in more ways than one. The construction and plan involved a maximum of common sense and convenience, while the management, in going as far west as Tenth street, showed an ability to read the signs of the times, which subsequent patronage has proved to have been exceedingly valuable. The newest of St. Louis' first-class theaters is the Germania, which is still farther west, being situated at the corner of Fourteenth and Locust streets. Here are represented German plays of

high character, and the patronage of the house is a tribute to the power of appreciation of the German element in St. Louis' population, an element which has done so much to maintain the stability of the city.

St. Louis is also exceedingly well cared for in the matter of summer opera. The oldest summer-garden theater in St. Louis is Uhrig's Cave, which dates from six or seven years prior to the war. During the summer evenings light opera is produced here by companies of established reputation, and empty seats are seldom seen. Close to the Cave is the Pickwick Theater, a favorite house of the numerous amateurs of promise of St. Louis. On the south side Schnaider's Garden, with its commodious and indeed luxurious summer theater, provides entertainment for dwellers in the southern wards. The new Sportsman's Park is also so arranged as to make it available for operatic and spectacular performances during the summer evenings. In the southern portion of the city Liederkranz Hall is very popular for high-class entertainments, and there are now in course of construction several additions to the entertainment halls and ball-rooms of the city.

CLUBS AND CLUB LIFE. New St. Louis is rich in the extreme in the matter of clubs. Of the Commercial, the Mercantile and the Noonday clubs mention has already been made. The two latter have been spoken of more in their business or commercial aspects, but they are also important factors in the society appointments of this great city. Since moving into its new building the Mercantile has carried the war into Africa in a most dexterous manner. From time, the memory whereof man knoweth not, ladies have looked upon clubs as their natural enemies, and have censured their sweethearts and husbands in no mild terms for allowing the luxuries of the smoking and billiard-room to lure them from the fireside in winter, or the front-door step in summer. The directors of the Mercantile, who it is not suggested have been censured in like manner as the immense majority of their fellow-men, decided to disarm the criticism of the ladies by making them, as it were, *particeps criminis.* To do this, they fitted up ladies' rooms in the most luxurious style, and not only made it admissible for members to bring their own, or other men's, sisters to the club, but even encouraged them to do so. Hence, the Mercantile Club, in addition to being one of the most influential commercial organizations in the West, is also one of the most delightful society and social clubs in the world, as popular with the wives and daughters of members as most clubs are unpopular. Mr. George D. Barnard, the president of the club, has earned much praise by his able completion of the work of reconstruction which was commenced and carried on so zealously by his predecessor, Mr. J. B. Case.

The St. Louis Club is luxurious in its appointments, and has an air of exclusiveness about it which is in accordance with the ideal of high-toned club life. Its home is in a magnificent building on the southwest corner of Ewing avenue and Locust street, and its four hundred members include representative men of every type which can be regarded as consistent with the requirements of the upper-ten.

The Fair Grounds Jockey Club has its home inside the Fair Grounds, and is a popular resort, especially in the summer-time. Its membership is very large, and its banqueting hall is taken advantage of frequently for the purposes of entertaining strangers. Had a phonograph been inserted in the walls of this hall it could have bottled up enough eloquence to have educated the rising generation from time to time on almost every point of interest and importance.

The University Club was erected by scholars for scholars, and all the learning and erudition of the city is represented within its walls. Its members can talk in a greater number of languages than the men who commenced to erect the Tower of Babel. Of recent years the qualifications of members, so far as University graduation is concerned, has been relaxed, and there are now several members who confess to knowing little Latin and less Greek. The club continues to be a high-toned social organization, popular in the extreme with gentlemen of refined tastes.

EXCLUSIVE ORGANIZATIONS.

The Marquette Club has its home in a very attractive and suitable building on Grand avenue and Pine street. The constitution of the club states that its primary objects are to unite the prominent Catholic gentlemen of St. Louis; to organize them into a body that shall represent, watch over, vindicate and further Catholic interests; to establish it in an unobjectionable club-house, and by placing the club on a lasting basis to perpetuate a union of Catholics in the city of St. Louis. The club has carried out its original object very successfully.

The Harmonic Club was established in the forties by several of the then prominent Hebrew citizens of St. Louis. The club is still somewhat of a religious institution, though it is a very high-class social club. It rents a fine building on the corner of Eighteenth and Olive streets, and it is its proud boast that bonds and indebtedness of any kind are absolutely unknown to the club or its management. The Columbia Club has just completed a very handsome building on Lindell boulevard, just west of Vandeventer avenue, in which 135 members will establish themselves and run a club similar in every respect to the Harmonie.

The Union Club has a home on the south side, at Lafayette and Jefferson avenues, in which there is crowded more provision for home comfort than has perhaps ever been seen under one roof before. Every club is established to fill a long-felt want, but few of them have done their work so thoroughly as the Union, which in its new location is a distinct boon to residents on the south side. The new building is quite unique, both externally and internally, and every member is individually proud of it.

The Liederkranz is also a south side club. It owns a very handsome building on Chouteau avenue and Thirteenth street, and its membership of 650 includes some of the most able singers in the city. The German element predominates strongly, and there are in addition to large and small entertainment and rehearsal halls, dining-rooms and club apartments of every character. Liederkranz concerts and entertainments are always leading social events.

Only members of the Order of Elks are eligible for the Elks Club, which has its home in the Hagan Opera Building, on Pine and Tenth streets. There are about a hundred members who make use of the club, both for business and social purposes. Athletics of every description are encouraged by the management, and the club has also a special reputation for hospitality, very elegant suppers being tendered to visitors to the city, especially those who have made a reputation elsewhere in their respective professions.

There are also several very successful ladies' athletic and cycling clubs and semi-religious associations.

HOTELS AND ACCOMMODATIONS FOR GUESTS. The autumnal festivities attracts so many visitors that during the fall season the hotel accommodations of St. Louis of recent years have been found scarcely adequate, and in order to increase the facilities for taking care of large carnival and convention crowds, the $2,000,000 hotel already described is being constructed. It will be opened in the course of a few months, and will make the down-town hotel facilities very complete. The Southern Hotel, a substantial fireproof structure, has for many years been regarded as the leading hotel in the city and among the foremost in the West, its rotunda being one of the most extensive in existence. The Lindell Hotel, a few blocks farther north, is another establishment first-class in every respect. The Laclede Hotel is looked upon as an ideal family hotel, and is also exceedingly popular with politicians of every shade. The number of caucuses that have been held in and around it is very large, and the hotel management has a reputation extending from Maine to California for going out of its way to accommodate individual visitors and delegations in every conceivable manner. Adjoining the Laclede is Hurst's new hotel, another very fine structure; and nearly opposite the Lindell is the Hotel Barnum, a very popular house.

The tendency to move westward, which has resulted from the rapid transit facilities, has also been marked in the hotels. A few years ago the idea of first-class hotels west of Twelfth street would have been ridiculed, but now there is on Fortieth street, or Vandeventer avenue, a hotel known as the West End, whose appointments are first-class in every respect, and which is very popular both as a hotel proper and a family boarding-house. On Grand avenue the Hotel Beers and Grand Avenue Hotel are further exponents of this western idea; and early in the ensuing spring another very handsome edifice for hotel purposes is to be erected on the same thoroughfare. In the vicinity of the New Union Station, also far west of what has up to recent years been regarded as out of the way of business and travel, two and probably three very fine hotels are about to be erected, sites having been obtained for that purpose. When they are added to the present hotel equipment of the city, St. Louis will be able to handle a convention crowd of almost any magnitude without the necessity of special bureaus for the placing of guests in boarding-houses and private residences.

BENCH AND BAR OF ST. LOUIS. St. Louis is not a litigious city, and arbitration for the settlement of commercial disputes has always been very popular. There are, however, in the city a large number of lawyers and attorneys who find sufficient employment to yield them good incomes and who display marked ability in the exercise of their profession. The bar of St. Louis to-day knows no superior in the West, and among the gentlemen practicing law there are several whose fame extends to distant points. In the early history of St. Louis the laws of England, France and Spain were all partly enforced, and there were many complex questions in regard to titles which called for the exercise of the greatest possible care and ingenuity. Those days have passed now, and the business falling into the hands of the attorneys of the city is of an entirely different nature. On the bench there are to be found many lawyers of exceptional experience, and many decisions have been made here which have been recognized as irreproachable law. Quite recently the city gave to the nation for a cabinet office one of its prominent attorneys; and other members of the St. Louis bar have distinguished themselves in various parts of the country. In another part of this work there will be found records of the careers of some of the most prominent members of the St. Louis bar, including sketches of some of the judges whose ability and integrity has made them more than famous.

The Bar Association of St. Louis was established in 1874. Col. Thomas T. Gautt was temporary chairman of the meeting called to "consider the propriety and feasibility of forming a bar association in the city of St. Louis." A committee of five was appointed, consisting of Alexander Martin, Henry Hitchcock, R. E. Rombauer, George M. Stewart and Given Campbell. The first president was Mr. John R. Shepley, who in his first address emphasized the fact that the object of the association was to "maintain the honor and dignity of the profession of law, to cultivate social intercourse among its members, and for the promotion of legal science and the administration of justice." It would be difficult to overrate the good influence of this association, or its effect on the tone of the bar and its members.

DOCTORS OF MEDICINE. St. Louis is such a healthy city that it is anything but a doctor's paradise, and the number of physicians in the city is not large, when the population is taken into account. Among the physicians who have made their home in St. Louis, there are several whose reputation extends beyond the confines of Missouri and Illinois, and even beyond the boundaries of the United States. Some of our surgeons are requisitioned from very distant points, when exceptionally complicated cases call for exceptional skill; and the city has also specialists who rank so high in the medical world that they are summoned for consultation to cities 1,000 miles distant. It would be interesting to trace the early history of medicine in the city, but it must suffice to say that at the present time nothing is

needed in this respect, and that all that science and skill can do to ameliorate suffering and to prolong life can be and is done in St. Louis. The medical press is well represented, and the medical journal which has the largest circulation in the world is published from this city.

Almost every known school of medicine is represented, not only by practitioners, but also by medical colleges. The number of these latter is very large, and the work they do in educating and preparing young men for the profession is influential for much good. There are several hospitals in the city, some of them connected with religious and other bodies, and others which are entirely independent and catholic in their work. It is to be regretted that the exigencies of space prevent a detailed description of the hospitals and medical colleges, but such would require an entire volume to even do the subject partial justice.

NEWSPAPERS OF NATIONAL INFLUENCE. The newspapers of St. Louis speak for themselves, two, at least, of them having national influence and importance. Following the plan generally adopted in this book, the early history of the newspapers will be but very briefly mentioned. The *Globe-Democrat* is probably the best newspaper in the United States west of New York, and it is certainly by far the best newspaper in the country west of New York and south of Chicago. It is the survival of the *Globe* and the *Democrat*, which papers were consolidated in 1875. Two years ago the *Globe-Democrat* moved into the magnificent building on the corner of Sixth and Pine streets, which it erected for its own home. The building is a model newspaper office in almost every respect, and it has few equals and still fewer superiors in the United States. The policy of the *Globe-Democrat* politically is Republican, but national affairs are looked upon in a very liberal manner, and measures, rather than parties, are analyzed and discussed from a critical standpoint. Mr. Joseph B. McCullagh is the editor-in-chief of this great newspaper, which, during the eighteen years which have elapsed since its publica-

9

tion under its present name, has been edited daily under his personal supervision, the aggregate number of days of his absence from the office during that period being about equal to the time occupied by the summer vacation of the ordinary professional or business man. The *Globe-Democrat* is conspicuous for the absence of trumpet-blowing of its own achievements, and when it moved into the "Temple of Truth," the only announcement made in its columns of its change of location was included in the single sentence: "We have moved."

The early history of the *St. Louis Republic* has already been given in these columns. It is now one of the most influential Democratic newspapers in the United States, and although old in years and experience, it is still young in enterprise and vigor. In addition to an excellent telegraphic and news service from outside the city, it makes a specialty of local news, which it covers with great accuracy and judgment. Since it changed its name and reorganized, its circulation has increased with great rapidity, and the growth of its influence has been quite on a par with its financial boom.

There are three evening newspapers in St. Louis published in the English language—the *Post-Dispatch*, the *Star-Sayings* and the *Chronicle*. The *Post-Dispatch* is the largest of these, and it publishes a Sunday issue which is really a magazine and compendium of current literature in addition to a first-class newspaper. It is edited by Mr. Florence White, and both the daily and Sunday issues are bright exponents of the New St. Louis idea.

The *Star-Sayings* is edited by Mr. John Magner, an able and conscientious journalist, who has succeeded in largely increasing the influence and importance of the paper. The *Star-Sayings* is enjoying a great renewal of prosperity, and makes itself heard on all questions of importance.

The *Chronicle* is the only one-cent daily paper in the city. Its editor, General Hawkins, has completely remodeled and rejuvenated the paper, which is popular in the extreme, and which claims to have a larger local sale than any other paper published.

The German papers are almost as prominent as those printed in English. The *Westliche Post* and the *Anzeiger des Westens* are quoted as authorities in all parts of the United States; and the *Amerika*, *Tribune* and *Tageblatt* have each their own field to fulfill in a satisfactory manner.

The magazine press of St. Louis is less conspicuous than the daily, and although there are several publications, there are none of sufficient national repute to make a detailed reference to them necessary.

The immense size of the Sunday newspapers and the large amount of space devoted to literary and scientific questions, has made it difficult to establish weekly papers on a paying basis in St. Louis. For many years the *Spectator* prospered and contributed to local literature a great deal of valuable and interesting matter. Its long career has, however, terminated, and the *Sunday Mirror* is now* practically in exclusive control of the weekly press. The *Mirror* differs in its make-up and character from any other western publication. It knows neither friend nor foe in its columns, and is original and fearless in its style and policy, supplying, in a way never filled before, a field which ought not to be overlooked in a city of 600,000 inhabitants.

*December, 1893.